Theatrical anecdotes; or, Fun and curiosities of the play, the playhouse and the players

Herman Diederik Johan van Schevichaven

Digitized by Microsoft ®

THEATRICAL ANECDOTES

THEATRICAL ANECDOTES

OR

FUN AND CURIOSITIES

OF THE

PLAY, THE PLAYHOUSE, AND THE PLAYERS

By JACOB LARWOOD

AUTHOR OF

"THE HISTORY OF SIGNBOARDS," "CLERICAL ANECDOTES," "FORENSIC ANECDOTES," ETC.

London

CHATTO AND WINDUS, PICCADILLY

1882

PREFACE.

It has been observed that in books of theatrical anecdotes there is probably more unscrupulousness and falsehood to be found than in any other miscellanies. On the other hand, it may be safely concluded that very few stories, however absurd, relative to plays and players, are to be pronounced absolutely incredible. They may have been a little rouged or burnt-corked *secundum artem*, but what of that? Too great a regard for truth has taken the point out of many a good story, and to weigh evidences concerning the "flying words" of a theatrical anecdote is a waste of critical acumen equal to the feat of breaking a butterfly on the wheel.

THEATRICAL ANECDOTES.

CRANIOLOGY.

THERE was a low comedian, familiarly called Dick Hoskins, who used to play in small country theatres in the north of England, and who was a practical joker on the stage. He played one night the Gravedigger at the Rochdale Theatre, to the Hamlet of a Mr. C——, a most solemn and mysterious tragedian of the cloak-and-dagger school. The theatre was built on the site of an old dissenting chapel, in which a preacher named Dr. Banks had formerly held forth, and in the small graveyard attached to which Dr. Banks had been laid to rest some twenty years before, his name being familiar yet among the audience. After answering Hamlet's question—"How long will a man lie in the earth ere he rot?" Dick proceeded to illustrate his answer by Yorick's skull, and taking it up, he said, in the words of the text, "Now, here's a skull that hath lain you in the earth three and twenty years. Whose do you think it was?" "Nay, I know not," replied Hamlet, in his sepulchral tragedy-tone. "This skull, sir," said Dick; "this skull, sir, was Doctor Banks's skull," and he pronounced the last word like *skooll.* The house roared with laughter, whilst the victimized tragedian stamped and fumed about the stage, exclaiming, "Yorick's, sir; Yorick's!" "No," said Dick, coolly, when the tumult had subsided, taking up another skull. "*This* is

Yorick's skull, the king's jester; but t'other's Doctor Banks's, as I *told* you." This was too much. The incensed Hamlet jumped prematurely into the grave, seized the (very) low comedian by the throat, and a most fearful contest ensued, in which Dick succeeded at length in overpowering the tragedian, whom he held down in the grave with one hand, while he flourished "Doctor Banks's skull" in triumph over his head with the other.

IMPROVING SHAKESPEARE.

MR. GEOFFRY GALWAY was a hairdresser by trade and an actor by profession, famous for playing little parts. His best parts were the Murderer in *Macbeth*, the Apothecary in *Romeo and Juliet*, and the Player King in *Hamlet*, upon his success in which he would plume himself with as much pride as though he had performed the heroes of the dramas. He had received his dramatic tuition under that human curiosity immortalized in the pages of Bernard's *Retrospections*. On one occasion, when representing the Player King, he stepped forward to repeat the lines—

> "For us and for our trage-dy,
> Here stooping to your clemen-cy,
> We beg your hearing patient-ly."

There he should have rested with Shakespeare, but genius was on the wing, and he could not bring the eagle-bird to earth; so he continued—

> "And if on this we may re-ly,
> Why, we'll be with you by-and-by."

At which Whiteley, the manager, who lay on the ground as Hamlet, snarled out, loud enough to be heard by all the audience—

> "And if on pay-day you re-ly,
> Take care I stop no sala-ry"

Thus justifying the rhyme by a very serious reason.

A SAVING FAITH.

SAMUEL SPRING, after having been head waiter at White's, became box-keeper of Drury Lane Theatre, in the reign of George IV. Like all such theatrical appendages, he was a most devoted and loyal adherent to the particular "concern" to which he belonged. Spring placed an almost religious reliance upon a high and superintending care, which especially protected the interest of his particular theatre. But it was not enough that Drury Lane flourished; Covent Garden must be in ruins, or it was but half a victory gained. One night he entered with unusual animation the green-room of Drury, having just witnessed at the rival establishment the condemnation of a new piece, and, addressing Mr. Wroughton, the then acting manager, with a triumphant air and the sly, habitual touch of his hat, said, in his tone of quaint humility, "Beg pardon, sir. I come to tell you that Providence has been very kind to us to-night at the *Garden.* New play, sir, *quite damned;* not even attempted to be given out, sir, for another night! Providence takes care of *the Lane,* sir!"

TRACTION AND ATTRACTION.

"DUMMY ALLEN," Edwin Forrest's costumer, and latterly keeper of a restaurant near the Bowery Theatre, New York, was a great character. He had a sublime contempt for all English stars, and could never listen to their praises with patience. One day John Povey met him, with the announcement that an extraordinary attraction had been engaged for the next season. "'Traction!" rejoined Allen, who was deaf and affected with a chronic catarrh; "what sort of 'traction? Legs, I s'pose; that's the thig dow-a-days. The bore you can hubbug the people the bedder." "Legs!" said John, rubbing his hands with satisfaction; "imagine not.

Better than that." Then, speaking confidentially through his hands, "We've secured Macready!" "Bah!" said Allen, with contempt; "he's dobody—can't speak decet Egglish; bere bounteback, sir, bere bounteback;" and he took snuff fiercely. "Well, mountebank or no mountebank," replied Povey, "he's sure to draw—a great card, sir." "Ay," growled Allen, with importance, "can *draw a cart*, eh? Bedder stick to his trade, then—pay him much bedder;" and, with a conclusive thump of his walking-stick, he turned away.

AN UNLICENSED HOUSE.

ONE day while Charles Bannister was under examination as a witness in the Court of King's Bench, the Lord Chief Justice retiring caused a temporary suspension of the proceedings. One of the learned counsel, by way of pleasantry, asked Charles for a song. "With all my heart," he answered, "if I can have an accompaniment." The barrister replied that they had no music there. "I wonder at that," said Bannister, "for you seem to have the *band* under your nose."

COCK-BRAINED.

IN some town where George Frederick Cooke was performing, he obtained a suit of clothes from a stage-struck tailor, who proposed that instead of receiving money for his goods, he should be allowed to play Catesby to Cooke's Richard. The tragedian was overjoyed at such an easy mode of discharging the debt, and accepted the arrangement, after having assured himself that the man knew the part. On the evening of his *début*, the tailor spouted and stamped agreeably to the most orthodox fashion, and elicited some applause. For the tent scene, Catesby as well as Richard had screwed up all their energies; and when Richard started from his knees, at the conclusion of the comments on the dream, exclaiming,

"Who's there?" the *amateur*, in his excitement, stammered out his answer, and abruptly stuck in the middle of his phrase—"'Tis I, my lord, the early village cock . . ." Cooke surveyed the stultified aspect of his officer for several seconds with a sardonic grin, as if enjoying his agony, and at length growled out, in a very audible tone, "Why the devil don't you crow, then?"

A MODERN ABSALOM.

BENSLEY, the tragedian, was a solemn, pompous actor of the old school, with a sepulchral voice, a stiff, stalking gait, and who delighted in a full, flowing wig. One evening, when he came on in the Dublin Theatre for his first soliloquy in Richard III., a nail at the wing caught the bottom of his majestic wig, and dismounting his hat, suspended the former in the air. An Irish gallery know how to laugh, even in a tragedy. Bensley caught his hat, as it fell, by a feather, and replacing it on his nob "shorn off its beams," advanced to the front and commenced his soliloquy, amidst a volley of importunities to resume his wig: "Mr. Bensley, me darling, put on your jasey! Bad luck to your politics—will you suffer a *whig* to be hung?" etc. The tragedian, however, considering that such an act would have compromised in some measure his dukely dignity, continued his meditations in despite of their advice, and stalked off at the conclusion as he had stalked on. An underling then made his appearance, and released the captured hair, with which he exited in pursuit of Richard, to as loud a demonstration of approval as Richard himself.

A GLORIOUS MARTYR.

MUNDEN was a great actor, heart and soul in his vocation. He was particularly great in the character of Obadiah in the *Committee; or, the Honest Thieves*. There is a scene in that piece wherein Teague plies the hypocrite

Obadiah with wine, when it was customary to use a black quart bottle, and to pour from its neck the contents down the throat of the actor, in spite of his resistance and repeated declaration of "No more, Mr. Teague." One night Munden's struggles against the readministration of the doses were found to be unusually vigorous, and therefore more exciting to the administrator. Nevertheless, he gulped the liquid down at each application of it, under which operation his contortions of face were so extremely comical that even Johnstone, who played the part of Teague, was convulsed at his brother comedian's extra-drollery, and the audience absolutely screamed with laughter. At length the scene ended, and Obadiah was borne off the stage in the usual manner. The moment Munden found himself out of sight and hearing of the audience, he sprang upon his legs, and broke out into the most passionate exclamations of disgust and anger, swearing that he had been poisoned, and calling for a stomach-pump. Pressed by all around him for a solution of the mystery, he cried out in an agony of disgust, pointing to the empty bottle still in Johnstone's hand, "Lamp-oil, lamp-oil, every drop of it!" The property-man had mistaken a bottle half-filled with the rankest lamp-oil for the quart bottle, in which usually some sherry and water was employed to drench the luckless actor. When the sufferer had in some degree recovered from the nausea caused by the accident, Johnstone marvelled why Munden, after his first taste of the liquor, should have allowed him to pour the whole of the disgusting liquid down his throat. "My dear boy," gasped Munden, "I was about to do so, but there was such a glorious roar in the house at the first face I made upon swallowing it, that I hadn't the heart to spoil the scene, by interrupting the effect."

PERSEVERANCE.

AFTER George II. had ceased to visit the theatres, Macklin's farce of *Love à la Mode* having been acted with much applause, he sent for the MS. He had it read out to him by a sedate old Hanoverian gentleman, who, being but little acquainted with English, spent eleven weeks in puzzling out the author's words; as for the meaning, they probably never got at that.

A CRUEL HOAX.

POPE, the actor, well known as a gourmand and for his attachment to venison, received an invitation to dinner from an old friend, accompanied by an apology for the simplicity of the *menu*—a small turbot and a boiled edgebone of beef. "The very thing of all others that I like!" exclaimed Pope. He went, and ate till he could literally eat no longer, when the word was given and a haunch of venison was brought in. Pope saw the trap which had been laid for him; but he was fairly caught, and after trifling with a delicious slice, he laid down his knife and fork, and gave way to a hysterical burst of tears, exclaiming, "A friend of twenty years' standing, and to be served in this manner!"

TIT FOR TAT.

WHILE Farquhar, the dramatist, was in Trinity College, Dublin, he sent to another student to borrow Burnet's *History of the Reformation;* but that gentleman sent him word he never lent any book out of his chamber; if, however, he would come there he should make use of it as long as he liked. A little while after, the owner of the book sent to borrow Farquhar's bellows. The future dramatist returned him the compliment: "I never lend my bellows out of my own chamber, but if the gentleman pleased to come there, he should make use of them as long as he liked."

"ROARING LIKE A SUCKING DOVE."

BILLY BATES at one time was at the head of a strolling company which occasionally visited Bristol, but when a permanent theatre was opened in that city by Powell and Holland, he enlisted in their company in an inferior capacity. At the opening performance a tragedy was given, in which Holland did a king at the head of his army, and Bates was condemned to a messenger, who gave notice of the enemy's approach. This character comprehended but one entrance and five lines of diction; but these five lines were precious, and Bates, having a throat like a speaking-trumpet, rushed on at rehearsal and roared them forth, taking at the same time a stage-effective but rather indecorous sweep of the boards, from the fourth wing to the footlights. "Mr. Bates," said Holland, with a stare of surprise, "you surely don't intend to deliver that message in that manner at night?" "Yes, but I do, Mr. Holland." "You are too loud, sir!" "Loud, sir! not at all, sir; 'tis only energetic. *I've got a benefit to make as well as you, Mr. Holland.*"

FRIENDLY ADVICE.

A TRAGICAL actor of Covent Garden Theatre requested Mr. Harris, the manager, for a renewal of his engagement, at the same time requiring a high increase of salary. Mr. Harris referred the actor to the following well-known laconic epitaph:—

"Lie still, if you are wise;
You'll go down if you rise."

"HE WOULD BE AN ACTOR."

ONE of the *pia vota* of the elder Mathews was that his son should become a clergyman. He was even credited with a declaration that "not even a dog of his should set feet upon the stage." But young Charles declined the Church, and avowed his intention to become an architect, for which purpose he was articled for four years to Pugin, the architect. After a while, however, the father recognized his son's histrionic skill and capacity, and perceived the slenderness of his chances of ever prospering as an architect. Being asked at that period what he was going to do with his son, his answer was, "Why, I mean him to *draw houses*, like his father."

A COOK'S REVENGE.

MRS. Jordan, having reasons of complaint against her Irish cook, one morning summoned the professor of gastronomy to her presence, paid her a month's wages, and discharged her. The *cordon bleu* was offended at such an unceremonious dismissal, and indignantly taking up a shilling, and banging it on the table, exclaimed, "Arrah now, honey, sure and you think yourself mighty grand! But, look 'ee, with this *thirteener* won't I sit in the gallery, and won't your royal grace give me a curtsey, and grin and caper for me? and won't I give your royal highness a howl and a hiss into the bargain?"

POTENTIAL AUTHORSHIP.

M. J. B. GONDELIER, the printer in the Passage du Caire at Paris, figures on the playbills as the author of four pieces, without having written one single word in any of them. On the evening of the first representation of one of these pieces, *La Mère au Bal et la Fille à la Maison*, he was taking his *ponche* in the Café du Theatre du Vaudeville. One of his friends asked him if he was one of the authors of the new piece. "I don't know yet," was the answer. "I am waiting for Théaulon, and have brought a thousand-franc note to become one of the authors." Théaulon was the real author, and M. Gondelier merely wished to figure on the bills in order to have his *entreés* behind the scenes. This process of putting one's name to plays written wholly or in part by others, in English theatrical slang is called "devilling."

QUIN'S SARCASM.

DINING one day at a party in Bath, Quin uttered something which caused a general delight. A nobleman present, who was not remarkable for the brilliancy of his ideas, exclaimed, "What a pity it is, Quin my boy, that a clever fellow like you should be a player!" Quin fixed his flashing eyes upon his interlocutor, and contemptuously replied, "What would your lordship have me be? A lord?"

HER NEXT SITUATION.

GEORGE COLMAN'S severity as a censor of plays is well known, yet in his conversation he would frequently make remarks which would not have passed muster in a comedy. Elliston and Alfred Bunn once went to him, in the hope of persuading him to remove some objections he had made to part of a play, as bordering on the profane, but he was immovable. "And now," he said, rubbing his hands, after all arguments had been exhausted, "let us go into the next room and have a glass of wine." They did so, and in the course of the conversation he inquired after his former partner in the Haymarket Theatre. "His wife is dying, I fear," said Elliston. "Dying! bless my soul, I'm sorry for that! Let me see, if I recollect rightly, she was his servant?" observed Colman.

"I have heard so," responded the lessee. "Then I hope," said the censor, "she'll carry a *good character to her next place!*"

SHORT, BUT SWEET.

AS Bannister was standing one night unobserved in the scenes, he heard some scene-shifters discuss the various impersonations of Hamlet they had witnessed. One admired Henderson, another Kemble, a third Kean, and each commended his own favourite. At last one of them said, "You may talk of Henderson, and Kemble, and Kean, and the rest of them; but Bannister's Hamlet for me, for he has always done twenty minutes sooner than anybody else."

"PATIENCE."

THERE was a silk-mercer in the last century who had frequented Bury St. Edmund's fair many years, and was remarkable for his imperturbable complacency; his patience surpassed Job's. Lewey Owen, the actor, took a bet that he would ruffle the worthy dealer's temper. He walked to the booth, and inquired for a particular silk. It did not suit him, when shown, and he desired to see another. That was nearer the colour, but a shade too light. A third, that was the right colour, but of too fine a texture. A fourth, too coarse; a medium texture would suit. A fifth, no; a sixth, a seventh, an eighth were taken down, rolled out, and inspected—all rejected. Still the mercer's patience was as inexhaustible as his stock. Lewey persevered. After looking over nearly every piece in the booth, and heaping the counter, the chairs, every available place with rolls of silk, paper, strings, half unrolled pieces laying about in chaotic confusion, Lewey at length pointed to a roll high up on the topmost shelf, which he desired to have a look at. The obliging mercer mounted a ladder, and with infinite difficulty obtained it, naturally expecting from the trouble his customer gave that he intended to purchase a good many yards. Having placed it before Lewey, he unrolled it, at his request, to the very end. When the roller made its appearance, Lewey took it in his right hand like a truncheon, and flourishing it gravely about his head, stuck it in his side. "Come," he said, "that will do; we've got it at last!" "What will do?" exclaimed the mercer, with profound astonishment. "Why, you must know, sir," replied Lewey, "that I'm the principal tragedian in Mr. Griffith's company; and having to perform *Richard the Third* to-night, which you must be aware can never be played without a good truncheon, I didn't see one in the stock to suit me, and have come out to buy one. Pray, what's the price of this?" The mercer's virtue was of no longer being. He positively foamed with rage, and, jumping over the counter, it is probable would have broken the roller over Lewey's head, had he not tumbled over his silks, which gave the actor time to make good his escape.

"TRIFLES THIN AS AIR."

MADEMOISELLE SARAH BERNHARDT once made an ascent in Giffard's captive balloon, and, inspired by her journey, the enthusiastic artist wrote a book, entitled *Impressions d'une Chaise*, illustrated by her fellow-traveller in this ascent, the painter Clairin. Whether this book be good, bad, or indifferent is neither here nor there, but the jokes of the Parisians about her ascent were perhaps a little overdone. The unkindest cut of all came, of course, from a friend. "You are a lucky woman," said Got to her; "you can mount into the balloon even whilst it is rising up in the air." "How is that, venerable dean?" inquired Sarah. "Why, don't you know?" was the reply. "The administration has ordered a winding staircase to be constructed, on purpose for you, *within the cable!*"

SUDDEN FORGETFULNESS.

AS "Gentleman" Johnstone was performing one night at the Lyceum Theatre, the "gods" thought proper to call for their favourite song, "The Sprig of Shillelah." Johnstone came forward, with his usual alacrity and good humour, to comply with the wishes of the house; accordingly, the band struck up, but Johnstone stood silent and apparently confused. This scene was repeated three times over, still the actor did not commence the song. At last he stepped forward, and thus addressed the house: "Ladies and gentlemen, I have sung this song so often that I have quite forgotten the first line." A universal roar of laughter ensued, and about two hundred voices began at once to prompt the actor, who, seeing escape impossible, thereupon sang with the usual applause.

MADAME CATALANI'S APPLES.

MADAME CATALANI having been engaged at Covent Garden Theatre, Mr. Harris, the manager, determined that she should make her first appearance in *The Free Knights.* The O. P. riots were at that time at their worst, and the celebrated artist was informed that on the first night of her appearance, she would probably be pelted with apples. "Ah, mon Dieu, sare!" she exclaimed, with the greatest earnestness and *naïveté;* "I hope dey vil be *roasted!*"

A DEAD HERO.

"ONE of the most ludicrous attempts to follow out the stage directions of the author at the least possible expense, that I ever had the ill-luck to witness," writes Macready, in his *Reminiscences,* "was at Kendal. The *corps dramatique* arrived in the town too late for the rehearsal of *Virginius*, and I had to undergo during the two first acts a succession of annoyances, in the scenic deficiencies and in the inaccuracies of the players. My unhappy temper was seriously tried under the repeated mortifications I experienced; but in the third act, where Siccius Dentatus should be discovered on a bier, with a company of soldiers mourning over it, I saw the old man who represented the Roman hero lying on the ground, and two men standing near. This was too absurd! the body having to be borne off in sight of the audience. I positively refused to go on. 'Oh pray, sir,' urged the manager, 'go on. The men have rehearsed the scene, and you will find it all right.' In vain I represented that the men could not carry off the dead Roman. 'Oh yes, indeed, sir,' reiterated the manager, 'they perfectly understand it.' There was nothing for it but submission. After some delay the scene was drawn up, and disclosed the trio as described. On I went, and uttered my lamentation over the prostrate veteran; but when I gave the order, 'Take up the dead body; bear it to the camp,' to my agony and horror, the two men, stooping down, put each an arm under the shoulder of the dead Dentatus, raised him upon his feet—he preserving a corpse-like rigidity, his eyes closed, and his head thrown back—and arm-in-arm the trio marched off at the opposite side of the stage, amid roars of laughter of the convulsed spectators."

"MY FACE IS MY FORTUNE."

LISTON was a remarkably ugly man. Once he played the character of the Elder Figaro in *The Two Figaros*, and it fell to his lot to speak the tag of the piece which included an adaptation of two well-known lines of Pope. The audiences of those days had some slight acquaintance with literature, though the opportunity of being erudite in music-hall matters was denied them; and when Liston came forward and said—

"If to my share some human failings fall,"

the house, ever recognisant of the actor's grotesqueness of features, and knowing the second line of the quotation, burst into roars of laughter that lasted some minutes. Not a muscle of his countenance did Liston move, not an attempt did he make to go on, till perfect quiet was restored; and then he spoke, with most correct intonation, gravely, and as if there was or could be nothing comic in the application, the second line—

"Look in my face, and you'll forget them all."

THE DEATH OF MOLIÈRE.

THE chief personage in one of Molière's best plays, *Le Malade Imaginaire*, is a hypochondriac who pretends to be dead. On the fourth night of the performance of this piece, Molière represented that character, and consequently, in one of the scenes, was obliged to act the part of a dead man. "It has been said," continues Bayle, from whom I take this account, "that he expired during that part of his play where he is told to make an end of his feint; but he could neither speak nor arise, for he was dead." But it is said, in the *Life of Molière's Wife*, from whom Bayle quotes farther on, that this sudden attack commenced in the part "when he speaks of rhubarb and senna, in the scene with the physicians; when, blood pouring from his mouth, to the great terror of the spectators and his friends, he was immediately carried home, when he expired a few hours after." On this occasion, the following smart epitaph was written:—

"Ci-git qui parut sur la scène
Le singe de la vie humaine;
Qui n'aura jamais son égal;
Qui voulant de la mort ainsi que de la vie
Etre l'imitateur dans une comédie,
Pour trop bien reussir y reussit fort mal;
Car la mort en étant ravie,
Trouva si belle la copie,
Qu'elle en fit un original."

HOW TO PREVENT A PANIC.

THE facetious Joe Hall, the original Lockit in *The Beggar's Opera*, in the year 1739, when the scene-room at Covent Garden was on fire and the audience greatly alarmed, was ordered by Rich, the manager, to run on the stage and explain the matter, which honest Joe did in the following extraordinary address:—"Ladies and gentlemen, for heaven's sake, don't be frightened; don't stir—keep your seats. The fire is almost extinguished; but if it was *not*, we have a reservoir of one hundred hogsheads of water over your heads, that would drown you all in a few minutes."

A PRETTY COMPLIMENT.

HAYDN, the composer, was a great admirer of the silver-toned Mrs. Billington. When Sir Joshua Reynolds showed him his celebrated picture of this lady, where she is represented as St. Cecilia listening to the heavenly choir, he observed, "It is a very fine likeness, but there is a strange mistake in the picture. You have painted her listening to the angels; you ought to have represented the angels listening to *her*."

SHYLOCK'S DOG.

IN 1838 an actor at a small theatre in the Bull-ring, Birmingham, tried a novel experiment to obtain a good house for his benefit. Round the neck of his dog he tied a label, with the words "Come and see, to-night! Bow, wow! Only sixpence." This and the actor dressed in Shylock's gaberdine paraded the streets, and certainly drew attention, if not a full house.

"HAMLET" IN HAMBURG.

IN 1776 Shakespeare's *Hamlet* was played in German in Hamburg. The play was thus announced by Herr Tegener: "*Hamlet, Prince of Denmark; or, the Comedy in the Comedy*," which was followed by this note: "To-day the *Connaisseur* cries, to old and young, 'Listen, listen to Hamlet's nervous thoughts. But all, all of you be attentive, so that you lose nothing of their beauty by unbearable noise. (*Nota Bene.*—The three actors in the little comedy are extra players.) Madame Gödel will to day, in the part of Ophelia, show the great effect of which the art of acting is capable; and Herr Gödel will excite enthusiasm by his masterly acting as Hamlet; the director, in the difficult part of the Ghost, will also show himself not unworthy the applause of a highly gracious audience. Oh, excellent public, come and see! Then you will find what a difference it makes when *Hamlet* is played by real actors or by bunglers, and when care is bestowed on dress and decorations." The Herr Director seems, however, to have been less successful as the Ghost than he had anticipated, for we hear that, owing to some defect in the machinery by which the Ghost was to disappear, the director—a bullet-headed, fat little man—remained suspended in mid-air, kicking, and vainly endeavouring to descend into the "vasty deep," amidst shouts of laughter of the audience.

AMENITY.

FOR many years there was a bitter feeling between Macklin and Quin, and the latter occasionally made very bitter remarks on his brother comedian. One of the most ill-natured things perhaps Quin ever said of Macklin, and to his face, was upon the following occasion. When Macklin brought his tragedy of *Henry VII.; or, the Popish Impostor* on the stage,

Quin told him it would not succeed. The event turning out pretty nearly as he had predicted, Quin said, "Well, sir, what do you think of my judgment now?" "Why, I think," says Macklin, "posterity will do me justice." "I believe they will, sir," replied Quin; "for now your play is only damned, but posterity will have the satisfaction to know that both play and author met with the same fate."

"HE WOULD [NOT] IF HE COULD."

A CURIOUS circumstance occurred when Templeton was singing *Elvino* to Mademoiselle Malibran's *Amina*. Templeton one evening, observing that Malibran treated him in a most unbecoming and rude manner, even while on the stage, asked advice of the manager as to the line of conduct he should pursue. He was advised to call upon the *diva*, state his feelings and ask if he had committed any offence that had incurred her displeasure. He did so next morning, when her reply, between an inclination to laugh and a disposition to be serious, was—"I thought you wanted, sir, to kiss me." At this moment, when she was the idol of the people, when peers would have given their coronets to press only the tips of her fingers, the Scottish songster alone remained calm. "Gude God," he exclaimed, "is that all! Make your mind easy; I would na kiss you for ony consideration;" and shaking hands, he left the house.

STAGE WHISPERS.

MRS. FANNY KEMBLE, in the journal of her tour in America, gives an amusing account of a performance of the last scene of *Romeo and Juliet*, with the whispered communications exchanged by the actors. Romeo, at the words "Quick, let me snatch thee to thy Romeo's arms," pounced upon his play-fellow, plucked her up in his arms, "like an uncomfortable bundle," and staggered down the stage with her. Juliet whispered, "Oh, you've got me up horridly! That 'll never do. Let me down; pray let me down!" But Romeo proceeds, with Shakespeare—

"There, breathe a vital spirit on thy lips,
And call thee back, my soul, to life and love!"

Juliet continues to whisper, "Pray put me down; you'll certainly throw me down if you don't set me on the ground directly." "In the midst of 'Cruel, cursed fate,' his dagger fell out of its sheath. I, embracing him tenderly, crammed it back again, because I knew I should want it at the end." The performance thus went on:—

"*Romeo.* Tear not my heartstrings thus!
They break! they crack! Juliet! Juliet!
[*Dies.*"

By-play, in whispers:

"*Juliet* (*to corpse*). Am I smothering you?

"*Corpse.* Not at all. But could you, do you think, be so kind as to put my wig on again for me? It has fallen off.

"*Juliet* (*to corpse*). I'm afraid I can't; but I'll throw my muslin veil over it. You've broken the phial, haven't you.

"*Corpse nodded.*

"*Juliet* (*to corpse*). Where's your dagger?

"*Corpse* (*to Juliet*). 'Pon my soul, I don't know."

AN ILL-BEHAVED CORPSE.

AS Congreve's *Mourning Bride* was being represented one night at the Smock Alley Theatre, Dublin, Mossop acted Osmin, and a subordinate actor Selim. Selim, stabbed by Osmin, should have remained dead on the stage; but, seized with a fit of coughing, he unluckily put up his hand and loosened his stock, which set the audience in a burst of laughter. The scene over, the enraged Mossop railed at his underling for daring to appear alive when he was dead; to which the man replied, that he must have choked had he not done as he did. Mossop retorted, "Sir, you should choke a thousand times rather than spoil my scene."

POLITE TOMMY HULL.

"TOMMY" HULL, the acting manager of Covent Garden, was always put forward to make announcements or apologies to the audience. In consequence of these duties he had acquired a habit of framing all his speeches in the precise style of his theatrical apologies. A ludicrous circumstance happened during the time when mobs nightly paraded the streets, on the occasion of Admiral Keppel's acquittal of the charges brought against him by Sir Hugh Palisser. Hull one night gave the mob in Martlett Court, Bow Street, where he then resided, a barrel of porter, and moblike, as soon as they had drank it, they began to break his windows in order to get more. Mr. Hull addressed the crowd in precisely the same urbane and gentlemanly tone and manner which he always so naturally assumed on the stage. "Ladies and gentlemen, I lament exceedingly to be under the necessity of offering an apology this evening; but I am obliged to state that all the *strong* beer has disappeared, and in this predicament, having at a very short notice procured a cask of *small*, we hope to *meet with your usual indulgence.*"

A VOICE FROM THE PIT.

MOODY early in life, before he went on the stage, had been to Jamaica, and worked his passage home as a sailor before the mast. One night, some time after he had been engaged at Drury Lane, when he was acting Stephano in the *Tempest*, a sailor in the front row of the pit got up, and, standing upon the seat, hallowed out, "What cheer, Jack Moody; what cheer, messmate?" This unexpected address rather astonished the audience. Moody, however, stepped forward, and, recognizing the man, called out, "Tom Hullet, keep your jawing tacks aboard; don't disturb the crew and passengers. When the show is over make sail for the stage door, and we'll finish the evening over a bowl of punch; but till then, Tom, keep your locker shut." When the play ended, Moody was as good as his word, and adjourned with his former messmate to the Black Jack, in Claremarket, where they spent a jolly night over sundry bowls of arrack punch.

DUMAS "KEAN."

THE elder Dumas has written much glorious nonsense, but his drama of *Kean, ou Désordre et Génie* ranks among his wildest productions. The hero is Edmund Kean, most erratic and most miserable of Mother Carey's chickens; and Dumas, with a truly Parisian disregard for exact facts, makes Kean indeed a tragedy hero. He lays the scene of the tragedian's glory at Covent Garden instead of Drury Lane; represents him a perfect Don Juan in the *beau monde*;* exhibits him as disputing the heart of the Countess Kefield, lady of the Danish ambassador, with no less a personage than the Prince of Wales, who—notwithstanding he is characterized as his intimate friend—for interfering with his Royal Highnesses's pleasurable pursuits, banishes him to America for one year. Thither the incorrigible Kean carries off the richest of English heiresses, yclept Miss Anna Danby: while in some intermediate scenes Kean is represented as challenging Lord Melville to

* The real Edmund's attachments to the fair sex were sufficiently numerous, though not always of quite so disastrous a nature as that to the wife of Alderman Cox. They all commenced with one love-letter; he had a circular, in fact, which he despatched to the successive objects of his affection. It may be added that Frederick Lemaitre was the original "Edmund Kean," and played the character, which was not unlike his own, to perfection. Sarah Bernhardt, in 1868, impersonated "Anna Danby," the heroine of the play.

mortal combat in a public-house ; as consenting to play Falstaff for a brother actor's benefit ; as addressing the audience after the fashion in which the king addresses his parliament, "My lords and gentlemen ;" and, to crown all, Kean's servant brings him a glass of—*eau sucré*. Now, Kean respected "a bumper of good liquor" as much as any subject in his majesty's dominions, and the chances are that if his servant had brought him a glass of *eau sucré* without adding thereto a considerable quantity of *eau de vie*, Kean would have broken every bone in the varlet's body.

A PROFESSIONAL BEAUTY.

THE remarkable beauty of Sophia Baddeley had obtained the early recognition of the public, and was long held to be almost a matter of general interest. When, in 1771, Foote produced his comedy of *The Maid of Bath*,* at the Haymarket, Mrs. Baddeley, by desire of the manager, occupied a prominent position in a box near the stage. About the middle of the play Foote, in the character of *Flint*, descanting upon the charms of the heroine, advanced to the footlights and exclaimed, "Not even the beauty of the nine Muses, nor even of the divine Baddeley herself, who is sitting here"—pointing to her box—"could exceed that of the Maid of Bath." This extravagance is said to have drawn extraordinary applause from all parts of the house. The actor was encored, and even called upon to repeat the words three times. The "divine Baddeley" affected to be confused ; she rose, and curtsied to the audience, and it was nearly a quarter of an hour before she could sit down again, the plaudits lasting so long. Her face was suffused with blushes, which remained apparent the whole evening ; for Mrs. Baddeley was not, we are assured, "according to the fashion of modern beauties, made up by art—she never used any rouge but on the

* A play based on the romantic incidents of the marriage of Sheridan with the beautiful Miss Linley.

stage." Her beauty, however, soon waned, her health gave way, she became very lame, was reduced to poverty, and died in Edinburgh, in 1786, the cost of her pauper's funeral being defrayed by the Edinburgh theatrical company.

IMPRISONMENT WITH HARD LABOUR.

TWO days previous to the first performance of *The Critic*, Sheridan had not written the last act. Dr. Ford and Mr. Linley, the joint proprietors of Drury Lane, began to be nervous and fidgety, and especially King, who was not only the stage-manager, but had to play a part in the piece. At last a night rehearsal of *The Critic* was ordered, and Sheridan, having dined with Linley, his brother-in-law, was prevailed upon to go to the theatre. While they were on the stage, King whispered to him that he had something particular to communicate, and begged he would step into the greenroom. Sheridan went, and there found a good fire, an armchair, and a table, with pens, ink, and paper, besides two bottles of claret and a dish of anchovy sandwiches. The moment he entered the room King left it, and locked the door, whilst Linley and Ford came up and told the author that, until he had finished the play, he would be kept where he was. Sheridan took the *ruse* in good part, finished the wine, the sandwiches, and the play, and was amused at the ingenuity of the contrivance.

AWFUL VISITORS.

AFTER the dreadful accident at Sadler's Wells, in 1807, during the run of *Mother Goose*, when twenty-three people were trodden to death, owing to a false alarm of fire, Joe Grimaldi met with a singular adventure. On running back to the theatre that night, he found the crowd of people collected round it so dense as to render approach by the usual path impossible. Filled with anxiety, and determined to ascertain the real state of the case, he ran round to the opposite bank of the New River, plunged in, swam across, and, finding the parlour window open and a light at the other end of the room, threw up the sash and jumped in, Harlequin-fashion. What was his horror, on looking round, to discover that there lay stretched in the apartment no fewer than nine dead bodies! These were the remains of nine human beings, lifeless and scarcely yet cold, whom a few hours back he had been himself exciting to shouts of laughter.

BIBLICAL CRITICISM.

AT the period when Mr. Morton was reader and "examiner of plays" to Drury Lane Theatre, a very popular author sent an adaptation of Halevy's opera of *La Tentation* under the title of *Temptation* to Alfred Bunn, the manager. He dispatched it to Morton, who, after examining it, returned the MS. together with his opinion on its merits, in the following humourous example of laconism: "Dear Bunn,—By not leading you into *Temptation*, I shall *deliver you from evil.* Truly yours.—T. M."

A SUPERFINE BULL.

THE first night of *The Stratford Jubilee* in Dublin, Robert Mahon had to sing the song of Shakespeare's Mulberry Tree, composed by the elder Dibdin, commencing with the words—

"Behold this fair goblet was carved from the tree
Which, oh! my sweet Shakespeare, was planted by thee."

He walked on, and began the song, holding in his hand a fine cut-glass rummer. The public looked at this "fair" glass "goblet" "carved from a tree" with much mirth, and soon hisses commenced. When the play was over Mahon had the folly to insist that he was right. "'Tis true," he said, "the property-man did stand at the wing with a wooden cup in his hand, which he wanted to thrust into mine; but could I appear before the audience with such a rascally vulgar thing in my hands? No; I insisted he should that instant go and fetch me an elegant glass rummer, and here it is."

A GOD FROM THE CLOUDS.

IT is told of one Walls, who was the prompter of a Scottish theatre, and occasionally appeared in minor parts, that he once directed a maid-of-all-work, employed in the wardrobe department of the theatre, to bring him a gill of whisky. The night was wet, so the girl, not caring to go out, intrusted the commission to a little boy who happened to be near. The play was *Othello*, and Walls played the Duke. The scene of the senate was in course of preparation; Brabantio had just stated—

> "My particular grief
> Is of so flood-gate and o'erbearing a nature,
> That it engluts and swallows other sorrows,
> And it is still itself."

And the Duke, obedient to his cue, inquired—

> "Why, what's the matter?"

when the little boy appeared upon the stage, bearing a pewter measure, and exclaimed, "Please, sir, it's just the whisky; and I could na git ony at fourpence, so yer awn the landlord a penny; and he says it's time you was payin' what's doon i' the buik." The senate broke up, amidst the uproarious laughter of the house.

EMPEROR AND PLAYERS.

WHILST Emperor Joseph II. was at Schoenbrunn, he had a first-rate French company performing there. They occupied apartments in the palace, and a plentiful table was allotted them. One day, while they were drinking their wine and abusing it, the Emperor passed by their dining-room, which opened into the imperial gardens. One of the gentlemen, with the innate modesty so peculiarly belonging to many individuals of his nation and profession, jumped up from the table with a glass of wine in his hand, followed his Majesty, and exclaimed, "Sire, I have brought your Majesty some of the thrash which is given us by your purveyor by way of wine. We are all disgusted at this treatment, and beg to request your Majesty to order something better, for it is absolutely impossible to drink it. He says it is Burgundy; do taste it, sire, I am sure you will admit it is not." The Emperor, with great composure, tasted the wine. "I think it excellent," he said; "at least, quite good enough for *me*, though perhaps not sufficiently good for *you* and your companions. In France, I dare say, you will get much better." He therewith turned on his heel, and sending for the grand chamberlain, ordered the whole *corps dramatique* to be discharged and expelled Vienna forthwith.

FOOTE'S OPINION ON GARRICK.

FOOTE had a low opinion of Garrick's literary abilities. He once received an anonymous letter, which pointed out to him a certain French play as an excellent subject for his theatre. The letter was well written, and contained quotations which proved classical learning in the writer. Somebody suggested that it had been penned by Garrick. "Oh no," replied the wit; "it is not Garrick's style, and I will prove this like Scrub. First, I am sure it's not Garrick's, because there is Greek in it; secondly, I am sure it is not Garrick's, because there is Latin in it; and thirdly, I am sure it is not Garrick's, because there is English in it."

AN OBSTINATE SKELETON.

AT the first production of *Blue Beard* at Drury Lane, in 1798, when the wife-murderer was slain by Selim, a most ludicrous scene took place. Whilst Blue Beard disappeared under the stage a skeleton rose, which, when seen by the audience, was to sink down again. But not one inch would that skeleton move. Kelly, the composer of the piece, who as Selim had just been killing Blue Beard, and whose blood was still up, gallantly ran with his drawn sabre, and pummelled the skeleton's skull with all his might, vociferating until it disappeared, loud enough to be heard by the whole house, "Down you go, d—n you! Why don't you go down?" The audience were in roars of laughter at this ridiculous scene, but good-naturedly appear to have entered into the feelings of an infuriated composer.

REALISM.

REALISM is a very good thing in its way, but it can be overdone, as appears from an instance in the *Memoirs of Ifland*. Whilst that celebrated actor was engaged at the theatre of Gotha, the stage-manager one summer night took a stroll with a friend, after the performance. It happened that they were at the foot of an ancient village steeple, just as the clock struck midnight. The play announced for the next day was *Hamlet*, and it struck them that the monotonous beating of the pendulum, and the gnarring sound of the wheels before the hour strikes, would make a very good and novel effect in the ghost scene. Consequently, next morning the machinist received instructions to imitate these sounds in the scene on the battlements; but it was omitted to communicate this novelty to the actors. So when the ghost stalked on the stage, a dismal and monotonous ticking began to accompany the speeches. Hamlet stared, the ghost looked uneasily round, Horatio and his friends sought for the cause, the audience began to smile. The machinist meanwhile steadily continued his exertions. The noise and the laughter increased, and the voices of the actors were completely drowned by this gigantic dead watch. On being spoken to, the machinist was inflexible, and pleaded his instructions, beating jealously all the time his two iron rods on a board. At last, when in addition to this the wheels began to creak and crunch, the ghost, unable to converse under such trying circumstances, returned whence he came, and the curtain fell, under storms of laughter and hisses.

ACTING OFF THE STAGE.

THE return of Palmer, the actor, to Drury Lane, after his secession to the Royalty, was a subject of importance to himself and to Sheridan, then manager of that theatre. Palmer made quite a scene of it. After his profound bow, he approached the author of *The School for Scandal* with an air of penitent humility, his head inclined, the white of his eyes turned up, his hands clasped together, and his whole air exactly that of Joseph Surface before Sir Peter Teazle. "My dear Mr. Sheridan," he begun, "if you could but know what I feel at this moment——" Sheridan, with inimitable readiness, stopped him. "Why, Jack, you forget; *I wrote it.*" Palmer, in telling this story, added that the manager's wit cost him something. "For," said he, "I made him add three pounds per week to the salary I had before my desertion."

CURSING DRAMAS.

AFTER Miss Bateman had, some years ago, aroused enthusiasm in certain quarters by her accomplished cursing in the drama of *Leah*, several pieces were written for her, in which her part consisted almost exclusively of curses. Thus she was, according to one dramatist, to ask a passer-by if he could kindly tell her the way to Regent Street; and when he smilingly replied, "You must take the first turning to the right, and go straight on," she was to answer, "Then may all the curses of an outraged woman," etc. With a good "square" curse in every scene, it was estimated that the drama must go better than *Leah*, which only had one curse in it really worth talking about.

SUCCESSFUL "GAG."

"POTIER, the famous comedian," writes Mr. Dutton Cook, in his *Book of the Play*, "was playing the leading part in a certain vaudeville, and was required, in the course of the performance, to sit at the table of a cheap café, and consume a bottle of beer. The beer was brought him by a mute performer in the character of a waiter, charged with the simple duty of drawing the cork from the bottle, and filling the glass of the customer. Potier was struck with the man's neat performance of his task, and especially with a curious comical gravity which distinguished his manner, and often bestowed upon the humble actor an encouraging smile or a nod of approval. The man at length urged a request that he might, as he poured out the beer, be permitted to say a few words. Potier sanctioned the gag. It moved the laughter of the audience. Potier gagged in reply, and there was more laughter. During subsequent representations the waiter was allowed further speeches, relieved by the additional gag of Potier, until at the end of a week it was found that an entirely new scene had been added to the vaudeville. Eventually the conversation between Potier and the waiter—not a line of which had been written or contemplated by the dramatist—became the chief attraction of the piece. It was the triumph of gag. The super, from this modest and accidental beginning of his career as an actor, speedily rose to be famous. He was afterwards known to the world as Arnal, one of the most admirable of Parisian comic actors."

"OLD HEADS AND YOUNG HEARTS."

NOT only did boys anciently enact women's parts, but they also played old men. Thus one Nathaniel Pavy, a boy who died in his thirteenth year, after having acted for three years, was so admirable a delineator of old men that Ben Jonson elegantly says the Fates *thought* him one, and, therefore cut the thread of his life. Ben's elegy on the death of this poor little fellow, for sweetness and tenderness, quite equals Catullus' complaint about Lydia's favourite sparrow :

"Weep with me all you that read
This little song ;
And know for whom a tear you shed
Death's self is sorry.

"'Twas a child that did so thrive
In grace and feature,
That heaven and nature seemed to strive
Which own'd the creature.

"Years he numbered scarce thirteen,
When Fates turn'd cruel ;
Yet three fill'd zodiacs had he been
The stage's jewel.

"And did act, what now we bemoan,
Old men so duly ;
As sooth the Parcæ thought him one,
He play'd so truly."

LIFE-STUDIES.

IT is told of Mrs. Siddons, that one day as she was passing in her carriage through St. Giles's, she saw two Irish vixens fighting. The tragedian ordered her coachman to stop, much to the amazement of the lady who was her companion on the occasion. Mrs. Siddons attentively watched the fight till its termination, when she told her servant to drive on. "You are astonished," she said to her friend, "at my stopping to witness a vulgar street-fight. But you must know I have never been satisfied that I exactly had caught the true facial expression for Lady Macbeth, when she talks of dashing out the brains of her babe. Now, one of those women struck me as having exactly the expression required, and I am determined to try it to-night, as I have to play the character." She did, and the effect electrified the audience.

LIKE CURETH LIKE.

PATERSON, a provincial actor of the last century, once pressed a brother actor for the repayment of a sum of two shillings, long due. "Let a fellow alone," was the reply; "I am sure to pay you ere long in some shape or other." Paterson answered good-humourously, "I shall be obliged to you to let it be as much *like two shillings* as you can."

SWEET DUCKS.

OLD Barry, the Dublin prompter, was an eccentric old humourist, who was on intimate terms with the most easy, impudent, and familiar audience of that theatre, and with the *habitués* of the shilling gallery. During the run of *Tom and Jerry*, which was played in Dublin some fifty or more nights successively, Barry's originally white Russia duck trousers, which he had continued to wear night after night, began to assume a rather dusky shade, indicating their long separation from soap and water. At last, when these long-enduring pants made their appearance about the twentieth night still encasing Barry's legs, one of the *habitués* cried out from the gallery, "Whist! Barry, you divil!" "What do you want, you blackguard?" said Barry, nothing moved by a style of address to which he was accustomed. "Wait till I whisper you," said the voice from above, whilst all were silent. "When did your *ducks* take the water last!" The house was uproarious, and the next night Barry's Russia-ducks were white as snow.

QUIN'S APOLOGY.

QUIN was one day stopped in the street by a person he had offended. "Mr. Quin," said he, "I—I—I understand, sir, you have been taking away my character!" "What have I said, sir?" "You—you—you called me a scoundrel, sir?" "Keep your character, sir," said Quin, and walked on.

BANNISTER'S BALCONIES.

IN 1797 Bannister removed from Frith Street to No. 2, Gower Street. It will be observed that this house is the only one in Gower Street which has balconies to the drawing-room windows. These had been constructed by order of Bannister, in violation, perhaps, to some clause in the building lease. The parish authorities, having no authority at all, came to remonstrate, alleging that it was contrary to an Act of Parliament. Bannister dumbfounded the dignity of the churchwarden by saying, "Sir, I have studied acts of plays, but I have never meddled with Acts of Parliament." The spiritual and temporal officer, for such is a churchwarden, retreated, and as the Duke of Bedford, or his agent, never took up the important question, the balconies remain even unto this day.

AN EYE TO BUSINESS.

MR. THORNTON, the manager of a provincial troupe, skilfully combined the duties of actor and manager. It was his general practice to take the money at the pit door, another actor officiating at the boxes. One evening, whilst he was committing a dramatic homicide on Richard III., the half-price was coming on. Thornton was never in the sublimest of his histrionic illusions, altogether so enveloped in Shakespeare that he forgot himself. His vigilant eye was cocked on the pit-entrance, to see that his substitute fulfilled his duties, or that the unprincipled villagers did not confound their individuality and pass in a group. He had concluded the soliloquy in the tent scene, and rousing at the words of Catesby, repeated the line, "Shadows, avaunt! you threaten here in vain!" when he suddenly espied a swain stealing in unobserved. The interest of Richard's situation was instantly forgotten in his own, and pointing at the offender, he exclaimed, "That man in the grey coat came in without paying!" He then subjoined, with a burst of truly rational triumph, "Richard is himself again."

A SENSATIONAL THEATRE.

"THE new theatre in Natchez," says Sol Smith, the American comedian, speaking about A.D. 1828, "was situated at the extreme end of the main street and in a graveyard. Two hundred yards of the street leading to it had been cut through 'this last receptacle of humanity,' and every day, in going to rehearsal, our sights were regaled with leg-bones sticking horizontally out of the earth ten or twelve feet above us, the rain having gradually washed away the clay and left them exposed. The dressing-rooms for the gentlemen were under the stage, where the earth was excavated to make rooms. Human bones were strewn about in every direction. The first night the lamplighter, being a little 'pushed' for time to get all ready, seized upon a skull, and sticking two tallow candles in the eye-sockets, I found my dressing-room thus lighted. In digging the grave in *Hamlet*, I experienced no difficulty in finding bones and skulls "to play at loggats with."

A HARMLESS WEAPON.

MISS O'NEIL, subsequently Lady Wrixon Becher, was playing her famous Juliet at Belfast. In the final tomb-scene, the property-man had forgotten to place a dagger for Juliet to stab herself when she finds her Romeo dead. What was she to do? how to kill herself? She clenched her hand, feigned to stab her fair bosom with an imaginary weapon, and died with her lover. Such was the respect of the audience for the great actress, that they took no notice of this anomaly until the curtain fell. Then, and only then, the long pent-up laughter burst from boxes, pit, and gallery.

MR. TOOLE'S GLOVES.

"SOME of my critics," observes Mr. Toole, "say that long-fingered Berlin gloves play very many powerful parts in my *repertoire*, but I will let that pass. There must be jealousy and envy in this wicked world. Many a good laugh have I got out of a good long-fingered greengrocer's glove as a muddled and puzzled waiter. But, bless you, it is not the glove that gets the laugh, but the art that arranges the fingers into comic attitudes. So long as the public laughs, I shall stick to the gloves as long as they stick to me."

BOY-ACTRESSES.

PREVIOUS to the time when actresses were admitted on the English stage, all the female characters were impersonated by boys and men, and to this the comparative insignificance of Shakespeare's heroines, and many of their peculiar characteristics, are frequently attributed. Such a boy-actress is to be found among the theatrical company Hamlet welcomes at Elsinore. "What, my lady and mistress!" says the young prince, "By'r Lady! your ladyship is nearer to heaven than when I saw you last, by the length of a *chopine.** Pray God your voice, like a piece of uncurrent gold, be not cracked within the ring," alluding to the curious, unequal sound of a boy who attains the age of puberty. So in George Chapman's Mask, *The Gentleman Usher*, 1606, Sarpego apprises the spectators—

> "Women will ensue,
> Which I must tell you true
> No women are indeed;
> But pages, made for need
> To fill up women's places,
> By virtue of their faces
> And other hidden graces."

The Puritans early took exception at the enormity of men attired like women. Dr. Reynolds, of Queen's College, for instance, was greatly shocked at the performance of a play at Christ Church, and, in 1593, published *The Overthrow of Stage Plays*. In this tedious invective he was especially severe upon "The sin of boys wearing the dress and affecting the air of women." Tom Nash, in his *Pierce Penniless*, again, praises the stage for not having, as they had abroad, women-actors—courtezans he called them; whilst the notorious Prynne, in his *Histriomastix*, cannot find words of abuse in sufficient quantity to express his horror at the appearance of women on the stage. After the death of Charles I., however, Prynne, disgusted with the violence of the parliamentary party, recanted, and, in his *Defence of Stage Plays*, proposed that women parts should be taken by women, and maintained that men's putting on of women's apparel was not warranted by Scripture.

It may be that the invectives of the Puritans against boys in woman's clothes helped to a change they would have regarded as still more deplorable—the appearance of female performers. At all events, we hear of a Mrs. Colman acting Ianthe in the

* A lady's high-heeled slipper.

first part of Davenant's *Siege of Rhodes*, in 1656. Immediately preceding the civil war, however, there were several male performers who distinguished themselves in this line of acting. Stephen Hammerton, who played at Blackfriars in the reign of James and the first years of Charles I., was then dead; he is stated to have been "a most noted and beautiful woman-actor." But there still were Burt, Shatterell, Clunn, Mohun, Charles Hart, and others. The latter was grandnephew of Shakespeare, and grandson of the poet's sister Joan.* He was celebrated for his impersonation of the Duchess in Shirley's tragedy of *The Cardinal.* Burt distinguished himself at the Blackfriars and Cockpit Theatres as Clariana in *Love's Cruelty.* In the Duke of Buckingham's play of *The Rehearsal*, one Abraham Ivory is mentioned, and the key to that work tells us that Ivory had formerly been "a considerable actor of woman's parts, but he afterwards stupified himself so far with drinking strong waters that he was fit for nothing but to go errands, for which and for mere charity the company allowed him a weekly salary." There was also one Alexander Goffe, "the woman-actor at Blackfriars." Of this man nothing is known but that, on the occasion of the furtive performances which occasionally took place at some distance from London, in the time of Oliver Cromwell, he used to make himself known to the persons of quality who patronized the plays, and give them notice of the time when, and the place where, the next representation would come off. At one of these performances, in 1655, Andrew Pennycuick played the heroine of Davenport's *King John.*

The ordinance of 1647 closed the theatres for nearly fourteen years; the boy-actors, with their elder *confrères*, took sides with the king, and several of them obtained commissions. Michael Mohun became a captain, and, after the death of Charles I., served in Flanders, when he held the rank of major. Hart was a lieutenant of horse in Prince Rupert's regiment, Burt a cornet

* The grandson of this player was alive at Stratford about the beginning of this century.

in the same, and Shatterell quartermaster. When the king had "his own again," the performers who, prior to the civil war, had personated the heroines of the drama, were too mature both in years and aspect to resume the tender office. As the prologue which introduced the first actress observed—

> "For, to speak truth, men act that are between
> Forty and fifty, wenches of fifteen."

And elsewhere—

> "Doubting we should never play agen,
> We have played all our women into men."

It is, therefore, not impossible that the happy consummation may have originated from necessity as much as choice; but, as the supply of actresses could not all at once keep pace with the demand, some of the lady-players of the old dispensation re-appeared for a while. It is thus that, after the Restoration, the gratifying spectacle was witnessed of "Major" Mohun—this title was always awarded him in the playbill—appearing as Bellamante, one of the heroines of Shirley's tragedy of *Love's Cruelty*. Yet at that time not less than thirty-five summers and a few campaigns had passed over the gallant major's head. This must have been a very unattractive exhibition, indeed, and an unlimited fund of *bonhomie* and good-humour was requisite in the spectators to accept the imperfect illusion, and to make abstraction of the square shoulders and baryton voice of the martial heroine.

The inequality of the supply to the demand will also explain the phenomenon of the appearance of a new boy-actress. This was Edward Kynaston, who had been a fellow-apprentice of Betterton at Rhodes * the bookseller's at Charing Cross, and who could know nothing of the methods and artifices of performance in use among the earlier boy-actresses. As he was the last, so he was perhaps the best of all the epicene stageplayers

* This Rhodes opened the first theatre after the death of Cromwell, the Cockpit, Drury Lane.

of the past. Downes, in his *Roscius Anglicanus*, describes him as so complete a stage beauty, "that it has since been disputable among the judicious, whether any woman that succeeded him so sensibly touched the audience as he." The testimony of the well-known Clerk of the Acts is not at variance with this. In April, 1661, he records that he saw Kynaston in the *Silent Woman* in three different characters, "which he did all equally well. First, as a poor woman in ordinary clothes; then as a rich lady in fine clothes, and in them was clearly the prettiest woman in the whole house; and lastly, as a man, and then likewise did appear the handsomest man in the house." "Kynaston at that time was so beautiful a youth," writes Colley Cibber, "that the ladies of quality prided themselves in taking him with them in their coaches to Hyde Park after the play, which in those days they might have sufficient time to do, because plays then used to begin at four o'clock, the hour that people of the same rank now (1739) are going to dinner. Of this truth I had the curiosity to inquire, and had it confirmed from his own mouth in his advanced age; and, indeed, to the last of him, his handsomeness was so very little abated that even at past sixty his teeth were all sound, white, and even as one would wish to see in a reigning toast of twenty."

An amusing though well-worn anecdote is related about Kynaston in his adult age. One day that Charles II. arrived at the theatre before his usual time, the play announced being *Hamlet*, he found the *dramatis personæ* not ready to appear. His Majesty, not choosing to have as much patience as his good subjects, sent one of his attendants to learn the cause of the delay. Knowing that the best excuse he could make to the merry monarch would be the truth, the manager went to the royal box, and plainly informed the king that the "queen was not yet shaved." "Odds fish!" replied his Majesty, good-humouredly, "then we'll wait till her barber has done with her."

The constant acting of female parts does not appear to have in the least destroyed the energy, grandeur, and manliness of the style of these old actors. Hart's acting in male parts, in style and character, resembled that of the late Macready. He was grave and stately, and in characters where weight, power, and passion were requested almost unsurpassed. Betterton said he had heard a courtier of the first rank remark, that Hart might teach any king on earth how to comport himself. Of Kynaston, Cibber asserts that he was "entirely master of real majesty in some of Shakespeare's parts, as in *Henry IV.*, where every sentiment came from him as if it had been his own." And further on, "This true majesty Kynaston had so entire a command of, that when he whispered the plain words to Hotspur, 'Send us your prisoners, or you'll hear of it,' he conveyed a more terrible menace than the loudest intemperance of voice could swell to."

A STORM IN A TEACUP.

IN the reign of Charles II., two beauties, Mrs. Barry and Mrs. Boutel, performed the two rival queens in Nat Lee's *Alexander the Great.* The two stage queens competed not merely for the same lover, but also in magnificence of raiment. A warm dispute about a veil arose behind the scenes, which, by the partiality of the property-man, was decided in favour of Mrs. Boutel. This offended the haughty Roxana, and during the course of the piece their rancour became inflamed by the speeches they had to deliver. At last when Statira, on hearing that the king approached, begs the Gods to help her, Roxana, hastening the designed blow, plunged her dagger with such force that, although the point was blunted, it made its way through her rival's stays and penetrated about half an inch into the flesh. About a century later, in the reign of George II., Peg Woffington and Mrs. Bellamy had a quarrel in the same play for somewhat similar reasons.

IN CHARACTER.

NOT a bad joke was uttered by Madame Vestris to Arnold, who told her that a *ci-devant* tailor had applied to him for an engagement at the English opera house. "You had better bring him out as *pantaloon*," said the beauty, laughing.

A PHENOMENON.

MADEMOISELLE MARS, the celebrated tragedian of the Théatre Français, long remained young in voice, figure, movement, action, and expression. In the days of passports, being about to make a foreign starring tour, she was asked what age should be inserted. Her answer was "forty-one;" her son, who accompanied her, being asked what was his, replied, "Just one year older than my mother." This lady held with a grip of iron to the girlish parts she had played for forty years, and never discovered that in some parts youth is better than experience. In her mellow age somebody spoke about her playing Juliet in her youth. "*Then* I could look, but not play the part," she said; "now I can *both play and look it.*" But the public were not altogether of this opinion, and one night some gallant Frenchman threw a wreath of immortelles upon the stage at her feet, by way of a delicate hint. It was on this or on a similar occasion that the poor old actress came in self-defence to the footlights, exclaiming, "Gentlemen, Mademoiselle Maria"—her part in the play—"is but seventeen years old; Mademoiselle Mars, alas, is seventy!"

A FEMALE BOHEMIAN.

COLLEY CIBBER had one daughter, a beauty, who married Richard Charke, an eminent violin-player, but the pair soon parted company. On the death of her husband, to protect herself from creditors, she gave a small sum to an old fish-hawker who had a stall in the Fleet-market, to marry her in the precincts of the Fleet. She obtained a certificate of the marriage and quitted the man. He was poor, old, and little better than an idiot, and it would have been madness to trouble him for the debts of his wife.

Though Mrs. Charke acted with some success in the Haymarket and Drury Lane Theatres, she is far more remarkable for her strange adventures and Bohemian existence. She was a sort of English Chevalier d'Eon, delighted in going about dressed in male attire, for which she insinuated that there were mysterious reasons. She also amused herself in fencing, shooting, riding races, grooming horses, digging in gardens, and playing upon the fiddle. Mrs. Charke was everything by turn and nothing long: a strolling actress, a grocer and oil*man* in Longacre, a gentleman's *male* servant, a waiter at the Kingshead Tavern, Marylebone; she kept a puppet-show in James Street, Haymarket, again was a sausage-seller, a public-house keeper in Drury Lane, employed in Russel's puppet-show in Brewer Street, and once more keeping a public-house in Islington. One day in affluence, the next in indigence; now confined in a sponging-house, presently released by a subscription of prostitutes. In her old age she wrote a novel. At that time she lived in most squalid poverty, in a thatched hovel, surrounded by the sweepings of the Metropolis, on the outskirts of Islington. In that place her death occurred on the 6th of April, 1760.

"OH, THE WOEING OF IT."

STEPHEN KEMBLE, the brother of John, was so stout that he could play Falstaff without "stuffing." He was no genius, though he played Falstaff and Lear tolerably, and also Richard the Third. In the latter play he once involved himself in an unforeseen dilemma. Having knelt to Lady Anne to declare his love, he found himself fixed to the floor by dint of his own gravitation. In this difficulty he was compelled to lay aside the tyrant, and sue to his victim for help. "Help me up, help me up!" he exclaimed in tones painfully energetic; and it became the Christian duty of the offended Lady Anne to set her crooked-backed lover on his legs again.

A DISINTERESTED MANAGER.

TATE WILKINSON had sundry peculiar habits. During his career as manager of the York Theatre, if any member of his company had obstinately refused to listen to his advice on any particular point of acting, he would mount some night into the gallery and hiss him most strenuously, an expedient which presently brought the trifler to his senses. On one occasion, being more than usually indignant at some very slovenly exhibition on the stage, his hiss was remarkably audible. The delinquent actor seemed, however, to have friends around him, for on a cry of "Turn him out!" poor Wilkinson was unceremoniously handed down from his own gallery and ejected into the street. Notwithstanding this misadventure, he afterwards still maintained this useful and very disinterested experiment.

BIRDS OF A FEATHER.

AT the time Moody and Sankey were starring it at Exeter Hall, a well-known West End pawnbroker happened to inquire the way to the Hall from J. W. Anson, who was returning from Ransome. The comedian, recognizing the "banker of the poor," informed him where the meeting was held, adding that the revivalists would be delighted to salute in him one of their colleagues. The astonished pawnbroker objected that he thought his interlocutor made a mistake, and took him for some other person. "Oh no," replied Anson; "are you not one of those who look after the *unredeemed?*"

LOVE'S LABOUR (NOT) LOST.

IN the cemetery of Lille, in Flanders, there is a black marble monument, surrounded with yew trees, bearing the simple inscription—

"À FRANCHOME.
UNE AMIE A PASSÉ PAR LÀ."

The story of this monument is pathetic. Franchome was the name of a youth of nineteen, brother of a musician, in the orchestra of the Comic Opera, in Paris. The youth, having seen Mademoiselle Déjazet in some of her most bewitching parts, fell desperately in love with the celebrated actress, and asked her in marriage. Mademoiselle Déjazet could only offer him her friendship, and the romantic youth returned to his native city, where, unable to forget his love, he soon after committed suicide. Three years after this unfortunate catastrophe Déjazet had an engagement in Lille, and knowing the sad end of her unhappy adorer, her first visit was to the cemetery, where she inquired for his grave. The sight of it broke her heart. It was a simple wooden cross, half hidden by weeds, the inscription almost effaced by rain and sunshine. "Does nobody look after this poor tomb?" she inquired from the gravedigger who accompanied her. "Nobody," was the reply. Déjazet at once ordered a handsome monument to be erected, yew trees to be planted; and when the stone-cutter entrusted with the labour inquired what inscription he was to cut on the monument, she tore a leaf from her pocket-book and wrote on it the two lines given above, simply recording that a friend had visited the lone tomb.

GRANDILOQUENCE.

A YOUNG actor named Hamblin made his first appearance in the character of Hamlet, under the management of Elliston, at Drury Lane, one night that the actor appointed for the evening had disappointed the public. After the performance, the magnificent manager called the neophite into the greenroom, and addressed him to this effect: "Young man, you have not only pleased the public, but you have pleased *me*; and, as a slight token of my regard and good wishes, I beg your acceptance of a small piece of plate!" It was beyond any question a *very* small piece of plate, for it was a silver tooth-pick.

THE *CORPUS DELICTI.*

A WAG, seeing a parcel lying on the table in the entrance-hall of a theatre, one end of which, from its having travelled to town by the side of some game, was smeared with blood, observed, "That parcel contains a manuscript tragedy;" and on being asked how he knew, replied, "Because the *fifth act* is peeping out at one corner of it."

UNASKED SUPERS.

WHEN John Bernard was manager of the theatre at Guernsey, Sir Sydney Smith happening one day to lie with his ship off the island, promised to attend a performance. The house on this occasion was filled with the navy; the officers occupied a box, whilst the pit was entirely taken up by the crew and marines, over whom a tall boatswain presided, to "look arter" their manners and expressions. To gratify their tastes the musical farce of *The Purse* was given, which contained a sailor, Will Steady. Bernard himself enacted this hero, and on concluding the first stanza of the famous drinking song, "Tol de riddle, dol de rido," gave the toast to his messmates on the stage, "The King! with three cheers." The tall boatswain in the pit, conceiving this to be equally addressed to himself and companions, sung out, "Ay, ay, sir," and clapping his whistle to his lips, brought all the tars on their legs with an ear-splitting hurrah. At the end of the second stanza, the toast was "The Duke of Clarence and the Navy!" The boatswain piped, and the hurrahing again ensued with equal enthusiasm. Concluding the third stanza, Bernard, in accordance with the injunctions of the book, hesitated awhile, and asked his brother tars on the stage whom he should give next, when the tall boatswain leaned over the stage-rail, and replied, "Sir Sydney Smith, to be sure." There was no help for it; the whistle went to work with a will, and the shouting was ten times more uproarious than ever.

IMPROVING THE LIKENESS.

THE first night of Macklin's *True-born Irishman* in Dublin, an eccentric gentleman, who had just come to a great fortune, sat with a large party in a stage-box. When Massink came on, as Pat Fitz-Mongrel, in the rout-scene, this gentleman in the boxes cried out, "Why, that's me! but what sort of rascally coat is that they've dressed me in? Here, I'll dress you!" With that he stood up, took off his own rich gold-laced coat, and flung it on the stage. Massink took it up smiling, stepped to the wing, put it on, and then returned to the stage. This play had a great success in Dublin, but was condemned in London, which caused Macklin to say that he had neglected "the geography of humour."

THE NATIONAL ANTHEM IN ITALIAN.

MADAME CATALANI could neither speak nor read English, yet occasionally when George III. honoured Drury Lane with his presence, she had to sing one or more stanzas of "God save the King." In order to render the national hymn pronounceable for the Italian tongue of the diva, it was penned out for her in this form, which must have given the songstress a great idea of the mellifluence and majesty of our language :—

"Oh Lord avar God arais,
Scaetter is ennemais
And meche tem fôl ;
Confaund tear politichs
Frosstre tear nevise trichs,
On George avar opes ui fichs,
God seve te kin."

A CHANGE OF NAME.

WHILST Harris was manager of Covent Garden, a singer of the name of Bowden made his appearance in *Robin Hood*, a part originally taken by Charles Bannister. Bannister was present at the performance, and a person sitting next to him, vehemently applauded Bowden. Between the acts he had the bad taste to say to Bannister, "Ay, ay, sir, Bowden is the true Robin Hood, the only Robin Hood." To which Bannister replied, "Sir, he may be Robin Hood this year, but next season he will be 'robbin' Harris.'"

A DOUBLE DESDEMONA.

ON the first night when Cooper performed at Louisville, United States, the fame of the great tragedian had drawn a crowded audience, and among the rest a young country lass, whom—not knowing her real name—we will call

Peggy. Peggy had never before seen the inside of a play-house. She entered at the time Othello was making his defence before the Duke and senate. The young girl was permitted to walk, unobserved, down the lobby until she arrived at the stage-box, which she entered. Staring a moment about her as if doubting whether she was in her proper place, she cast her eyes on the stage, and observed several chairs unoccupied. It appeared to her that the people on the stage seemed more at their ease than those among whom she was standing, and withal much more sociable. Just at that moment Othello, as fate would have it, looking in the direction of the place where she stood, exclaimed, "There comes the lady." The senators half rose in expectation of seeing the "gentle Desdemona," when lo! the maiden from the country stepped from the box plump on the stage, and advanced towards the expectant Moor. It is impossible to give any idea of the confusion that followed: the audience clapped and cheered, the Duke and the senators forgot their dignity, Othello joined in the general mirth. The blushing girl was ready to sink with consternation, until some compassionate soul helped her out of her unpleasant situation. It was agreed by all present, that no lady ever made her *debût* on any stage with more *éclat* than Miss Peggy.

THEATRICALS AND GASTRONOMY.

KELLY, in his *Reminiscences*, gives an amusing picture of Tate Wilkinson. That eccentric manager of Drury Lane had a small appetite, but was a great epicure, and had taken it into his head that Kelly was an authority in culinary art. When he had taken a few glasses of Madeira, he would mix his conversation about theatricals and eatables together in a manner at once ludicrous and incomprehensible. "I was sitting with him one night," says Kelly, "in high spirits after supper, and we spoke of Barry, the actor. 'Sir,' said he, 'Barry, sir, was as much superior to Garrick in

Romeo as St. Paul's is to a Methodist chapel—not but that I think that if lobster sauce is not well made, a turbot isn't eatable, let it be ever so firm. There was Mrs. Barry; Mrs. Barry was very fine and very majestic in Zenobia; Barry in the same play was very good—not but that wild rabbits are better than tame ones. Though Mrs. Barry was so great in her day, yet Mrs. Siddons—stewed and smothered with onions, either of them are delicious.' And on he went in that manner to the end of the chapter, until he talked himself asleep."

THE VIPER AND THE FILE.

WHEN Thomas Sheridan was manager of Smock Alley Theatre, Dublin, he was told one day that a gentleman wished to speak to him; a stranger entered, seemingly much agitated. "My dear sir," he exclaimed, "I have a thousand pardons to ask you, and hope for your forgiveness!" "Sir," said Sheridan, "I have not the pleasure of knowing you. What is the nature of the offence given me?" "Oh, sir, the irreparable injuries I have done to your professional reputation!" "Indeed! but how?" "Oh, sir, by my persisting in writing you down in a much-read popular publication"—mentioning the title—"I am sure I must have hurt your mind most exceedingly." "Hurt my mind! This is the first knowledge I ever had of the circumstance. And as to injuring my personal reputation—here! bring the box-book"—calling at the door; the box-keeper brought the book—"There, sir, look," continued Sheridan, "I play this night, and, as you see, every box is taken by persons of the first rank and consequence in Dublin; therefore, pray comfort yourself, as to having hurt either my mind or my reputation."

"HOME, SWEET HOME."

THIS popular song occurs in the opera *Clari*, written by John Howard Payne, an American actor and manager, dramatist and critic. The opera was first represented at Drury Lane in 1813, and made the fortune of every one connected with it, except the author. It gained for Maria Tree, eldest sister of Charles Kean, a wealthy husband; and filled the house and treasury of Charles Kean, the manager. It was estimated in 1853 that 100,000 copies of the song had been sold by the original publishers, whose profits two years after it was issued are said to have amounted to 2000 guineas. The author only received £30 for the whole opera. In 1832 Payne returned to America, and on the 29th of November received, at the Park Theatre, New York, the first complimentary benefit ever given by the citizens of that city. The receipts amounted to 4200 dollars. Payne was appointed consul to Tunis in 1841, and died there, April 10th, 1852, aged fifty-nine.

A PROPHECY.

CONGREVE'S brilliant comedy, *The Way of the World*, was damned offhand on the first night. The author came forward at the close, and coolly asked the audience, "Is it your intention to damn this play?" "Yes! yes! Off! off!" was the answer of the pit. "Then I can tell you," he rejoined, "that this play of mine will be a living play when you shall be all dead and damned." So far as we know, his prophecy proved true. *The Way of the World* continued one of the stock-pieces for more than a century.

THE SWORD IN THE PLAY-HOUSE.

IN December, 1702, a duel took place on the very stage of Drury Lane Theatre, between Mr. Goodyear and Beau Fielding, the well-known "Fribble" of that day. At a representation of *The Scornful Lady* for the benefit of Mrs. Oldfield, many persons of distinction were behind the scenes. Among others Beau Fielding came, and being always mighty ambitious to show his fine figure, he very closely pressed forward against some gentlemen, among whom was one Mr. Fulwood, a barrister of Gray's Inn, an acquaintance of Mrs. Oldfield's. Fulwood, being quick-tempered, told Fielding not to push him so rudely, upon which the beau laid his hand upon his sword. Fulwood drew instantly, and, apparently without any further ado, plunged his sword "twelve inches" (so says Curl, my authority for this occurrence) into Fielding's abdomen. This put the audience into great consternation, and Mr. Fulwood was with much entreaty persuaded to leave the place, which at length he did, "out of respect for Mrs. Oldfield." After this gallant feat Fulwood repaired to Lincoln's Inn Theatre, where he went into the pit, and in a very few minutes cast his eyes upon one Captain Cusack, whom he owed an old grudge. Having "his hand in" after the occurrence at Drury Lane, he there and then demanded satisfaction of Cusack. The Captain without the least hesitation obeyed the summons. They went into Lincoln's Inn Fields, and set to in good earnest. In less than half an hour word was brought into the house that Mr. Fulwood had been killed on the spot, and that Captain Cusack had made good his escape. Here we have a pleasing picture of manners in the now so-much admired time of Good Queen Anne! More sensational things than this even have been seen in the play-house. Langbaine the critic, writing in the time of Charles II., declares that he "once saw a real tragedy in the pit of Drury Lane Theatre, where Mr. Scrope received a mortal wound from

Sir. T. Armstrong, and died presently, after being removed to a house opposite the theatre."

A KIND TURN.

GEORGE BARTLEY was a sensible, unaffected actor, without any pretension to genius, but thoroughly dependable to the extent of his talent. When he first joined the Covent Garden Company, Fawcett was stage-manager, and in possession, of course, of all the best parts. One day he sent for Bartley, and said, "George, I'm going to give you a chance. Hamlet is put up for next week, and you shall play the 'First Gravedigger.' I've plenty to do, and it is but fair to give you a turn." Bartley expressed his gratitude. Fawcett shook hands with him and walked away, muttering to himself, but loud enough for Bartley to hear him, "There's a wind at night comes up that cursed grave-trap enough to cut one's vitals out!'

ASTRONOMICAL STUDIES.

DR. HERSCHEL, the astronomer, at one time was organist at the Octagon Chapel at Bath, and played an instrument in the orchestra of the theatre, whilst he occupied his leisure time with astronomical studies. One summer Mrs. Baddeley came down to Bath for a few nights, and, at the first rehearsal, when she walked in as Polly in the *Beggar's Opera*, Herschel, who had never seen her before, was so overpowered with her beauty that he dropped his fiddlestick and stared at her. When this was mentioned in the green-room, Edwin remarked, "Well, that was nothing strange ; he was *star*-gazing."

GARRICK'S OPINION OF BIRMINGHAM.

GARRICK was on a visit at Hagley, Lord Lyttelton's seat, when news came that a company of players were about to perform at Birmingham. "They will hear you are in the neighbourhood," said his lordship to Garrick, "and will ask you to write an address to the Birmingham audience." "Suppose then," replied Garrick, "I begin thus :—

'Ye sons of iron, copper, brass, and steel,
Who have not heads to think, nor hearts to feel——' "

"Oh!" exclaimed Lord Lyttelton, "if you begin thus, they'll hiss the players off the stage and pull the house down." "My lord," answered Garrick, "what is the use of an address if it does not come home to the *business* and *bosoms* of the audience?"

KEEP TO THE LAST.

FOTTEREL, or Jemmy Fotterel, as he was more familiarly called, was a great favourite with the Dublin gallery audience, and in private life notorious for his gambling propensities, which always kept him shabby and penniless. One of the terms used in Jemmy's favourite game of hazard, when the person has lost his right of throwing, is "Pass the box." One evening Jemmy had the King in *Hamlet* to play, owing to another actor's indisposition, and though a low comedian and apparently the most unfit man to assume the buskin, a stern necessity has no master. Jemmy, however, like many other comedians, had no mean opinion of his tragic powers, and resolved to electrify the audience. He took the trouble of studying that difficult speech of the King's which is generally omitted, and when the moment came, walked forward, commencing to utter it with the slow enunciation and ponderous gravity of Kemble. The audience were taken by surprise, and were silent; but a man in the gallery, who knew something of Jemmy and his habits, and had always been accustomed to see him in farce, grew uneasy at this dull exhibition, and when he saw the actor actually going to kneel down, he could not restrain his discontent, and roared out, "Oh, bother! Jemmy Fotterel, pass the box, pass the box."

HIS FAVOURITE SONG.

MR. CUSSANS was the son of an opulent West Indian merchant, and, though a gentleman of property, he was a considerable actor. He played frequently at Sadler's Wells, where he was much celebrated in the character song of "Oh! poor Robinson Crusoe." In this song he had as many encores as he pleased; and on a certain evening, having sang it three or four times, the curtain drew up for another part of the entertainment, when, to the astonishment and delight of the Sadler's Wells auditory, Cussans started up from the very centre of the shilling gallery, vigorously singing his favourite song. Nor would his admirers suffer the drama to proceed till he had again sung it twice from the same spot.

A GENTLE REPROOF.

ELLISTON was one of those who consider no behaviour towards the other sex worthy the term civility which falls short of a positive declaration of love. He used to relate a smart rebuke he once received in a stage-coach. Addressing a fair fellow-traveller in language somewhat savouring of "Young Wilding," and perceiving the lady less enraptured at his advances than he expected, he made a sort of apology, and concluded by hoping that he had not exceeded "the bounds of decorum." "Perhaps not, sir," replied she; "but your limits of decorum are so extremely uncertain, that you may possibly lose your way in the excursion."

THE JUDGMENT OF PARIS.

ONE night, while Frederick Reynolds, the dramatist, was sitting in the front row of the balcony-box at the Haymarket Theatre, during the performance of the *Son-in-Law*, in the scene of the equivoque between Cranky and Bowkit, when the former, after making objections to the other's offer to marry his daughter, observes, "Besides, you are such an ugly fellow!" "Ugly!" repeated Edwin, who played Bowkit, "ugly!" Then coolly advancing towards the footlights, he exclaimed, "Now, I submit to the decision of an enlightened British public, which is the ugliest fellow of the *three*, I, old Cranky, or"—pointing to Reynolds—"that gentleman in the front row of the balcony-box." Reynolds, seeing himself the object of scrutiny and pointing fingers, hastily fled, amidst the roars of the aforesaid enlightened British public.

THE OPERATION OF A JOKE.

JOHN KEMBLE was slow at catching a joke. One night Parsons told a rich comic story at which all laughed. Kemble alone preserved a fixed, grave, classical countenance; but when Dodd afterwards sang a pathetic ballad, which excited general interest, Kemble, in the middle of it, burst into an odd fit of laughter, and in a tone tremulous from excessive gaiety, exclaimed, "I beg your pardon, gentlemen, but I have *just taken* Parson's joke—ha, ha! and it is really—very good!"

AN INSANE OPHELIA.

MRS. MONTFORD, the widow of the actor Montford murdered by Captain Hill, had an annuity of £300 a year settled on her by Lord Berkeley, on condition that she never should remarry. Booth, the actor, asked her in marriage, but though she loved him she loved her annuity better, and refused him. Thereupon Booth married her friend Miss Santlow, a celebrated dancer and tolerable comedian, the favourite of Secretary Craggs. This marriage so shocked Mrs. Montford that she gave way to despair, which soon deprived her of her senses. In this condition she was brought to London, in order that the best advice might be procured. As she was not outrageous, even in the most violent paroxysm of her disorder, she was not placed under any rigorous confinement, and allowed to go about the house. One day, during a lucid interval, she asked her attendant what play was to be performed that evening, and was told it was *Hamlet*. In this tragedy, whilst on the stage, she had ever been received with rapture as Ophelia. The recollection struck her, and with that cunning which is often associate with insanity, she eluded the care of her keepers, and hurried to the theatre, where she concealed herself until the scene in which Ophelia enters in her insane state. She then pushed on to the stage, before the lady who had performed the previous part of the character could come up, and exhibited a more perfect rendering of madness than the utmost exertions of mimic art could effect. She was, in truth, Ophelia herself, to the amazement of the performers, and the astonishment of the audience. Nature having made this last effort, her vital powers failed her. On going off she exclaimed, "It is all over!" She was immediately conveyed back to her late place of security, where a few days after,

"Like a lily drooping, she bowed her head and died."

SOUPE GRASSE.

MONSIEUR VÉRON, director of the Académie Royale de Musique at Paris, visited this country in 1837 for the purpose of engaging Fanny and Herminie Elssler. He gave them a splendid dinner at the Clarendon, and when the dessert was put upon the table, the centre-piece was a large salver with jewelry, for each of the sisters to select one trinket from, of a given value, in addition to the theatrical engagement he offered them. It was not only an elegant, but a very politic mode of arranging business, for while they would have otherwise been disputing upon a question of a few hundred francs, a bauble or two of not half the value decided it at once. Véron's astonishment, however, at the bill for this dinner was a treat, not at its general amount--which, considering the splendour of the "spread" for sixteen guests, was very reasonable, being under £40—but at an item of £8 8*s.* for soup! He could not understand that the usual charge of half a guinea a head, when turtle is put on the table, was anything short of imposition, averring, with an ambiguous smile, that £8 8*s.* would nearly purchase all the soup in Paris.

SUDDEN DEATH.

CHARLES L. UNDERNER was the leader of the orchestra at the Trimble Opera House, Albany, United States. On January 3, 1869, he entered the musicians' room as usual, and seeing a looking-glass broken, exclaimed, "Ah! somebody is going to die! I hope it is not I." In less than half an hour afterwards he was seen, while leading the band, to drop his head. He was taken from his seat and found to be dead.

KEMBLE'S SOLEMNITY.

J. P. KEMBLE exhibited an almost regal solemnity—an exalted oddity which was most amusing, and which never forsook him for a moment under any circumstances. The contrast between his genuine seriousness and the grotesque situations in which he sometimes found himself is exceedingly diverting. Murray, the Edinburgh manager, told

Moore that when Kemble was playing Coriolanus in "Old Reekie," a raw actor forgot his part at the passage—

> "For that he . . .
> Has envied against the people, seeking means
> To pluck away their power."

And, after staring at Kemble, substituted "And that he is always going about the streets, making every one uncomfortable!" After the play the fellow apologized; but the great tragedian looked at him with ineffable scorn, and merely ejaculated the uncomplimentary monosyllable, "Beast!"

A BLACK DRAUGHT.

"ONE evening," says Mrs. Mowath, the American actress, "when I was playing Juliet, the property-man forgot the bottle containing the sleeping-potion for the fair girl of Verona. The omission was only discovered at the moment the vial was needed. Some bottle must be found for the Friar, or he cannot utter the solemn charge with which he confides the drug to the perplexed scion of the Capulets. The property-man, confused at discovering his own neglect, and fearful of the fine to which it would subject him, caught up the first small bottle at hand and gave it to the Friar. The vial was the prompter's, and contained ink. When Juliet snatched the fatal potion from the Friar's hand, he whispered something in an undertone. I caught the words 'so, take care,' but was too absorbed in my part to comprehend the warning. Juliet returns home, meets her parents, retires to her chamber, dismisses her nurse, and finally drinks the potion. At the words, 'Romeo, this I drink to thee!' I placed the bottle to my lips, and unsuspiciously swallowed down the inky draught! The dark stains upon my hands and lips might have been mistaken for the quick working of the poison, for the audience remained ignorant of the mishap, which I myself only half comprehended.

When the scene closed the prompter rushed up to me, exclaiming, 'Good gracious! you have been drinking from my bottle of ink!' I could not resist the temptation of quoting the remark of the dying wit under similiar circumstances. 'Let me swallow a sheet of blotting-paper.'"

CRITICISM DEFEATED.

ONE of the happiest retorts ever made upon a critical assailant by a badgered manager, was that given by Mr. Edward Henry to the self-sufficient representative of an obscure weekly in Manchester. Mr. Henry was at that time the manager of the Queen's Theatre, and on one occasion Byron's *Old Soldiers* was produced by a travelling company. The piece did not please our critic at all. As soon as the act-drop had descended he pounced upon Mr. Henry, vented his noble indignation, swore that he would tear the piece to tatters, annihilate its author, etc., etc. "All right," answered the manager, with the most imperturbable coolness; "we change the bill on Friday, and your paper does not appear till Saturday. Fire away, my boy."

PNEUMATICS.

ON one occasion when Mrs. Billington was singing a passage with an obligato for the trumpet, her husband, who was the conductor, thought the trumpeter might play louder, and so repeatedly urged the musician that at last the Teutonic exclaimed, "Louter! louter! eh? Mein Gott, vere is de vint to come from?"

A PROLIFIC GENIUS.

A COUNTRY manager once took upon himself to bring out Macklin's *Love à la Mode* at his theatre. Macklin wrote to him that if he attempted to do so, he would send him sheets of parchment that would reach from Chancery

Lane to the next gooseberry-bush, the nearest verge of Yorkshire to John O'Groat's house. The manager's answer to Macklin ran thus: "*Your Love à la Mode*, sir! I'm not going to play *your Love à la Mode;* I have twenty *Love à la Modes.* I could write a *Love à la Mode* every day in the week; I could write three hundred and sixty-six *Love à la Modes* in a year."

MARS AND NAPOLEON.

THE celebrated Mademoiselle Mars was a great admirer of Napoleon I., and after the emperor's return to France in 1815, she constantly wore the Napoleonic violet on some part of her dress. One of her admirers observed, "I do not wonder at it; the emperor has always considered Mars as the first of the gods." "Yes," she replied; "and Mars regards the emperor as the first of mortals." M. Papillon de Ferté, superintendent of the theatres, said to her, in a tone at once gentle and gallant, "Charming rose, when will you cease to be a violet?" "When the butterfly (*papillon*) becomes an eagle!" was the punning reply. It may be added that the admiration was mutual. Frédéric Lemaitre relates, in his *Souvenirs*, that when the troops defiled before the emperor, on his return from Elba, Mademoiselle Mars was present to witness this grand spectacle. She was perceived by the emperor, who had taken his stand under the Pavillon de l'Horloge. An aide-de-camp was at once despatched to the *tragedienne*, and when she approached, Napoleon shook her by the hand, and made her take a seat among the ladies of his court.

COOKE'S TOE-BONE.

GEORGE FREDERICK COOKE drank himself to death in New York, and was buried there. When Edmund Kean some years after visited America, he caused the body to be taken up and removed to another place, where he erected a monument over it. In the transition from the old grave to the new, Kean abstracted one of the toe-bones of the great actor, which he preserved as a relic and brought back with him to England. On his return the Drury Lane company went to meet him at Barnet, in order to grace his entry into the metropolis. Elliston led the procession, the other actors followed according to rank. On encountering Kean, they were about to welcome him, when he stopped them. "Before you say a word, my merry men," said he, with a serious air, "behold! Fall down and kiss this relic! This is the toe-bone of the greatest creature that ever walked the earth—of George Frederick Cooke. Come, down with you all, and kiss the bone." The little black relic, not unlike a tobacco-stopper, was produced. Elliston, between doubt and reverence, fell upon his knees and kissed it. Stout Stephen Kemble dropped down with difficulty; then another came, and another, and actor after actor followed, from the beginning to the end of the line, till all had performed the ceremony.

The ridiculous relic was preserved for many years by Kean with the greatest reverence, until one day Mrs. Kean, in a moment of passion, flung it from the window into a dry well in the Duke of Portland's garden, where it probably still lies up to this present writing. Kean never knew the culprit, but after a long search, he gravely and sadly observed to his wife, "Mary, your son has lost his fortune. In possessing Cooke's toe-bone he was worth £10,000; now he is a beggar."

MY LORD MAYOR'S DUCKS.

WHATEVER opinions Tate Wilkinson, the eccentric manager of Drury Lane Theatre, may have entertained of Michael Kelly's abilities, it is certain that he took it into his head that Kelly's skill in the culinary art was great. He hardly ever discussed any subjects but those of cooking and eating with him. At one time when he was making an agreement with Kelly, the latter wanted twenty guineas more than Wilkinson was willing to give. At length the manager exclaimed, "Well, young Apicius, twenty guineas shall not part us—you shall have it your own way; but confess now honestly, didn't you think the ducks were over-roasted yesterday at my Lord Mayor's?"

THE YOUTH OF A GENIUS.

COMBE, the author of *Doctor Syntax's Tours*, told Samuel Rogers, the poet, that "he recollected having seen Mrs. Siddons when a very young woman, standing by the side of her father's stage and knocking a pair of snuffers against a candlestick, to imitate the sound of a windmill, during the representation of some Harlequinade." Who dreamt then that that candlestick-rapping little girl would in after years prove such a spirit-wrapper, and that her candlestick-scene in Macbeth would one day knock so terribly at many throbbing hearts, as she muttered in her tortured sleep "to bed! to bed! to bed?"

A MODERN DIOGENES.

SOWERBY had, by sundry applications of too much "spiritual comfort," incurred the severest displeasure of the Manchester public, which they marked in a signal manner by keeping away from the theatre on his benefit night. Just as the curtain was about to rise, Sowerby went up into the gallery, carrying a lantern at the end of a pitchfork, and stumbling over the only two individuals there seated, viz. the fruit-woman and her boy, he exclaimed, "Don't be alarmed, my worthy people, I am come upon the errand of Diogenes, but with this difference in our pursuit—that he went about the world looking for an honest man, and I am looking in vain for any man at all."

BEEF AND PICKLES.

DURING Dr. Arne's residence at Thames Ditton, he received a visit from Garrick, paid chiefly with the view of hearing Miss Brent, whose musical taste the Doctor had cultivated with uncommon pains, and on whose talent he justly set a high value. Garrick readily acquiesced in her superior merit, but at the same time told Arne, that all his geese were swans. "Tommy," he said, "you should consider that music is at best but pickle to my roast beef." "By——, Davy," replied the Doctor, "your beef shall be well pickled before I have done." Miss Brent accordingly made her first appearance at Covent Garden in the *Beggar's Opera*, which ran with such success during the whole season, that the Drury Lane house was nearly deserted, except on those nights when Garrick himself appeared. Roscius had to work so hard all that winter, that he was obliged to make a journey to Italy in order to recruit his health; and at his return he thought it advisable to pickle his beef after Dr. Arne's fashion, by engaging Miss Wright as the only rival who could be opposed to Miss Brent with success.

A PART FOR THE WHOLE.

SUZANNE LAGIER was a good actress, but extremely stout. She was one night enacting a part in a melodrama with Taillade, the original Pierre of *The Two Orphans*, and this actor had at one moment to carry her fainting off the stage. He tried with all his might to lift the "fleshy" heroine, but although she helped her little comrade by standing on tip-toe in the usual manner, he was unable to move her an inch. At this juncture one of the deities cried from the gallery, "Take what you can, and come back for the rest."

"*NE TOUCHEZ PAS À LA REINE.*"

SIR RICHARD FANSHAW translated, in 1671, Mendoza's play, *Querer pro solo Querer*, under the title of *To Love for Love's sake.* The original was a Spanish court-play, in which the characters, males, giants and all, were played by ladies of the highest order of grandeeship. Appended to the drama, the length of which may be judged from its having taken nine days in the representation, is a poetical account of the fire which broke out in the theatre on one of the nights of its acting, when the whole *dramatis personæ* were nearly burnt, because the common people out of "base fear," and the nobles out of "pure respect," could not think of laying hands on the "great donnas," till the young king broke the charm of etiquette by snatching up the queen, and bore her through the flames upon his back; the grandees, dilatory Æneases, followed his example, and each saved one Anchises-fashion, till the whole courtly company were got off in tolerable safety.

LOVE AND COMEDY.

IT appears from Reid's "Biographia Dramatica; or, The Companion to the Play-house," that up to 1810 there were 243 plays in the English language, the title of which commenced with "Love" or "Lover." This is as it should be. The elder Dumas once said that in a comedy there is always a question of love and matrimony; the problem is to be worked out, whether to marry or not to marry. Will he marry her? Will she marry him? Those are the questions the interested playgoer has to ask himself when he goes to see a comedy. Somebody is on the brink of marriage, there you have the first act; in the second, an incident takes place which prevents marriage; a new method of bringing about the happy conclusion is exhibited in the third act; an obstacle arises in the fourth, which is removed; and, as everything must have an end, the fifth act terminates the play with connubial bliss all round.

BLIND AND SEEING.

CHARLES S. PORTER was the leading actor at the Old South Street Theatre in Philadelphia, in his younger days. On one occasion, the play being *The Blind Boy*, he was obliged to apologize to the audience for the young man who was to have played the Blind Boy, and another was called upon to read the part. His first appearance was on a bridge, where he was seen threading his way, with a cane in one hand and the play-book in the other. Whilst his eyes were riveted on the book, his cane was busily engaged in feeling his way. This was too ludicrous, and poor Edmund, the blind boy, had no sympathy from the audience that night. As good a sight was witnessed in London in 1668, when Kynaston, disabled by a caning received from Sir Charles Sedley's bravos, was unable to appear in *The Heiress*. Beeston had to take his part and read it. He caused considerable amusement to the pit by having for that purpose to use a candle, in a scene supposed to be acted in pitch-dark.

CASUISTRY.

WHEN G. F. Cooke was playing in Liverpool, the managers found great difficulty in keeping him sober. After repeated transgressions he solemnly promised "not to cause any more trouble, as he had given over drinking in a great measure." In the evening of the day upon which this promise was made, Cooke was not to be found when wanted for Sir Pertinax MacSycophant. The audience grew impatient, the manager stormed, and after a long search discovered him at a pot-house near the theatre, drinking with great composure and perseverance out of a small glass. On the irritated manager upbraiding Cooke with breach of his solemn promise, the incorrigible player answered with the most provoking coolness, "I certainly made that promise, and I have kept it; I *have* given over drinking *in a great measure*," and he held the small glass up triumphantly.

THE TITILLATING DUST.

THE following advertisement is a curious instance of the shifts theatrical managers had recourse to, at a time when the licensed houses alone were allowed to perform "stage entertainments." It was inserted in the papers in 1756, when Theophilus Cibber appeared at the Richmond Theatre:—

"CIBBER AND Co., snuff merchants, sell at their warehouse on Richmond Hill most excellent cephalic snuff, which, taken in moderate quantities, in the evening especially, will not fail to raise the spirits, clear the brain, throw off all ill humours, dispel the spleen, enliven the imagination, exhilarate the mind, give joy to the heart, and greatly invigorate and improve the understanding. Mr. Cibber has also opened at the aforesaid warehouse, late called the Theatre, on the Hill, an histrionic academy for the instruction of young persons of genius in the art of acting, and proposes, for the better improvement of such pupils, and frequently with his assistance, to give public rehearsals without hire, gain, or reward."

Snuff was sold in very small quantities at the various entrances, and for the money thus paid the purchaser obtained gratis admission to the hall. It may be added that it was at this theatre that Charles Dibdin, the song-writer, is said to have made his *début* as an actor, in 1762.

FEELING v. STUDY.

QUINTILIAN mentions having seen actors, after performing pathetic characters, weep for a time on laying aside their mask, and go home in tears. A still more remarkable anecdote of the manners of the ancient tragedians is transmitted to us. A tragedian, in the play of *Electra*, actually brought on the stage the urn containing the ashes of his own son, as an additional excitement in his scenic effects. Modern actors prefer to remain perfectly cool and collected. Mrs. Siddons, after rushing off the stage in apparently the most excruciating anguish, in Belvidera or Mrs. Beverley, was accustomed to walk quietly to the greenroom, thrusting up her nose enormous quantities of snuff, in perfect composure. After commending Kelly's acting in *The Deserter*, she gravely added, "But, Kelly, you *feel* too much; if you feel so strongly, you will never make an actor." Mounet Sully, of the Comédie Française, is an instance of an actor who plays by feeling, and as his feelings change from day to day, he rarely plays the same part twice alike. This is a sure sign of imperfect art, for thus a part cannot be worked out in all its details. When M. Emile Augier gave that artist the leading part in *Jean de Thommeray*, he found this acting from impulses a great drawback. "Great heavens!" cried the exasperated author, at last, "try to have a little less genius and a little more talent."

A HIGHWAY WOMAN.

MRS. CHARKE, the eccentric daughter of Colley Cibber, had long lived on unpleasant terms with her father, by whom she was treated with just severity for her total disregard of all social duties and common decorum. Being one day greatly irritated by the dramatist's refusal to honour her drafts, she equipped herself after the style of a "gentleman of the road," and hiring a suitable horse, actually waylaid her father in Epping Forest, by stopping his chariot, presenting her pistol, and desiring him to deliver. The affrighted Colley parted with his money, observing, "Young man, young man! this is a sorry trade; take heed in time." "And so I would," replied his daughter, "but I've a wicked old hunks of a father, who rolls in money and mistresses, yet denies me a guinea, and has had the impudence to make so worthy a gentleman as you answer for it."

ILLUSTRATING A PROVERB.

ON one of the pantomime nights at the Surrey, when Elliston was manager, the harlequin, in jumping through a window, fell with considerable violence on the other side of the scene, owing to the neglect of the carpenter in not having placed the wadded bedding to receive him. The unhappy pantomimist uttered a tremendous cry, but was not materially injured. When Elliston was apprised of the circumstance, he observed, "Ay, there was much cry and little wool."

SIGNS OF A BREWING STORM.

WHEN Ducrow was at the head of Astley's, it was his custom to purchase a new hat the last day of rehearsing a new piece. He would craftily call attention to its gloss, shape, fit, etc., enlarging at the same time upon its cost. When he came to his grand effects, and anything went wrong, he would deliberately give his hat a crushing blow, and cry, "There goes *7s. 6d.*! Try again." They generally did it better the second time. Failing in another effect, he would take off his hat, and, rubbing it furiously the wrong way, growl, "There goes *15s.*, darn it! Try again." But when the climax came, and did not succeed to his satisfaction, he would dash the unfortunate hat down, and, vigorously trampling on it, yell out, "There goes one guinea. Try again, and *do it*, or, darn ye, I'll smash the lot!" And they did try, and generally did it well.

TOO LITERAL.

IN Settle's play, *The Conquest of China by the Tartars*, Jevon, an actor of the time of Charles II., acted a Chinese prince and commander of the Chinese army. Being vanquished by the Tartars, he was to fall upon the point of his sword and kill himself, rather than be made a prisoner by the enemy. Jevon, instead of falling on the point of his sword, laid it in the scabbard at length upon the ground, and fell upon it, saying, "Now I am dead," which put the author in such a fret (says the prompter Downes, on whose authority rests this story), that it made him speak treble instead of double. Jevon's answer was, "Did you not bid me fall upon my sword?"

KEAN'S EFFECTIVE ACTING.

THE surprising energy of Kean's acting may be judged by the effect of his impersonation of Sir Giles Marrall, in Massinger's *New Way to Pay Old Debts*. In 1816, Kean acted that part in his best style, and the conclusion seemed so terribly real that it threw ladies in the side-boxes into hysterics, and Lord Byron himself into a "convulsion fit." Mrs. Glover, a leading actress of long experience, at the dying speech, fainted outright on the stage; Mrs. Horn staggered to a chair, and wept aloud at the appalling scene; and Munden, who sustained Marrall in a manner worthy of his leader, stood so transfixed with astonishment and terror, that he was taken off the stage by the armpits, his legs trailing, and his eyes fixed with a species of fascination on Kean's darkened and convulsed countenance.

A CLERICAL ACTOR.

IN the year 1768, a gentleman in holy orders presented himself upon the Dublin Stage as Scrub, in Farquhar's play, *The Beaux' Stratagem.* On that occasion Walker wrote to Garrick: "We have a parson to appear as Scrub, with Mr. Mossop as Archer; such an extraordinary metamorphosis will no doubt excite curiosity. The town cannot now complain that they have had no novelty; this is perhaps the greatest the stage ever knew—though it is thought the canonical gentleman will be so scandalized as to influence a party against him; but however it happens, it will bring one great house at least, perhaps several, and if we can but escape civil, we do not much mind ecclesiastical, censure. Excommunication is not half so terrible to our state as an execution."

RICHELIEU IN A PASSION.

EDWIN FORREST was once playing an engagement at Pittsburg. Dressed for the character of Richelieu, he was in the act of going on the stage in the first scene, when he discovered that the sleeve of the dress he wore was either too short or drawn up. He called to his dresser, and told him to pull the sleeve down. The man commenced pulling the robe instead of the undersleeve, when Forrest, in a loud voice, exclaimed, "Hell and fury! what are you about? The undersleeve, you fool!" Being near the first entrance his voice was heard in front, and a round of applause followed, the audience imagining it part of the play. "What are they applauding?" inquired Forrest. The prompter readily replied, "Your first speech, sir, off the stage."

REACTIONARY.

VANHOVE, Talma's father-in-law, was a very mediocre actor who played stage kings. Stationary in the midst of the revolution introduced by his son-in-law in theatrical costume, his wonder and remarks were the amusement of the greenroom. When, in the name of progress, he was compelled to discard the velvet coat and the lengthy embroidered satin waistcoat in which he was wont to impersonate Agamemnon, he exclaimed, "What a beau-tiful progress! There is not even a side-pocket in your Greek costume to put the key of one's box in!"

SUPERIOR NONSENSE.

MACKLIN objected very strongly to performers throwing in words of their own. Lee Lewis one morning, at the rehearsal of *Love à la Mode*, in which he played Squire Groom, added some gag which he thought very smart. "Hoy! Hoy!" said Macklin. "What's that?" "Oh," replied Lewis, "'tis only a little of my nonsense. "Ay," retorted Macklin; "but I think *my* nonsense is rather better than *yours*, so keep to *that*, if you please, sir."

OUR MERCURIAL NEIGHBOURS.

ON the evening of the second entry of the allied armies into Paris, the popular melodrama *La Pie Voleuse* was being acted at the Porte Saint Martin. There was one thousand eight hundred francs in the house, which at that time was considered a handsome receipt. During the performance the doors were closed, because the rumbling noise of the cannon rolling over the stones interrupted the interest of the dialogue, and it rendered impossible the sympathetic attention of the audience. Disgusted at this elasticity of the Parisian public, a French writer, who recorded the fact, added, "I take pleasure in hoping that we may never again be subjected to the same trial, and that, in any case, we may bear it in a more dignified fashion." How Paris bore it when the terrible event occurred again, is too well known to be retold.

A PLACE IN A BOX.

SOL SMITH, the American actor and manager, had a funny story to tell of what happened through his inordinate craving for the theatre. Under the protection of a couple of boys, sons of supers, he used to steal in by the back door, but after these boys were gone this became more difficult. Having been turned out once or twice, he crept in one night unperceived, hid himself in a large box, which he found in the carpenter's gallery, and closed the lid. For more than an hour he lay concealed, waiting for the curtain to go up. When it did, he was delighted to find that, by lifting the cover of the box, he could see all that was going on below. The play was *Richard III.*, and all went well till the second act, when he heard four or five men making their way directly to his hiding-place. He had barely time to close the lid, when they took up the box, and, profanely remarking on its great weight, proceeded to take "King Henry's coffin" downstairs. Upon the stage they went, followed by Lady Anne and the troop of mourners. She lamented loudly, and Sol perspired in secret. Through all the famous courting-scene he managed to keep quiet, but as the live corpse was carried "to Whitefriars," and upstairs again, the awkward supers turned and tumbled and tipped the coffined majesty so that they hurt him severely, and he cried out. The passage was dark, the bearers were frightened, and, dropping their precious burden, gave poor Sol a chance to slip out of his coffin and into the street. The intelligent auxiliaries were certain there was a ghost in the box; and Smith, with a keen appreciation of the necessity for a dramatic ending of this story, solemnly asserted that the four supers never entered the playhouse again, but immediately joined the Church, and one of them became a famous preacher, whose special hobby was the sin of theatre-going, against which he assured his hearers he had, when a young man, a most mysterious and supernatural warning.

AN EPISCOPAL PLAY.

MRS. SIDDONS once played in Miss Burney's tragedy *Elvira*. This play, owing to the presence of no less than *three* bishops among the *dramatis personæ*, caused much merriment. At that time bishop, a compound of hot claret, sugar, and spices, was in high esteem, and when jolly fellows met at a tavern, the first order to the waiter was to "bring in the bishop." Unacquainted with this fact, Miss Burney made her King exclaim, "Bring in the Bishop," and the summons filled the audience with as much hilarity as if they had partaken of the exhilarating beverage. They continued in the best possible humour throughout the piece. The dying scene made them still more jocose, when a passing stranger proposed to carry the expiring heroine to the other side of a hedge. This hedge, though remote from any dwelling, nevertheless proved a very comfortable retreat, for in a few minutes afterwards the dying lady was brought from behind it on an elegant couch, and after dying was removed once more behind the hedge. The solemn accents of Siddons herself were unavailing against this ludicrous circumstance, and she was carried off on her couch amidst roars of mirth.

PAPER OR GOLD?

THE French public occasionally are very sensitive. In 1837 F. Lemaitre, in one of his favourite parts—that of the needy adventurer, Robert Macaire—took a dirty paper from his pocket, from which he offered his stage-friend Bertrand a pinch of snuff. The public hissed him for this. Lemaitre knew his audience, threw the paper away, and produced a golden snuff-box, from which he offered a second pinch to Bertrand. Thereupon the public applauded. "Excuse me, gentlemen," said Frédéric, addressing himself to the pit. "The bit of paper was better; it was more in keeping with the character. You ought to hiss the golden snuff-box."

PLEASANT REMINDERS.

JOHN Palmer, "Plausible Jack Palmer," the original Joseph Surface, was excellent in characters of liveliness and impudence, the bucks, bloods, and saucy footmen of the past. His grand presence and lofty airs contrasted somewhat with the humbleness of his origin. He was thought to be too forgetful that his father had been doorkeeper and bill-sticker to Drury Lane Theatre; at any rate, his professional brethren took care to remind him of the fact. On one occasion he entered the greenroom wearing a valuable pair of diamond kneebuckles, the gift, it was alleged, of an admiring lady of quality. "Palmer, I perceive, deals in diamonds," observed William Parsons, the inimitable "Mr. Crabtree" of that day. "Yes," said Bannister; "but I can well remember the time when he dealt only in *paste*." Thereupon Parsons whispered to Palmer, "Why don't you *stick* him to the wall, Jack?"

EN ATTENDANT.

JOHN KEMBLE once went to Dicky Peake's house half cocked, at half-past nine in the evening. Sheridan, he said, had appointed to meet him there, and he would not neglect being in time for the world. Peake sat him down to wine with Dunn the treasurer. The three got exceedingly drunk, and all fell asleep, Kemble occupying the carpet. The tragedian was the first to wake. He arose and opened the window-shutter, and, dazzled by the morning sunlight, roused his two companions, and, their watches being all run out, wondered as to the time of day. They soon heard eight strike. "Eight!" exclaimed Kemble. "This is too provoking of Sheridan; he is always late in keeping his appointments. I don't suppose he will come at all now. If he *should*, tell him, my dear Dick, how long I waited for him!" Therewith *exit* John Kemble.

FOLLOW YOUR LEADER.

FREDERIC LEMAITRE relates, in his *Souvenirs*, that one evening as he was playing Georges to Madame Dorval's Amelia, in *The Gambler* (*Trente Ans ou La Vie d'un Joueur*), the lady's lace bonnet caught fire by touching the flame of one of the candles on the writing-table, in the scene when Amelia signs the document by which she makes over her jointure. Lemaitre, quick as thought, without saying a word, tore the bonnet off her head, and crushing it to extinguish the flames, put it into his pocket. The action was so sudden that Madame Dorval herself had no idea what it meant; it had been observed, however, by many of the spectators, who rewarded Lemaitre's presence of mind with a round of applause. Among those who had seen this necessary by-play there was a provincial actor, who, not having observed that the bonnet was in flames, thought it was some original "effect" of the great actor, and hearing the hearty applause, muttered to himself, "I must remember that." When, soon after, he was called to play the same part at a provincial theatre, he did not forget the interesting episode, and at the moment when Amelia was about to sign the fatal document, he wrenched off her bonnet and put it into his pocket. The audience was astonished, began to whisper, thought it was a case of sudden madness; whilst the actor, not hearing any applause, muttered, "The blockheads! they don't understand it." After the play, one of his friends complimented him on the remarkable manner in which he had played the character of Georges de Germany. "But," said he, "what on earth did you mean by tearing off Amelia's bonnet?" "What!" was the reply, "Don't you know? That is one of the great effects of Frédéric Lemaitre."

THE BITTER CUP.

FORMERLY there stood a small private theatre, the Sans Souci, in Leicester Street, on the site now occupied by Russell and Hampton's furniture warehouse. Here an old actor of the name of Southey, brother of the Laureate, had consented one evening to play old Hardcastle, in *She Stoops to Conquer*. His conditions were five shillings remuneration, and the special stipulation that the tankard, which Diggory brings on, should be filled according to his own prescription. In accordance with this agreement, a "cup" of egg-wine and spice was prepared, regardless of expense, at the Leicester Hotel opposite, and sent over in a handsome silver tankard. But, alas! "between the cup and the lip there is many a slip." When Diggory brought it on and placed it in the hands of Southey, who was to have the first pull at it, his gaze of horror, when he lifted the lid, spoke for itself. The poor man let the lid fall on the empty tankark, and fairly wept. The carpenters, through whose hands the cup had passed, smelling the warm, spiced beverage, had been unable to resist the temptation, and, passing it from hand to hand, had drunk every drop of the precious liquor.

A DUTCH MIRACLE PLAY.

WHETHER "based on fact," or a flight of the imagination, the following description of the stage arrangements of a Dutch miracle play occurs in Chetwood's *General History of the Stage*. I omit some of the details, as too graphic and "unfit for publication." "The heavy Dutch have plays in their own language, but they are generally planned on the Old Testament. I had a description of one given me from an English spectator. It was the story of Abraham sacrificing his son Isaac. But Abraham was armed with a gun, instead of a sacrificing knife. The angel, to prevent the gun from firing, sprinkled some water on the priming in a manner not fit to be described. The ram in the brake, which was represented by boughs of laurel, was a plump, fat Dutchman, with fair brow-spread antlers on his head, fixed artificially; and all the decorations were of a piece." If such were the appliances of the Dutch stage in the first half of the eighteenth century, the Hollanders may be said to have progressed with giant strides—witness the Dutch performance at the Imperial Theatre, in 1880.

KNOW THYSELF.

SECRETARY CRAGGS, when very young, in company with some of his friends, went, with Estcourt, to Sir Godfrey Kneller's, and whispered to him that a gentleman present was able to give such a representation of many among his most powerful patrons as would occasion the greatest surprise. Estcourt accordingly, at the artist's desire, mimicked Lords Somers, Halifax, Godolphin, and others, so perfectly that Kneller was delighted, and laughed heartily at the impersonations. Craggs gave a signal as concerted, and Estcourt immediately mimicked Sir Godfrey himself, who cried out, in a transport of ungovernable conviction, "Nay, there you are out, man! By G——, that is not me!" Richard Steele, in the *Tatler*, August 6, 1709, adverts to Estcourt's surprising powers of personal imitation, under the name of Tom Mirror. Colley Cibber says of the same, "This man was so amazing and extraordinary a mimic, that no man or woman, from the coquette to the privy councillor, ever moved or spoke before him but he could carry their voice, look, mien, and motion, instantly into another company."

THE FIRST ACTRESSES.

CORYAT, in his *Crudities*, published in 1611, tells us that he saw female performers at Vienna, adding that he had heard that females had acted on the stage in London. Beyond this vague allusion, nothing is known of these performances. It is certain, however, that in 1629 actresses made their public appearance in London, in the persons of some French women, belonging to a French company which visited the metropolis in that year. The Puritanical, stage-hating Prynne boiled over with indignation at such an indecorous innovation; and even some years afterwards, when he published his *Histriomastix*, almost choked himself with the utterance of invectives at these unfortunate predecessors of Sarah Bernhardt. In a marginal note to the above work, he writes: "Some French women, or monsters rather, in Michaelmass term, 1629, attempted to act a French play, at the playhouse in Blackfriars—an impudent, shameful, unwomanish, graceless, if not more than wh——h attempt." The novelty did not take, and the opinion of the general public coincided with that of the self-appointed censor, as appears from the following curious passage in a letter, dated November 8, 1629, addressed by one Thomas Brande (possibly the owner of the Globe Theatre), probably to Bishop Laud, now in the Lambeth Library:—

"Furthermore, you should know that last day certain vagrant French players, who had been expelled from their own country, *and those women*, did attempt, thereby giving just offence to all virtuous and well-disposed persons in this town, to act a certain lascivious and unchaste comedy, in the French tongue, at the Blackfriars. Glad I am to say, they were hissed, hooted, and pippin-pelted from the stage, so as I do not think they will be ready to try the same again."

The ill-reception of the French ladies did not deter them from renewing the attempt. A fortnight afterwards, on November 22, they appeared for one day at the Red Bull. The reception appears once more to have been too warm. More than three weeks elapsed before they ventured a third time to face an English audience, when, on the afternoon of December 14, 1629, they gave a representation at the Fortune playhouse. Sir Henry Herbert, Master of the Revels, magnanimously abated them one pound from the usual two pounds fee to which he was entitled for permitting them to perform. In a memorandum subjoined to the entry of one pound for allowing them to play at the Fortune, he adds, "I should have had another piece (*i.e.* pound), but in respect of their ill fortune, I was content to bestow a piece back."

The next French company which visited London early in the spring of 1635, appears to have comprised no actresses, and the innovation was probably but little imitated on the English stage before the Restoration. It is clear that it was considered open to grave doubts, even by persons who were warm friends of the theatre. At the same time, it should be remembered that in the masks at court, ladies constantly took part as performers; as when, in 1632, the queen and her ladies acted in a pastoral, *The Shepherd's Paradise*, at Whitehall.

That actresses began to be seen more and more on the stage of the time of Charles I., would appear from a passage in Brome's *The Court Beggar*, v. 2 (1632), "The boy is a pretty actor, and his mother can play her part. Women-actors now grow in request, sir."

These, however, appear to have been sporadic cases. But on

Saturday, the 8th of December, 1660, an English actress appeared on the stage of the Vere Street Theatre, Clare Market, and from that time the custom was established; boy-actresses fell into the background, and ere long disappeared. The lady played Desdemona, and a certain Thomas Jordan, an actor and the author of various poetical pieces, provided for delivery upon this occasion a "Prologue to introduce the first woman that came to act on the stage, in the tragedy called *The Moor of Venice.*"

"I come, unknown to any of the rest,
To tell the news. I saw the lady drest—
The woman plays to-day. Mistake me not:
No man in gown, or page in petticoat;
A woman to my knowledge, yet I can't,
If I should die, make affidavit on't.
Do you not twitter, gentlemen? I know
You will be censuring; do it fairly, though.
'Tis possible a virtuous woman may
Abhor all sorts of looseness, and yet play—
Play on the stage, where all eyes are upon her.
Shall we count that a crime France counts an honour?
In other kingdoms husbands safely trust 'em,
The difference lies only in the custom;
And let it be our custom, I advise,
I'm sure this *custom's* better than th' *excise*,
And may procure us *custom*. Hearts of flint
Will melt in passion when a woman's in't.
But, gentlemen, you that as judges sit
In the star-chamber of the house—the pit,
Have modest thoughts of her; pray do not run
To give her visits when the play is done,
With 'Damme, your most humble servant, lady,'
She knows these things as well as you, it may be;
Not a bit there, dear gallants, she doth know
Her own deserts—and your temptations too.
But to the point. In this reforming age,
We have intents to civilize the stage.
Our women are defective, and so sized
You'd think they were some of the Guard disguised.
For, to speak truth, men act that are between
Forty and fifty, wenches of fifteen;

With bone so large, and nerve so incompliant,
When you call "Desdemona," enter giant.
We shall purge every thing that is unclean,
Lascivious, scurrilous, impious, or obscene;
And when we've put all things in this fair way,
Barebones himself may come to see the play."

Who this Desdemona really was is still an open question. The gossiping Pepys is silent on the subject, there being no entry in his Diary on that day.* Betterton, in his *History of the English Stage*, says that a Mrs. Norris (who subsequently became the mother of "Jubilee Dickey" Norris) was "the first woman who ever appeared on the stage." But this statement is questioned, and Mrs. Ann Marshall, "leading lady" of Killigrew's troupe; a Mrs. Hughes, a member of the same company; Mrs. Betterton, then known as Mrs. Saunderson; and a Mrs. Coleman, mentioned by Pepys as a "pleasant, jolly woman," all have been brought forward as the first female Desdemona. On the whole, Mrs. Hughes seems to have the support of more probabilities than any of the other ladies. Very little is known concerning this lady—who is not once remembered by Pepys—except a few parts she played, and that she was taken from the stage by Prince Rupert. He bought for her, at a cost of £20,000, the once magnificent seat of Sir Nicholas Crispe, near Hammersmith, better known at a later date as Brandenburg House, and the residence of the unfortunate Queen Caroline. By the prince Mrs. Hughes had a daughter, who after her father was named Ruperta, and married to Lieutenant-General Howe. She survived her husband, and died at Somerset House in 1740. Grammont's *Memoirs* is almost the only work from which any information may be gleaned concerning Mrs. Hughes. She is there described as an impertinent gipsy, and accused of pride. The king, we are told, was "greatly pleased" with Prince Rupert's entanglement with the actress, for which "great re-

* On January 3, 1661, Pepys says: "To the theatre, where was acted *Beggars' Bush*, it being very well done; and here, for the first time, I saw a woman come upon the stage."

joicings" were made at the then fashionable Tunbridge. "Nobody," says Grammont, "was bold enough to make it the subject of satire, though the same constraint was not observed with other ridiculous personages." Upon the temper of the prince she appears to have had a beneficial influence, for she is stated to have "brought down and greatly subdued his natural fierceness. . . . From this time adieu alembics, crucibles, furnaces, and all the black furniture of the forges ; a complete farewell to all mathematical instruments and chemical speculations : sweet powders and essences were now the only ingredients that occupied any share of his intention."

As might have been expected, female performers soon became highly popular, and some plays were represented entirely by women, as they had previously been by men. Such was *The Parson's Wedding*, a comedy by Killigrew, which was wholly performed by females, although there were seven male and only six female characters in the piece, exclusive of servants.*

AN ENTHUSIASTIC PLAYGOER.

WHEN *The Dramatist* was being represented at Covent Garden, Frederick Reynolds, the author of that comedy, then a Templar, treated the porter of the Temple to a seat in the gallery. The next morning Reynolds asked him how he had enjoyed himself. "Pretty well, as for that," replied the man ; "but, you see, your honour has forgotten to pay me." "What!" exclaimed Reynolds ; "I gave you a shilling last night." "Faith, now, you are right," Murphy rejoined, "and indeed, I paid it at the door of that winding gallery. But that's not my maning. It's the *porterage*, sir ! Arrah, the porterage—all the way from here to Covent Garden and back ; and for that, and the trouble, and the great loss of time, I think your

* Pepys' Diary, October 11, 1664 : "Luellin tells me what an obscene, loose play this *Parson's Wedding* is, acted by nothing but women, at the King's House."

honour yourself will allow I cannot ax you a farthing short of another two shillings."

A "BOB ACRES."

AT the time when England went in constant fears of a landing of Napoleon's armies, George Colman, among many thousands of his countrymen, was called upon to serve in the militia. A form was forwarded him, containing many inquiries, one of which ran as follows:—"State your reasons for declining to serve." The wit complied with this injunction by writing in the place left open for the explanation of his want of patriotism—"Old, lame, and a coward."

A SLIDING SCALE.

THERE was one Hambleton, a good bass singer in his time, who lived to a great age, and latterly played old men in provincial theatres. One day, when travelling on the top of a stage-coach, it was overturned, and he rolled down a steep bank into a ditch below. His fellow-travellers, who had landed on the roadside, thought him dangerously wounded, if not killed. They descended the slope in great haste, but their fear subsided when they found him lying on his back, running the gamut. Coming to the lowest note, he exclaimed, "I thank God my G is all right!" Fear gave way to laughter, and the vocalist was lifted out of the mud by light hearts and willing hands.

NOT SUCH FOOLS.

MR. Gilbert, the dramatist, once heard that his *Trial by Jury*, renamed and slightly altered, was being given at a certain hall; and not liking to be swindled, he called upon the manager. The author opened proceedings by inquiring whether the hall was not let for amateur theatricals.

sometimes. It was certainly, any evening, if not already engaged, and the manager inquired what his visitor proposed to play. "Well, there's a piece called *Trial by Jury*. I was thinking of that," the visitor replied. "And a very good piece too," the manager kindly assured him; "sure to take." "I know who could play the principal parts very well," Mr. Gilbert said, "but I was doubtful about the chorus. Could you help me in this, do you think?" "I think I could—in fact, I'm sure of it; you need not trouble about a chorus that knows the music," the manager replied. "Thank you; you are very kind," Mr. Gilbert gently answered; "but," he continued, "by the way, are there not some charges—fees—of some kind to be paid for the right of playing pieces of this sort? I fancy I have heard something to that effect." Then the manager grew very confidential indeed. He looked sly; he even winked; and he said, "Never you mind about that. I don't. Why, we play the very piece you're talking about every night; only we don't call it *Trial by Jury*. We ain't such fools. Gilbert and Sullivan don't know anything about it, and ain't likely to. You leave it to me, and you'll be all right!" It was now Mr. Gilbert's turn, and he quietly replied, "I think you've made a slight mistake in my name. I am Mr. W. S. Gilbert, and I had heard that you were good enough to play my piece without mentioning it; so I came to see." Mr. Gilbert declares that the man shrank visibly. From a huge creature six feet high he seemed to descend to the dimensions of a child in petticoats; but Mr. Gilbert mercifully spared him, for the sake of the fun he had afforded.

ANOTHER BROTHER OF OPHELIA.

SAYS O'Keeffe, in his *Recollections:* "In my youth I often saw Glover on the stage. He was a surgeon, and a good writer in the London periodical papers. When he was in Cork, a man was hanged for sheep-stealing, whom Glover smuggled into a field, and by surgical skill restored to life, though the culprit had hung the full time prescribed by the law. A few nights after, Glover being on the stage acting Polonius, the revived sheep-stealer, full of whiskey, broke into the pit and in a loud voice called out to Glover, "Mr. Glover, you know you are my second father; you brought me to life, and sure you have to support me now, for I have no money of my own. You have been the means of bringing me back into the world, sir; so, by the piper of Blessington, you are bound to maintain me." The sheriff was present at the time, but appeared not to hear the appeal; and, on the fellow persisting in his outcries, he, through a piece of clemency, slipped out of the theatre. The crowd at length forced the man away, telling him that if the sheriff found him alive, it was his duty to hang him over again.

A COMEDY IN NEWGATE.

THE day after the unfortunate Dr. Dodd had been convicted of the offence for which he was subsequently executed, he wrote a note to Woodfall, the printer of the *Morning Chronicle*, requesting an immediate interview. The latter at once complied with the request, and, on being ushered into the doctor's presence, commenced sympathizing with him about his unfortunate position. Dodd interrupted him with apparent composure, and informed the publisher that in his earlier days he had been a lover of the stage. "I sketched out a comedy," he said, "based upon the character of Sir Roger de Coverley in the *Spectator*. This piece I finished since my *residence* in Newgate, and if you be so good as to revise it, and give me your interest with the manager of one of the theatres, I shall feel much obliged to you." Woodfall complied with the doctor's request, and corresponded with him on the subject of this play until the week before the doctor's execution. The comedy was placed in the hands of Harris, then manager of Drury Lane, but was never acted or published. Nor was this the only play written by Dr. Dodd. Whilst he was an undergraduate at Cambridge, he had produced a tragedy called *The Syracusian*, but, like his last work, it was still-born, and never appeared before the public. It had been sold in 1750 to Watts, the printer; but in the next year, on the author's taking orders, he withdrew the copy from the hands of the managers, and returned the money the printer had advanced. It was founded on a fictitious story, and was intended to be performed with chorusses.

A DOUBLE STAR.

RICHARD WINSTONE spoke his farewell address on his benefit night at the theatre in King Street, Bristol, on the 11th of June, 1784. He was then about eighty years of age, and so afflicted with deafness that it was impossible for him to "catch the word" from the prompter at the side of the stage. To assist him, therefore, in the delivery of his farewell address, one of the performers, provided with a copy of the address, was stationed behind the veteran actor, and instructed to keep moving forward and backward with him, following him in all his movements like his shadow. The whimsicality of this "star," with his satellite moving in the same orbit, may be imagined.

PLAYBILL CURIOSITIES.

REVALARD, after having for some time played the part of tyrants and brigands in the Ambigu Theatre, became manager of a provincial company. The bills he issued in that capacity were sometimes remarkable. One night a sensational melodrama was represented, in which there occurred the bombardment of a town, when a person in the pit was slightly injured by a piece of wadding. The next day Revalard, afraid that this accident might have a disagreeable influence on the receipts, added to the playbills: "The ladies and gentlemen who intend to honour us this evening with their presence, are informed that henceforth the bombardment will only take place at the point of the bayonet." On another occasion he gave several representations in small towns, which were very scantily attended. The day before the company took its departure, he concluded his playbill in these words: "The company of M. Revalard, deeply touched by the warm and cordial reception they have daily met with from the public of this city, has the honour to inform its patrons that, instead of leaving next Saturday, as was notified yesterday, he and his companions will leave this city to-morrow at six o'clock."

HEAD AND FOOTE.

FOOTE'S natural and ready wit, was mixed with an unpleasant dash of unsparing maliciousness. When one of his friends, on a certain occasion, only quoted in jest some trifling circumstance about a "game" leg, Foote, who had a wooden leg, maliciously replied, "Pray, sir, make no allusion to *my* weakest part. Did I ever attack *your* head?"

BLIND PERFORMERS.

IN 1744 a performance took place at Drury Lane, in behalf of Dr. Clancy. Deprived of sight in 1734, which rendered him incapable of following his profession as a physician, this gentleman amused himself with writing two or three plays, which were acted at Smock Alley Theatre, Dublin. Patronage at last procured him a benefit in London. In allusion to his infirmity, the playbill was headed with the line from Milton—

> "The day returns, but not to me returns."

The play was *Œdipus*, and the part of the blind prophet Tiresias was undertaken by Dr. Clancy. "As this," observed the advertisements, "will be the first instance of any person labouring under so heavy a deprivation performing on the stage, the novelty as well as the unhappiness of his case will engage the favour and protection of a British audience." This painful performance attracted a very numerous audience, proving the fact that an appetite for "the sensational" was not altogether unknown among the playgoers of the last century. Dr. Clancy's performance does not appear to have been particularly striking, nor was it repeated. His case, however, ultimately moved the pity of George II., who granted him for life an annual pension of £40, from the privy purse.

About the year 1792, one Briscoe, the manager of a Staffordshire company of comedians, was struck with blindness. His theatrical labours had not been very successful, when he could see, but he still fancied he could act, notwithstanding his affliction. He announced to the public that, although being stone blind, he would play Tamerlane on one night and Oroonoko on the next. On the first occasion Mr. Briscoe had a crowded audience, on the next night the house was too small to contain his admirers. All the world now flocked to see the blind actor, who was far more indebted to the loss of his eyes than to all the foresight of his former days.

NAPOLEON DISBANDING HIS ARMY.

ON the first night of *Little Red Riding Hood* at the Olympic Pavilion in Wych Street, December 21, 1818, every thing failed; not a scene could be induced to close or to open properly, and the curtain fell amidst a storm of disapprobation. Elliston, the proprietor, was fuming, and sent round an order to the prompter that not one of the carpenters, scene-shifters, or property-men were to leave the theatre till he had spoken to them. As soon as the house was cleared, the curtain was raised, and all the culprits assembled on the stage in front of the scene, representing the interior of a cottage, having a door in one half and a latticed window in the other. The Napoleon of managers took up his position in the centre, with his back to the footlights, harangued his army in the most grandiloquent language, expatiated on the enormity of their offence, their ingratitude to the men whose bread they were eating, the disgrace they had brought upon the theatre, the cruel injury they had brought on Mr. Planché, the young and promising author of the play. Then, pointing in the most tragical attitude to his wife and daughters, who remained in a private box, bade them look upon the family they had ruined; and, burying his face in his handkerchief, to stifle his sobs, passed slowly through the door in the scene, leaving his auditors silent, abashed and somewhat affected, yet rather relieved by being let off with a lecture. The next minute the casement in the other flat was thrown violently open, and thrusting out his head, his face scarlet with fury, he roared out, "I discharge you all!" No words can convey an idea of the glorious absurdity of this ludicrous scene.

MISPLACED PITY.

COLLEY CIBBER being one day in the green-room, and observing his son Theophilus to enter, dressed in a black satin coat and breeches, with white satin facings, and a waistcoat trimmed with silver frogs, he inquired of him what character he performed that night. To which the young man, who had then attained his fiftieth year, replied, "None, sir." Struck with the oddity of his son's appearance, the father, having taken a pinch of snuff with a very solemn air, such as would have become Sir Novelty Fashion, then asked what made him appear in so singular a dress. "Taste, sir; taste," answered the son, with his usual airy pertness. Upon which the sire, now highly exasperated at the absurdity and impudence of his son, exclaimed, "Then I pity you!" "Don't pity me, sir," replied Theophilus, turning upon his heel with the utmost effrontery; "pity my tailor." Theo, it must be remembered, never paid for anything he had obtained on credit.

HIS WEAK POINT.

CHARLES DIGNUM, the singer and comedian, was the soul of good humour, but he had one foible—he was desirous of being thought very intelligent, and that people should attribute his frequent fits of vacuity to profound mental abstraction. He was thus in the habit, in the greenroom and elsewhere, of placing his finger to his forehead, in the manner Lawrence Stern is represented in his portrait, and pretending to be unconscious of what was passing around him. Some one observing Dignum in his usual meditative posture, called Sheridan's attention to it. "Look at Dignum; he is thinking again." "No," replied Sheridan; "he thinks he thinks."

URSA MAJOR.

PHILIP LEWIS had been an actor of considerable eminence in his day at Dublin and Edinburgh. In his old age, it was a source of misery to him to remember how many men whom he considered his inferiors had become metropolitan favourites. As he used openly to complain about this misfortune, few of his former acquaintances chose to associate with him. Mr. and Mrs. Webb, of Covent Garden Theatre, however, who had been among his early companions, invited him one Sunday to dinner in their cottage somewhere on the banks of the Thames. Lewis was on his good behaviour, and was unusually good tempered throughout the day. After dinner, Webb produced a bottle of excellent Madeira, filled Lewis's glass, and asked his opinion of it. The veteran put the glass to his lips, smacked them, looked at Webb for an instant, and burst out in tears. Distressed at this sight, the worthy host exclaimed, "My dear Philip, what can be the cause of this distress?" "The cause," blubbered Lewis; "why, to think, Dicky, that such a blockhead as you should have your country house, and be able to drink this Madeira, when I am forced to live in an attic, and thank my nephew for scraps!"

PURITANICAL HERRINGS.

THE following curious fact is related in Walter Donaldson's *Recollections of an Actor*, as having happened early in the present century:—"A circumstance in Moss's career as a manager happened in Whitehaven. He opened the theatre with some degree of success; but in less than a week—on a Saturday night—Moss and his troupe were conveyed to the lock-up. There they remained all Sunday, in durance vile. On Monday morning they were taken before the magistrates, and a most novel charge was brought against them. An inhabitant of the town, called respectable and rational, came forward in open court to denounce the actors as a curse to society in general, but to Whitehaven in particular. This wiseacre declared, 'Before the theatre opened there was an immense take of herrings, but since the players entered the town they have all fled, and the fishermen are now suffering. This misfortune he ascribed entirely to the actors, who always bring a curse wherever they appear.' The magistrates looked over their books, and consulted the man that generally knows something—the town clerk. They then found nothing could be done in the business but to shut up the theatre, and to send the sons of the 'wicked one' away. This is no romance, but an actual fact."

"THINK OF MY FEELINGS."

WHEN Stephen Kemble was playing at Taunton, he came to rehearsal one morning without his coat. The manager inquired the cause of this strange appearance. "Sir," said Kemble, "the landlord of the house where I was reading the paper, charged me double for my ale. I told him he had cheated me, and would not pay him. He seized me, and pulled off my coat; so, rather than submit to his extortion, I came away without it." "But, Mr. Kemble," said the manager, "walk through the streets without your coat!" "But, Mr. Hughes," said Stephen, "pay sixpence for my ale!" "But your coat, Mr. Kemble!" "Curse my coat, sir; think of my feelings!" The story got wind, and Kemble's words became for a time a saying in the west of England, where, whenever a man determined to set appearances at nought, he would invariably exclaim, "Oh! curse my coat; think of my feelings!"

DIAMOND CUTS DIAMOND.

FULLER, the manager of the Old Pearl Theatre, Albany, United States, was anything but "square," and generally managed to cheat everybody. On the last night of the season, the printer, Henry D. Stone, held a claim of 125 dollars against the theatre. There was a great rush on that night to see Edwin Forrest play Metamora, and the regular ticket-office was besieged. By a standing arrangement the printer had the privilege of giving written passes, which were charged to his account. Knowing that it was only by sharp practice that the "artful dodger," as Fuller was called, could be made to settle, Stone had a lot of passes prepared, and opened an opposition ticket-office next door to the theatre, in a confectionary store. The news spread among the crowd that tickets could be had there, and a large number were speedily sold. The next morning, instead of the manager owing the printer, the printer owed the manager just seventy-five cents.

HARD WORK.

ON Saturday, April 19, 1817, Junius Brutus Booth played Sir Edward Mortimer in three different towns. At 11 a.m., he played at Cirencester; at 4 p.m., in Gloucester; and at 8 p.m., in Cheltenham. For this arduous achievement he received about £30.

UNSOOTABLE COMPANY.

BLACK coats are *de rigueur* at the Italian operas, and predominate in the stalls of all the West End theatres; but a coat may be ever so black, and yet objectionable. Witness the following touching appeal to Elliston, at the time when he was lessee and manager of the Surrey Theatre, the authenticity of which is vouched for by his biographer:—

"August 10th, 1827.

"SIR,—I really must beg to call your attention to a most abominable nuisance which exists in your house, and which is, in a great measure, the cause of minor theatres not holding the rank they should amongst playhouses. I mean the admission of *sweeps* into the theatre in the very dress in which they climb chimneys. This not only incommodes ladies and gentlemen by the obnoxious odour arising from their attire, but these sweeps take up twice the room of other people, because the ladies, in particular, object to their clothes being soiled by such unpleasant neighbours. I have, with my wife, been in the habit of visiting the Surrey Theatre, and on *three* occasions we have been annoyed by these sweeps. People will not go, sir, where sweeps are; and you will find, sooner or later, these gentlemen will have the whole theatre to themselves, unless an alteration be made. I own, at some theatres the managers are too particular in dress. Those days are past, and the public have a right to go to theatrical entertainments in their morning costumes; but this ought not to include the sweeps. It is not a week ago since a young lady, in a nice white gown, sat down on the very spot which a nasty sweep had just quitted, and when she got up the sight was most horrible, for she was a very heavy lady and had laughed a good deal during the performance; but it was no laughing matter to her when she got home. I hope I have said quite enough, and am your

"WELL-WISHER.

"R. W. Elliston, Esq."

HEART[H]LESS JOKE.

IN 1809 Drury Lane was destroyed by fire. Sheridan, its then proprietor, at the time of the conflagration was at the House of Commons, which voted an immediate adjournment when the disastrous news arrived, though Sheridan himself protested against such an interruption of public business on account of his own or any private interests. He went thither, however, in all haste, and, whilst seeing his property in flames, sat down with his friend Barry in a coffee-house opposite, to discuss a bottle of port, coolly remarking, in answer to some friendly expostulation, that "it was hard if a man could not drink a glass of wine by his own fire."

TRANSITORY GLORY.

COLLEY CIBBER relates, that on one occasion a young gentleman, who, like Bayes in *The Rehearsal*, "only wrote for fame and reputation," got a comedy of his placed on the boards. On the second day of his Muse's public triumph, he marched, in a stately full-bottomed periwig, into the lobby of the house, leading a lady of condition by the hand. Raising his voice to the true pitch of the Sir Fopling Flutter sound, he called out, "Hey, box-keeper, where is my Lady Such-a-one's servant?" the man having been sent to keep a place for her ladyship, in those benighted days when reserved seats were not. Judge of the dismay of the young poet, when John Trott, the box-keeper, calmly replied, "Sir, we have dismissed. There was not company enough to pay for the candles."

THE WORST PUNISHMENT.

TAYLOR, when proprietor of the Haymarket Opera-house was once dining with some friends, when the subject of capital punishments was started, during the discussion of which he remained in a reverie. A gentleman at table strongly advocated the abolition of capital punishment in all cases. "What would you inflict, then, on a criminal of the worst kind?" asked another. "By ——" said Taylor, starting up, "make him manager of the opera-house. If he deserved a worse punishment, he must be a devil incarnate."

PLAY AND EARNEST.

THE following anecdote is related by Mr. Robert Lloyd:— "When I was engaged as a utility gentleman at Greenock some years ago, an incident occurred which the actors in it may remember. The piece was *The Anchor of Hope*. Towards the end of the second act, a band of smugglers attack a captain. An old Jew pedlar appears opportunely on the scene, and helps to knock the smugglers down. This is all very well for the actors, when they know what is coming; but, alas! on this occasion they did not. It happened that the Channel Fleet at the time lay moored at Greenock, and the sailors were enjoying themselves in the town. On this especial occasion, the somewhat nautical name of the piece seeming to have struck their fancy, the gallery and pit were full of them. When the time came for the captain to be assaulted, there were suddenly to be seen sailors finding their way from the gallery to the pit, and thence on to the stage, others from the pit following suit. Indignant at seeing a captain subjected to ill usage, they knocked every smuggler down; and, not content with that, put their feet on the poor utilities' chests, daring them to move, amid the excitement of the whole house. It was only with difficulty that Mr. Calhaem, who acted the Jew pedlar, when the act-drop came down, could convince the gallant tars that it was 'only acting.'"

"LOVE'S LAST SHIFT."

"TO let you see," says Chetwood, in his amusing old-fashioned style, "how formerly even tragedy heroes were now and then put to their shifts, I'll tell you a short story that befell Mr. Thurmond, one of the Drury Lane company. It was the custom, at that time, for persons of the first rank and distinction to give their birthday suits to the most favoured actors. I think Mr. Thurmond was honoured by General Ingoldsby with his; but his finances being at the lowest tide of ebb, the rich suit was put "in buckle" (*i. e.* in pawn). One night notice was given that the General would be present with the Government at the play, and all the performers on the stage were prepared to dress out in the suits presented. The spouse of Johnny Thurmond tried all her arts to persuade Mr. Holdfast, the pawnbroker (as it fell out, his real name), to let go the clothes for that evening, to be returned when the play was over. But all arguments were fruitless; nothing but the ready, or a pledge of fully equal value. Well, what must be done? The whole family in confusion and at their wits' end. At last Winny, the wife, put on a composed countenance, though with a troubled heart, stepped to a neighbouring tavern, and ordered a very hot negus to comfort Johnny in the great part he was to perform that night—begging to have the silver tankard with the lid, because, as she said, "a cover and the vehicle silver would retain heat longer than any other metal." The request was complied with; the negus carried to the play-house piping hot, popped into a vile, earthen mug; the silver tankard travelled *incognito* under her apron, popped into the pawnbroker's hands in exchange for the suit, which was put on and played its part with the rest of the wardrobe. When its duty was over, it was carried back to remain in its former depository, the tankard to its owner; and when the tide flowed with its lunar influence, the stranded suit was wafted into safe harbour again, after paying a little for dry docking, which was all the damage received."

RATHER DISTRAIT.

WALKING one day with a brother dramatist, Mr. Bayle Bernard, in Regent's Quadrant, Sheridan Knowles was accosted by a gentleman in these terms: "You're a pretty fellow, Knowles! After fixing your own day and hour to dine with us, you never make your appearance, and from that time to this not a word have we heard from you!" "I could not help it, upon my honour," replied Knowles; "and I've been so busy ever since, I haven't had a moment to write or call. How are you all at home?" "Oh, quite well, thank you. But, come now, will you name another day, and keep your word?" "I will—sure I will." "Well, what day? Shall we say Thursday next?" "Thursday? Yes, by all means—Thursday be it." "At six?" "At six. I'll be there punctually. My love to 'em all." "Thank ye. Remember, now—six, next Thursday." "All right, my dear fellow; I'll be with you." The friend departed, and Sheridan, relinking his arm with that of Bayle Bernard, said, "Who's that chap?" not having the least idea of the name or residence of the man he had promised to dine with on the following Thursday, or the interesting "family at home," to whom he had sent his love.

ANTI-SEMITICISM OF CHARLES MATHEWS.

THE late Charles Mathews, one evening in his youth, after playing the part of the Jew Mordeana in Macklin's *Love à la Mode*, in Dublin, was invited to supper by G. F. Cooke in his rooms. After supper whiskey punch was introduced, and Cooke paid his respects to this pleasing beverage so assiduously, that at last he became outrageously drunk, and smashed everything in his room because the landlady would not let him have any more punch. Mathews tried to make his escape, when Cooke dragged him to the window, and called for the watch. A watchman, who had been attracted already by the noise, asked the cause of the disturbance, when, to the horror of his struggling guest, Cooke exclaimed, "I give this man in charge; he has committed a capital offence—he has committed a murder." Mathews protested violently. "Yes," continued Cooke, "to my certain knowledge he has been this night guilty of a cruel, atrocious murder in cold blood. He has most barbarously murdered an inoffensive Jew gentleman of the name of Mordeana, and I charge him with it, in the name of Macklin, author of *Love à la Mode*." At this moment Mathews managed to make his escape, and bolted down the stairs, Cooke throwing the candlesticks after him, with the words, "Well, if you *will* go, you sha'n't say I sent you to bed without a light." It took some time to convince honest Dogberry that no "inoffensive Jew gentleman" had been killed and murdered.

YOUR MONEY OR YOUR LIFE.

BICKERSTAFF, a comedian, whose benefit Steele, as being his relation, in the third number of the *Tatler* good-naturedly recommended to the public, enjoyed a weekly salary of £4. In an economical moment, Cibber retrenched one-half of it. The impoverished actor at once called on his manager, represented the largeness of his family, and concluded by flatly informing him that, as he could not subsist upon the narrow allowance to which he had reduced him, he felt compelled to call the author of his distress to account, for that he would rather perish by the sword than die of starvation. The affrighted Cibber, considering discretion the better part of valour, referred the incensed actor to the next Saturday for answer, when Bickerstaff found his stipend restored to its usual amount.

MOONSTRUCK.

AS an instance of the enormities inflicted upon the manager of a theatre by candidates for stage honours, Alfred Bunn, manager of Drury Lane, mentions the following: "A tragedy of nearly six hundred *pages*, written by an author totally unknown, and likely ever to remain so, was sent by one particular friend of mine, and strongly recommended by three others. It commenced with a moonlight scene, and in the opening soliloquy thereof the hero, gazing on the unclouded glory of Diana, accused her, despite her beauty and alleged chastity, of intriguing—with whom? With the *Man in the Moon*."

UTILITY WITH A VENGEANCE.

THOMAS KING, the original Sir Peter Teazle in the immortal *School for Scandal*, used to relate: "I remember that when I had been but a short time on the stage, I performed one night King Richard, sang two comic songs, played in an interlude, danced a hornpipe, spoke a prologue, and was afterwards harlequin, in a sharing company, and after all this fatigue my share came to threepence and three pieces of candle." A biographer adds that King on the same occasion had journeyed from Beaconsfield, in Bucks, to London, and back again, in order that he might obtain certain "properties" essential, as he considered, to his appearance as King Richard.

DRESS CLOTHES INDISPENSABLE.

A CAPITAL story is told of Mr. Hollingshead's method of dealing with people who make impudent requests for gratuitous admission to his theatres. A so-called "gentleman" wrote to the manager of the Gaiety some time ago to say that, as people in evening dress gave a tone to the house, the writer and a friend would be glad to go to the Gaiety, and would promise to appear in evening dress and white ties, if Mr. Hollingshead would give them a couple of seats. Mr. Hollingshead was good enough to send them a couple of admissions—to the upper gallery—dress clothes indispensable.

NO ACCOUNTING FOR TASTES.

THE father of Sir Watkin William Wynn, being fond of theatricals, erected a theatre at his seat at Wynnstay, and employed Austin, of the Chester Theatre, to assist him in the cares of management. A play was selected, the parts allotted, and a rehearsal called. "Clear the stage," said the amateur manager, "and call Lord A——." "His lordship's gone shooting," a servant answered. "Call Sir B. C——." "He's gone a-fishing, Sir Watkin." "Request Lady D—— to come." "Her ladyship has just gone for a drive." "Who the devil would be a manager?" cried Sir Watkin, impatiently. "Not I, if I had your lordship's money," retorted the Chester manager.

HONEY AND WAX.

MRS. HONEY, a beautiful actress in the first quarter of this century, possessed that most uncomfortable adjunct, a jealous husband. Rumours were current that he occasionally laid hands on her, when Othello was particularly strong within him. On this presumption, the witty James Smith, one of the authors of the "Rejected Addresses," made the following epigram :—

"This pair in matrimony
 Go most unequal snacks ;
He gets all the *Honey*,
 And she gets all the *Whacks*"

PROFESSIONAL JEALOUSY.

"DURING the performances of some distinguished amateurs in behalf of the projected Guild of Literature and Art," says Mr. Buckstone, "my dresser, named Parsons, was employed to superintend the costumes and the dressing of the various characters to be represented. Wishing to know how they had acquitted themselves, the following dialogue took place: 'Well, Parsons, how did the amateurs get on?' 'Never see such a set of muffs in my life.' 'What do you mean? Are you aware who and what the gentlemen were?—great authors, artists, barristers, and others eminent in literature and science.' 'I don't care for that,' said Parsons; "they were all regular muffs.' 'What do you mean?' 'Mean! why, they *couldn't button nothing*.'"

PATERNAL PRIDE.

YOUNG VESTRIS, now best known as the husband of the celebrated lady of that name, had learnt dancing from his father, the ballet-master of the Haymarket Opera House. On some nobleman remarking to the latter that his son was a better dancer than he, old Vestris replied, "Very true, my lord; but my son had a better master than I had."

THE DAY OF REST.

AT the time when David Morris was proprietor of the Haymarket Theatre, the position of stage-manager was held by Tom Dibdin, one of the sons of the celebrated nautical poet, and himself the author of many popular dramatic pieces. Mr. Dibdin had engaged to write a comedy for the Haymarket, and some weeks having elapsed without its being forthcoming, Morris stopped him one day as he was passing through the box office. "Mr. Dibdin! How about that comedy you promised me?" "My dear sir, what opportunity have I for writing? I am on the stage all day, from ten or eleven in the morning till four in the afternoon; run home to my dinner, and back again to see the curtain up, and remain till it finally falls, long after midnight. I never have any time for composition." "No time! Then what do you do on Sundays?"

ALL TRUTH NEEDS NOT BE TOLD.

AT a rehearsal of the beautiful quartet in the second act of *Pietro l'Eremita*, Madame Camporese, in the character of Agia, had to sing *Mi manca la voce*. When she uttered these words, Madame Ronzi de Begnis, in a whisper not too gentle for Camporese to overhear it, observed, "*È vero*." This remark produced a retort courteous, somewhat more than verging on the limits of decorum: it was said even that the sound of a box on the ear was repeated by the echoes of Old Drury.

A PERFERVID ADMIRER.

A CURIOUS occurrence happened at the first representation of *Statira*, in Paris, in 1679. Pradon, the author of the piece, was present, muffled in his cloak; he had taken a seat in the pit, in order to witness the fate of his work. Hisses were heard during the first scenes, which increased as the play progressed. Pradon could not stand it, and was about to protest, when a friend whispered, "Don't make yourself known; hiss like the rest." The author, for want of better advice, followed his friend's recommendation. Unfortunately, a mousquetaire seated by his side admired the play, and, annoyed by the loud hisses of his neighbour, he rudely pushed him, exclaiming, "Why do you hiss, sir? This is an excellent piece, and the author is a man of good position." Pradon, annoyed at the guardsman's rudeness, told him to mind his own business, and that he would hiss as much as he liked. Off went his hat and wig, which the mousquetaire flung on the stage, in return for which insolence Pradon boxed his ears. Thereupon the enraged mousquetaire drew his sword and belaboured the dramatist with the flat of it to his heart's content, after which Pradon, beaten but happy, left the house, and adjourned to an apothecary's to have his wheals and stripes seen to.

COMPARISONS ARE ODIOUS.

WHEN M. Favar was appointed first ballet-master of Drury Lane Theatre, Soderini, one of the violin players, went on the stage after the first rehearsal, and said to him, "Allow me, my dear sir, to introduce myself to you. You are the dearest friend I have on earth; let me thank you a thousand times for the happiness you have conferred on me by coming amongst us. Command me in any way, for whatever I do for you, I can never sufficiently repay you." The ballet-master, who had never seen or heard of Soderini before, was astonished. "Pray, sir," said he, "to what peculiar piece of good fortune may I attribute the compliments and professions you favour me with?" "To your unparalleled ugliness, my dear sir," replied Soderini; "for before *your* arrival, I was considered the ugliest man in Great Britain."

WISE AS THE SERPENT.

IN Marmontel's tragedy of *Cleopatra*, represented in the last century in the Théâtre Français, when the Egyptian queen was about to commit *felony-de-se*, she held in her hands a mechanical asp of cunning workmanship devised by Vaucanson, the ingenious mechanician. This venomous reptile reared its head, and, before plunging its apparent fangs into the arm of the actress, gave a shrill hiss. A spectator hereupon arose, and left the house, with the simple but expressive remark, "I am of the same opinion as the asp."

BARTERING SEATS.

MRS. BAKER was an eccentric notoriety in her theatrical circuit. This lady manager never allowed but one pay-place for box, pit, and gallery, and but one cash-taker, namely, herself. She was always to be seen in *propria persona* at her station from the opening to the closing of the doors. No "reasonable offer" was refused by her, and at the lag-end of an evening performance, the little vagabonds who hovered about the entrance, children of tender age, would sometimes tender threepence, sometimes fourpence, to be admitted to the closing scenes of the entertainments, which small remuneration the lady, provided she was in good humour, would graciously accept. Nay, not unfrequently would she deign to smile upon other proffers than the current coin of this realm, from these little stage-struck vagrants, such as a penknife, a pair of scissors, a nut-cracker, or any such tangible and useful article. By this system she became a sort of unlicensed pawnbroker, for such articles were generally deposited for seats in the gallery, redeemable, however, without interest, at the earliest convenience of the pledger. A pet dove was once offered by a little girl, anxious for admission to the gallery on any usurious terms, and was accepted on the agreement that the bird was to be redeemed the next morning *before its breakfast-time* at pit price.

A TIMELY RESCUE.

THE experienced actor is prepared for all accidents, cool upon all occasions, equal to every emergency. Some five and twenty years ago a sensational drama was played at the Gaieté Theatre, in Paris, entitled *Le Fils de la Nuit.* The chief attraction in this piece was a naval engagement between a pirate brig and two small boats. During the first performance of this effective scene, brilliantly illuminated by electric light, a ludicrous accident almost totally spoiled the whole effect. One of the fifty supers who worked the stormy undulations of the ocean, managed to push his head through the canvas waves. For the sake of coolness, he had divested himself of his upper garment, and there he stood, head and bust in the brilliant light, exposed to the full view of the spectators. Fechter, who represented the pirate captain, and commanded on board the brig, did not lose his presence of mind, but immediately called out, "A man overboard!" Aided by the crew, the amazed super was hauled on board, amid the applause of the gratified spectators, who fancied that this rescue from a watery grave formed part of the play.

A QUEEN OF FASHION.

ORIGINALLY known as "Nosegay Nan"—a flower-girl in the Mall, St. James's Park, and a ballad singer at tavern doors—Fanny Barton, in 1735, made her *début* in Theophilus Cibber's company, at the Haymarket Theatre, as Miranda in *The Busy Body*. In 1759 she married her music-master, and then became Mrs. Abington. The union, however, was not a happy one, and ere long husband and wife parted company not to meet again. Step by step Mrs. Abington ascended to the head of her profession, and when a few years after her *début* she appeared in Smock Alley Theatre, Dublin, she at once was declared the Queen of Fashion. "Even so early," says Chetwood, the historian of the Irish stage, "did she discern a taste in dress and a talent to lead the *ton*, that several of the ladies' most fashionable ornaments were distinguished by her name, and the Abington cap became the prevailing rage of the day." Five years later she took all the leading characters in comedy at Drury Lane, where for eighteen years she delighted the town with her ladies of fashion and grand coquettes—Lady Townley, Lady Betty Modish, Lydia Languish, Lady Teazle, and such like fluttering embodiments of fashion and frivolity.

Her pay was £12 a week, besides £60 a year for her wardrobe, and a benefit night. All her spare time was occupied in running about London to give advice to aristocratic ladies on the all-important subject of dress and new fashions. She was consulted like a doctor, and feed in a most liberal manner. No marriage, drawing-room, masquerade, or entertainment took place but Mrs. Abington's assistance was requested, in order to regulate dress and decoration. In this manner alone she made over £2000 a year. Her attire on and off the stage was always perfection, and much studied and copied. In this she displayed more than art: it was true genius; and as the disciples of Pythagoras imposed silence on all cavillers by the words, "The master has said it," so it was sufficient in London to say, "It is like Mrs. Abington's," to stop the mouth of grumbling husbands and fathers. Mrs. Abington has been not less than four times portrayed by Sir Joshua Reynolds—in the character of Roxalana in *The Sultan*, of Miss Prue in *Love for Love*, of Lady Teazle in *The School for Scandal*, and as the "Comic Muse." This once celebrated beauty outlived her popularity. She died in 1815, "the world forgetting, by the world forgot."

WAR AND SONG.

EMPRESS CATHERINE of Russia, being desirous of engaging Catarina Gabrielli, the celebrated Italian vocalist, for the Imperial Theatre at St. Petersburg, sent an agent to Milan to inquire from the *diva* what would be her terms. "Fifteen hundred pounds sterling per annum, besides a house and private carriage." The Empress's agent remonstrated with her on the unreasonableness of so enormous a salary, assuring her that it was the pay of a Field-Marshal. "Very well," objected the *diva;* "then Her Majesty had better make her Field-Marshals sing."

A SPARE DIET.

MESSRS. J. PAIN and Bouilly, two French playwrights, produced, by joint authorship, some pleasing pieces, the best of which was *Fanchon la Vielleuse*, which was a great success. This was followed by many other productions of the same authors, which, however, were not near so good; the public thereupon remarked that "*Fanchon n'eût pas tant maigri, si jamais elle ne se fût nourrie qui de Pain et de Bouilly.*"

THE GALLOWS-BUILDER.

IN 1792, Colman's *Surrender of Calais* was produced at the Haymarket, in which a scene occurs between two carpenters who had to build the gallows upon which the unhappy patriots were to be executed. Parsons played the chief workman, in which character he had to say, "So the king is coming; an the king like not my scaffold I am no true man." One night, when George III. was present, the humorous player gave the passage a different turn. Advancing very near the royal box, he exclaimed, "An the king were here, and did not admire my scaffold, I would say, 'D—— him! he has no taste.'" This innovation, accompanied with his usual grimace and horizontal protrusion of his leg, produced an irresistible effect. The king burst into a fit of laughter, and was among the foremost to applaud and the last to desist.

A DEATHBED MARRIAGE.

THE witty George Farquhar's last play, *The Beaux' Stratagem*, was begun, finished, and acted in the space of six weeks; when he was almost dying—and, in fact, he expired, before the run of his comedy was over. Wilkes, the comedian, often used to visit him in his last days, and once told him that Mrs. Oldfield thought he had dealt too freely with the character of Mrs. Sullen in the play, in giving her to Archer, without a proper divorce. "To solve that question," replied the dying wit, "*I*'ll get a real divorce, marry her myself, and give her my bond she shall be a real widow in less than a week."

SUDDEN MADNESS.

WHEN Thomas Sheridan was at his zenith in Dublin, a tragic actor named Layfield was also held in high estimation. His distinguished parts were Ventidius, Iago, Cassius, Syphax, and Apamantus. One night, doing Iago to Sheridan's Othello, Layfield came out with—

> "Oh, my Lord! beware of jealousy;
> It is a green-eyed *lobster*."

After this the play could proceed no further. Layfield was at that moment struck with incurable madness, and died somewhat in the manner of Nat Lee, the tragic poet. The above "green-eyed lobster" was the first instance poor Layfield gave of this dreadful visitation.

A MUSIC LESSON.

AT the period the ancient ballad of "The Old English Gentleman" burst on the world, two publishers laid claim to the copyright as authors of the accompaniment. The case was tried in the Court of King's Bench, before Lord Denman, who acted as judge. Tom Cooke, the vocalist, was subpœnaed as a witness for one of the parties, and Sir James Scarlett was retained as counsel. In the course of the trial, Sir James elicited the following evidence:—

Sir James. Now, Mr. Cooke, you say the melodies are the same, but different?

Cooke. I said the notes in the two copies were alike, but with a different accent.

Sir James. What is a musical accent?

Cooke. When I explain anything in music I charge a guinea a lesson. (*Loud laughter in court.*)

Sir James (*rather ruffled*). Never mind your terms. I ask you what is a musical accent? Can you see it?

Cooke. No.

Sir James. Can you feel it?

Cooke. A musician can.

Sir James. Now, sir, don't beat about the bush, but tell his lordship and the jury, who are supposed to know nothing about it, the meaning of what you call an accent.

Cooke. The accent in music is a stress laid on a particular note, as you would lay a stress on a particular word, for the purpose of being better understood. If I were to say, "You are an *ass*," the accent would rest on *ass*; but were I to say, "*You* are an ass," it would rest on *you*, Sir James. (*Reiterated shouts of laughter by the whole court, in which the judge and bench joined.*)

When silence was obtained, Lord Denman addressed the crest-fallen counsel: "Are you satisfied, Sir James?" Sir James had become *scarlet*, blushing like the rose, very unlike his brethren in general. And, considering the tenor of Cooke's evidence not in accordance with the harmony of his feelings, being instrumental in leading him up to ridicule, Sir James, in rather a *con-spirito* style, told the witty Thomas Cooke to go down, who retired amidst screams of laughter and applause.

SARAH BERNHARDT, FIRST OLD WOMAN.

IN September, 1876, it was proposed to produce *Rome Vaincue* at the Théâtre Français. There is an old man and an old woman in that piece, and the question arose who was to impersonate the old woman. Not every actress is willing to abdicate her charms for a whole night. Sarah Bernhardt, however, was ready to hide her youth and beauty under burnt-cork wrinkles and a white flaxen wig. She appeared as Posthumia, a blind old crone, wrinkled as a pippin in May. Mounet Sully impersonated an aged Gaul. Both were splendid, and acted their part to perfection. The success was immense; the public was fascinated, and the admiration of the talented actress nearly degenerated into sheer idolatry.

THE CORONET AMONG THE ACTRESSES.

"UNEASY lies the head that wears a crown," writes our great dramatist, and there is not an actress that does not know the line. They do not seem to apply it to the coronet, however, for not a few actresses have been willing to exchange the sock or buskin for the troubles attending upon greatness. Witness the following list:—

LAVINIA FENTON made her first appearance at the Haymarket Theatre in 1726, as Monimia, in Otway's tragedy of *The Orphan*, being then eighteen years of age. In 1728, *The Beggars' Opera* was first produced at Lincoln's Inn Fields, when she played Polly Peachum, at a salary of 30*s*. a week. The next year she retired from the stage under the protection of the Duke of Bolton, who promised her the succession to his wife. It was not till three and twenty years after that the duke could and did redeem his engagement. Lavinia died in 1760, aged 52.

HARRIET MELLON was the daughter of a poor strolling actress, and made her first appearance as Lydia Languish, in Sheridan's comedy of *The Rivals*, January 31, 1795. On January 8, 1815, she married Mr. Coutts, the opulent banker, then a widower of two months' standing. He died in 1822, leaving her an income of over £70,000 a year. On the 16th of June, 1827, she married the Duke of St. Albans, then in the twenty-seventh year of his age. The duke died in 1849; the duchess on August 6th, 1857.

ANASTASIA ROBINSON made her first appearance on January 27, 1714, in the opera *Creso*, before which time she had sung at concerts in York Buildings, and at her own house in Golden Square. The Earl of Peterborough, the hero of the expedition in Spain, in 1724 took her from the stage, and married her secretly, and, though the marriage was not made public for many years, she received the best company at Peterborough House, Fulham, and Bevis Mount, Southampton. The Earl died in 1735, aged 75. The countess survived him till 1750.

ELIZABETH FARRAN made her first appearance at the Haymarket, as Miss Hardcastle in *She Stoops to Conquer*, in 1777. A platonic affection, it is said, long existed between the Earl of Derby and this actress. When she played in *The School for Scandal*, his lordship sometimes crept up to her behind the screen, to the great amusement of the audience, who used to hope that it would fall a little too soon. Miss Farran during this *liaison* moved in the best society, and had to wait a score of years for the death of the countess. In less than three weeks after this event happened her marriage with the earl was arranged, an indecent haste that did not augur well for the happiness of the future. She quitted the stage, and on April 8, 1797, became Countess of Derby. She died in 1829, her brilliant marriage having ended in prosy fashion by divorce.

LOUISA BRUNTON made her first appearance at Covent Garden Theatre, as Lady Townley in the comedy of the *Provoked Husband*, on the 5th of October, 1803. She retired from the stage on May 26, 1808, when she married the Earl of Craven, and died, in the 78th year of her age, September 3, 1860.

MARIA FOOTE made her first appearance at Covent Garden Theatre, as Amanthis, in Mrs. Inchbald's comedy of *The Child of Nature*, in June, 1814. On the 7th of April, 1831, when she was about thirty-five, she became Countess of Harrington. Before that happy consummation she had "loved not wisely, but too well," and had two children by Colonel Berkeley. Nor was the earl her only suitor. During the years which she devoted to make the colonel happy, she had constant offers of marriage from wealthy suitors. One of these—Joseph Hayne, Esq., of

Burderop Park, Wilts—was accepted; but having changed his mind, he was mulcted in £3000 for breach of promise. Well might she sing, in the character of Phœbe in *Rosina*—

> "There's fifty young men have told me fine tales,
> And call'd me the fairest she."

The countess died in 1867.

KATHERINE STEPHENS made her first appearance at Covent Garden Theatre, as Mandane in Dr. Arne's opera *Artaxerxes*, in September, 1813. Twenty-five years after, Kitty, being then forty-five, married the Earl of Essex, who was 83. She died in February, 1882, at the age of 88, having been a widow for forty-three years.

MARY BOLTON made her first appearance as Polly Peachum, October 8th, 1806. She married Edward, Lord Thurlow, in 1813. He was nephew to the first Lord Thurlow, the judge, and was well known for some poems, not devoid of merit.

ELIZABETH O'NEILL, born in 1791, made her first appearance at Covent Garden Theatre, as Juliet, on the 6th of October, 1814. She retired from the stage, and married William Wrixon Becher, Esq., on the 18th of December, 1819. On the death of his uncle Mr. Becher succeeded to the baronetcy, and his wife became Lady Wrixon Becher. She died about 1875. Miss O'Neill and her relations, it is well known, suggested to Thackeray the Fotheringays and Captain Costigan.

LOUISA MORDAUNT, born in 1812, made her first curtsy to a London audience at Drury Lane, on October 16, 1829, as the Widow Cheerly in *The Soldier's Daughter.* Her first marriage took place in 1831; her husband, Captain John Alexander Nisbeth, of the Life Guards, died shortly after, killed by an accident with a buggy. On the 15th of October, 1844, she married Sir William Boothby, Bart., and was left a second time a widow in 1845. Being but slenderly provided for, she returned to the stage.

MISS ROBINSON, not the famous "Perdita," early in this century married Sir Charles Felix Smith, of the Royal Engineers.

Finally, MISS SAUNDERS, a provincial actress, some five and twenty years ago married Sir William Don, a Scotch baronet, who had taken to the stage as a profession.

Among actresses who have married younger sons, we find, in modern times—

SUSANNAH PATON, who made her first curtsy to a London public at the Haymarket Theatre, August 3, 1822, as Susannah in *The Marriage of Figaro.* In 1824 she married Lord William Pitt Lennox, a younger son of the Duke of Richmond. Divorced at her own suit, she subsequently became the wife of Wood, the singer, and died in 1864.

CAMILLE DUBOIS married, in 1877, the Hon. Wyndham Edward Campbell Stanhope, brother of the present Earl of Harrington.

A CANDID CONFESSION.

THE tenor Gabrielli, brother of the great female singer of that name, once appeared at the Teatro Argentini, in Rome. Before he had got through a dozen bars of his first song the critics began to hiss and hoot, and very deservedly, for he was execrable. Gabrielli thereupon came forward, and addressed the audience in these words :—"You fancy you are mortifying me by hooting me ; you are grossly deceived. On the contrary, I applaud your judgment, for I solemnly declare to you that I never appeared on any stage without receiving the same treatment, and sometimes much worse !" This appeal, though it produced a momentary laugh, could not procure a second appearance for the poor fellow.

A PROTEST.

ON the 23rd of January, 1793, a play was represented in Paris, entitled *Dumouriez à Bruxelles*, written by a notorious lady of doubtful character, Olympia de Gouges. At the conclusion, when, according to French custom, the audience inquired the name of the author, an elderly female with a shaggy, towzy head, surmounted by a bonnet put on awry, leant over one of the boxes. "Gentlemen," she exclaimed, "you desire to know the author: it is I, Olympia de Gouges. You have hissed my piece, not because it was bad, but because it was infamously played." This sally was received with roars of derisive laughter, and when Olympia protested, the uproar became so outrageous, that she had to fly. At the second representation, the pit thought proper to interrupt the performance. A "tree of liberty" had been inaugurated in the first scene, and in a moment a number of men made their way on to the stage, and commenced dancing the Carmagnole round the "property" tree with the same enthusiasm which characterized such patriotic performances in the streets of Paris.

PUBLIC DISCRIMINATION.

JACK BANNISTER, happening to be at Manchester, by way of amusement asked the manager of the theatre to advertise him under a feigned name for some small part in a comedy, announcing at the same time that between the play and the farce, the gentleman would "attempt a scene in *The Children in the Wood*, after the manner of the celebrated Mr. John Bannister, of the Theatre Royal, Drury Lane." Bannister acted his part in the play, and passed unnoticed; at the conclusion the curtain again rose for the imitation. On walked the mimic in suitable costume, as perfect a Walter as ever was seen, and went through the scene selected for the purpose after his best manner. But the interruptions were many, for scarcely had he spoken three lines, when he was saluted by a most distinct hiss. This was soon followed by cries of "Off! off! trash!—hiss, hiss!" announcing to the poor country "presumer" that he had entirely failed. In fact, he was completely condemned. He ventured to address the audience, but no, they would not hear him. They were thoroughly disgusted at the attempt at imitation, which a journal the next morning declared "the vilest that had ever been offered to the public."

THEATRICAL CRITICISM.

"A NEW comedy," says Reynolds in his *Life and Times*, "written by one of my particular friends, was put into rehearsal. On the very evening that it was to be produced, meeting a late leading critic of the day as he was going out of town, and asking him to speak good-naturedly of my friend's play, he kindly told me that I might write myself the theatrical criticism for the following morning's newspaper, but to be sure to confine my praise within rational bounds. Speeding post-haste with this good news to my friend, the author, he quietly heard my communication, and then replied, 'Pooh! *You* write the account of my piece! I shall write it *myself*.' He was as good as his word; and sending his precious *morceau* to the printer in my name, it was, according to the previous direction of the great critic and editor, inserted verbatim. The following morning I was not a little astonished when I read that 'The first four acts of the comedy of the previous evening were not inferior in point of plot, incident, language, and character to the greatest efforts of Beaumont and Fletcher and other old dramatists,' and 'that the last act might probably be considered one of the finest on the stage.'"

THE DEAR DEPARTED.

MACKLIN was very intimate with Frank Hayman, the historical painter, and happening to call upon him one morning, soon after the death of the painter's wife (with whom the latter had lived on but indifferent terms), he found him wrangling with the undertaker about the extravagance of the funeral expenses. Macklin listened to the altercation for some time; at last, going up to Hayman, he observed with great gravity

"Come, come, Frank; though the bill is a little extravagant, pay it in respect to the memory of your poor wife; for I am sure she would have done twice as much for you, had she had the same opportunity."

STAGE OATHS.

WE have the testimony of Uncle Toby that the officers in the army before Dunkerque "swore terribly," for which there was, no doubt, some reason in their minds. A similar bad practice appears to have obtained a hundred years before on the stage, for in 1606 it was thought necessary to refrain the use of big words in plays. An Act (3 Jas. I. c. 21) was framed "to prevent the profane use of the Holy Name of God, or of Christ Jesus, or of the Holy Ghost, of the Trinity, in any play, on a penalty of £10."

A STROLLING LUMINARY.

THE old theatre at Jacobs Well, Bristol, was situated a quarter of a mile from the city; and as there were no lamps in that quarter in the last century, the walk home in the dark, through a dirty road and a long, dreary rope-walk, was the reverse of exhilarating. This caused the periodical appearance of the moon to be hailed with general satisfaction, and the performer whose benefit happened to fall when that luminary was in the sky, took care to insert at the foot of the bill that it would be "a moonlight night." A cunning old fox, named Richard Winstone, bethought himself of a manner to make the full moon on the night of his benefit a cause of special attraction, and communicated the expected appearance of the luminous orb in the following words:—"And on this night Madame Cynthia will appear in her utmost splendour." Few of the Bristol public thought of consulting Lempriere's *Classical Dictionary;* the majority jumped to the conclusion that Madame Cynthia was some

French or Italian performer whom old Winstone had prevailed upon to take a part in his benefit. The house was crowded to suffocation, and at the end of each act all eyes were directed towards the stage-door from which madame was expected to make her entry. When the play ended, and even the hope that the illustrious foreigner was reserved to dance or sing at the end of the performance could no longer be entertained, the manager was vociferously called upon to explain why he had presumed to insert in his bill of fare the name of a performer whom he did not produce. "Ladies and gentlemen," said the old stager, after making his best bow to the house, "although Madame Cynthia does not think fit to appear on these boards, she will cheerfully lend you her assistance to get safely home; and I once more beg leave to congratulate you on its being a *fine moonlight night*."

STUFFED.

POPE the comedian's besetting sin was gastronomy. Amongst the many anecdotes related of him is a curious *équivoque* which he occasioned at Drury Lane Theatre. *The Suspicious Husband* was in rehearsal, in which Pope had gone through the character of Strickland; but the actor who had to sustain the part of his servant Tester "being suddenly taken ill," an understrapper was called on to fulfil his duties. This unhappy wight, being puzzled about the costume he had to wear, accosted Pope just as he was passing off the wing, on his way home to dinner. "Pray, sir," said he, with nervous abruptness, "how is it to be dressed?" Pope, whose thoughts were running on the turkey awaiting him, replied as abruptly, "Stuffed, to be sure; stuffed, by all means." On the evening of the play's representation, when "all ladies and gentlemen concerned" met in the green-room, ready to go on for their respective parts, in walks the Tester of the night, as complete a Falstaff in livery as could possibly have been accomplished. The shrieks of the assembled party can well be imagined. "In the name of all that's wonderful, what is this?" was the universal demand. "Why! why! Mr. Pope said it should be stuffed, and I can assure you I have had trouble enough to get it all in," replied the terrified votary of the Thespian art.

JULIET'S FALL.

A LAUGHABLE occurrence took place in the theatre at Wigan, when the present century was in its teens. The juvenile leading lady, a good actress—a very pretty woman by the way, and a young mother—was cast to play Juliet in *Romeo and Juliet*. Her baby had been placed in her dressing-room for security, and in order that it should be near its mother. But just before the balcony scene the young tyrant became unruly and impossible to control. What was to be done? A mother's tact hit upon the true soothing syrup; she nestled the infant to her breast, and from that moment the young villain became silent as a mouse. Juliet, being called, hastily mounted the supposed balcony, throwing a lace scarf over her shoulders, which concealed the little suckling; and leaning over the balcony, with her other arm pensively placed upon her cheek, she looked the picture of innocence and beauty. The scene opened and went glowingly. But, alas! Juliet has to appear and disappear three times, and in her effort to do so gracefully, and yet conceal the baby, she stumbled against the iron brace that supported the frail structure. Down fell the front of the balcony, and, lo! the love-lorn maid was discovered with a baby at her breast, seated on a tub, and at her foot, accidentally placed there by the thirsty carpenter, was a quart pot of beer. The said carpenter was discovered on all-fours, steadying with his back the rickety structure above. Shrieks of laughter from all parts of the house greeted the tableau, and of the play no more was heard that night.

SHERIDAN KNOWLES.

SHERIDAN KNOWLES was the most eccentric of men One day he said to Abbot, with whom he had been acting somewhere in the country, "My dear fellow, I'm off to-morrow. Can I take any letters for you?" postage being very expensive in those days. "You're very kind," answered Abbot; "but where are you going to?" "I haven't made up my mind," was the startling reply. On another occasion, seeing O. Smith, the popular melodramatic actor, on the opposite side of the Strand, Knowles rushed across the road, seized him by the hand, and inquired eagerly after his health. Smith, who only knew him by sight, said, "I think, Mr. Knowles, you are mistaken; I am O. Smith." "My dear fellow," cried Knowles, "I beg you ten thousand pardons; I took you for your *namesake*, T. P. Cooke!"

A THEATRICAL MRS. PARTINGTON.

PRADON, a very inferior rival of Racine, possessed neither genius nor education. The Prince de Conti, meeting him after the first representation of his tragedy *Tamerlan*, observed, "Why, Pradon, you have transported in your play a town from Asia to Europe." "I humbly beg your Royal Highness's pardon," said the dramatist, "but I must confess I don't understand anything about *chronology*."

MARRIAGES MADE IN HEAVEN.

IN Bannister's *Memoirs* a curious fact is related concerning the marriage of John Kemble. One of the daughters of Lord North, the statesman, had fallen in love with the graceful and showy actor merely from seeing him on the stage. Kemble was sent for by the father, and, to his astonishment, acquainted with the circumstance. The noble lord told him further that it was in Kemble's power to do him a great favour, relieving him effectually from all apprehension of the young lady's further indulging her fancy, by marrying any one else for whom he might have an attachment, in which case his lordship promised the actor's wife a dower of £5000. Kemble immediately proposed to Miss Brereton, daughter of Hopkins, the Drury Lane prompter, a pretty actress in the company, and the marriage took place without delay. Upon this happy event the afflicted and magnanimous father recovered his spirits instantly, but lost his memory. When Kemble applied for the promised thousands, my lord declared that he had no recollection whatever of the contract further than some general conversation on such matters, adding that if he was to pay £5000 for every whim of his daughter's, he would soon be a poor man. It is believed that Kemble never got a shilling from this sensitive nobleman, and that for the rest of his life he attached a new value to the vulgar etiquette of signing and sealing beforehand, even with the most plausible of mankind. It must be added, however, that Kemble, on seeing this story in print, declared it to be "a lie."

COURT AND COURTESY.

THE following is a pleasant glimpse of theatrical life in the time of "the Merry Monarch." It is from the *Sketches and Notes* of old Downes, bookkeeper, otherwise prompter, of Davenant's Theatre in Lincoln's Inn Fields. "*The Sullen Lovers* (a play by Shadwell) was a wonderful success, being acted twelve days together, when our company were commanded to Dover, in May, 1670, the king, with all his court, meeting his sister, the Duchess of Orleans, there. This comedy and *Sir Solomon Single* pleased Madam the Duchess and the whole company extremely. The French court wore then excessive short, laced coats, some scarlet, some blue, with broad waist-belts. Mr. Nokes having at that time one shorter than the French fashion to act Sir Arthur Addle in, the Duke of Monmouth gave him his sword and belt from his side, and buckled it on himself, on purpose to ape the French. Mr. Nokes looked more like a dressed-up ape than a Sir Arthur, which, upon his first entrance on the stage, put the king and court to an excessive laughter, at which the French looked very chagrined to see themselves aped by such a buffoon as Sir Arthur. Mr. Nokes kept the duke's sword to his dying day."

SLIPS OF THE TONGUE.

MR. LEATHES, in his entertaining volume *An Actor Abroad*, gives some amusing instances of what is called "getting the tongue into a knot." "I once heard," he says, "a very famous tragedian, when playing Claude Melnotte in *The Lady of Lyons*, speak of the box given to his 'grand-grand-great mother!' I have twice heard that common and ridiculous mistake made by a utility man in *Richard the Third*, 'Stand back, my lord, and let the parson cough,' instead of 'the coffin pass.' It is not difficult to make a nervous performer misplace a word; it is easy and unkind. I once chaffed a lady who was going to play the player Queen in *Hamlet*, and was nervous, into saying—

'Nor earth to me give heaven, nor food light.'"

THE FIRST PLAY IN AMERICA.

ON the 5th of September, 1752, the first play performed in America by a regular company of comedians was represented to a delighted audience at Williamsburg, the capital of Virginia. The piece was the *Merchant of Venice*, and it was followed by Garrick's farce of *Lethe*. Thus Shakespeare had the first place in time as in merit as the dramatist of the western world, and Garrick the honour of attending upon his master. *Lethe* was then new even in London, and a favourite afterpiece. William Hallam, who had failed, in 1750, as manager in Goodman's Fields, London, was the person who had enlisted the *corps dramatique* for a visit to the "western wilderness." His brother, Lewis Hallam, was appointed manager, and William, who stayed at home, was to be "viceroy over him" according to Trinculo's division of offices. The apostles who were to propagate the drama in America were twelve in number, and twenty-four plays and their attendant farces had been cast and put in study before leaving England. The reason that the company went to Virginia, in preference to the other American provinces, was because the first settlers in that state were of the established English Church, and more liberally disposed towards the drama than all other sects. Hallam, upon application to the Governor, obtained permission to erect or fit up a building for a theatre, and a long house in the suburbs of Williamsburg was metamorphosed into pit, boxes, gallery, and stage. It was situated so near the woods, that the manager could stand within the door and shoot pigeons for his dinner, which he more than once did.

A PROVOST'S INTERVENTION.

AN instance of accidental recognition occurred in Scotland, in 1793, which was not a little curious. Mrs. Cross, of Covent Garden Theatre, was in that year acting in Glasgow. On one occasion, the Provost being present, the lady had no sooner made her appearance on the stage, than the agitated functionary exclaimed, "Stop—stop the play! I would speak to that woman." Great was the consternation throughout the auditory at this occurrence, and the curtain being immediately lowered, the perturbed Provost made his way at once into the actresses' dressing-room. After a few hurried words, he discovered her to be his own wife, from whom he had been separated for nearly twenty years. Each had supposed the other dead! The magistrate, hereupon, bore off the lady to his house, and the next evening she took her place in the boxes, where she was quite as much a heroine as when sustaining the woes of Calista on the stage.

TWO ROMEOS.

A LADY of fashion being asked her opinion of the Romeo of Garrick and of Barry, said, "When I saw Garrick, if I had been his Juliet, I should have wished him to leap up into the balcony to me; but when I saw Barry, I should have been inclined to jump down to him."

PAINFUL COINCIDENCE.

SIMS REEVES, the great tenor, before he became a singer, was playing "little business," and occasionally "singing walking gentleman," at a salary of 35*s.* a week, in the Newcastle-upon-Tyne troupe. One evening he was playing the Squire in the pantomime of *Old Mother Goose*, and at the very moment when he was walking off the stage, singing—

"My wife is dead, there let her lie,
She's at rest, and so am I,"

A man tapped him hurriedly on the shoulder, and whispered, "You must come home directly; Mrs. Reeves is dead." He hurried home, and found it was but too true.

THE MOMENTOUS QUESTION.

JOHN ASHLEY, who at one time conducted the oratorios at Covent Garden, was a great lover of money. The keys of his strong box had much more harmony for him than the keys of the piano. Just before the performance of one of the oratorios, Ashley was suddenly seized by a fit of epilepsy, and fell down, as though stricken with death, in the green-room of the theatre. Medical aid was speedily procured, but for a considerable time it was doubtful whether or not the attack was fatal. The patient, however, was so far restored as to regain consciousness of things around him, when, earnestly clasping the hands of a friend who bent over him, he exclaimed, "In the name of Heaven, tell me what sort of a house it is?"

A PARALLEL TO A PARABLE.

IN the time when Thomas Sheridan was manager of the Dublin Theatre, a fashion prevailed amongst the *dessus du panier*-ladies of that city of benefiting distinguished players by the lady patroness attending in person early at the entrance of her box in the theatre, and receiving her company, as in her own drawing-room, who paid their respects to her before taking their places. Frequent jealousies arose among the leaders of fashion concerning the *éclat* on their respective nights. In the year 1758, a rich brewer's wife, ambitious of trying her strength in a higher sphere, was rash enough to take a patronizing lead for the benefit of some actor. She issued her cards accordingly in the fashionable world for a special night, and took her place early in the theatre for the general reception. To her great mortification, however, and no less of the poor beneficiary, her levée had but a gloomy appearance. Seated in solitary grandeur at the door of her box, she had little interruption to her own meditation, for no company arrived. She was in a high state of anger and nervous irritation, when at last the box-keeper, advancing with an aspect of encouragement, observed, "Your ladyship's gallery is excellent; your ladyship's gallery looks charming!" In the course of five minutes the man returned, contentedly rubbing his hands, and bowing, "Your ladyship's pit is improving; we don't despair of your ladyship's pit."

By this time the curtain was up for the comedy. Maddened

with rage, the lady now took her seat on her crimson chair in a side box, with an agreeable view of the whole dress circle perfectly empty, some twenty forlorn individuals in the pit, but "her ladyship's gallery excellent." Her state was positively volcanic. At the close of the first act, the box-keeper again advanced, observing, "Your ladyship's gallery is really tremendous—positively overwhelming; we can't contain them." "Send them here," ejaculated the lady, gasping with fury. "Send them here, if there are five hundred, and let the expenses be mine." The order was at once obeyed, and a body of ragamuffins was admitted, which, if quantity did not supply the absence of quality, was most satisfactory. The house was now a bumper. The benefit thus turned out a good one, but the lady patroness withdrew from that hour as a leader of fashion.

A NEW SPECIES OF RATANY.

THE late Désiré, of the Bouffes Parisiens, had a friend passionately fond of flowers and rare plants, and who considered himself a great judge of them. One day Désiré buried a dead rat in a flower-pot, and, allowing the tail to remain above the earth, tied it up to a training stick. He sent this pot to his friend as a very rare specimen of a cactus. After many days of great care and constant watering, which such a valuable exotic required, the victim of Désiré's pleasantry began to think that something might be amiss with the root of the plant. He pulled the prodigy from the pot, and—*smelt a rat.*

A GHASTLY DRIVE.

A RATHER singular occurrence once happened to Mrs. Bland, a celebrated ballad songstress, the delight of our grandparents. She had ordered a hackney coach to be in readiness at the door of Drury Lane Theatre to convey her home at the close of the evening's entertainment. In she got, but after some time perceived that the vehicle was proceeding in the contrary direction to the place of her residence. She pulled the check-string, but to no purpose; the driver heeded not. After a while, thoroughly terrified, she lowered the glass, and shouted for help; but the hackney at that moment was in some shady part of London, and her cries only were answered by derisive jokes. The passers-by fancied that the young lady was merely in company of too lively a companion. At length, however, some charitable soul stopped the horses, and it was then discovered that the poor driver—sat dead upon his box.

A PERTURBED GHOST.

AS Dowton one evening was playing the ghost in *Hamlet*, he was lowered by means of the trap in the stage, his face being turned towards the audience. Elliston and De Camp, who were concealed below, had provided themselves with canes, and whilst Dowton slowly descended to solemn music, they sharply and rapidly belaboured the thinly clad calves of his legs. Poor Dowton, whose duty it was to look as calm and dignified as a ghost usually does, could scarcely refrain from shouting. Choking with rage, he at length reached the lower regions under the stage, and looked round for his torturers. Elliston and De Camp had, of course, in time *decamped*. Just, then Holland, dressed for some part in the highest finish of fashion, issued from one of the rooms. The enraged Dowton, taking him for the offender, seized a mop immersed in dirty water, and, thrusting it in his face, utterly ruined ruffles, point-lace, and every particular of his elaborate attire. In vain Holland protested his innocence, and implored for mercy. His cries only whetted the appetite of the other's revenge; again and again the saturated mop was at work on his finery.

Somewhat cooled by this retaliation, Dowton at last left his victim; but by this time the prompter's bell had announced the commencement of the piece in which Holland was to appear.

What was to be done? The drama was proceeding; it was impossible for him to present himself in the condition to which he had been reduced. All was confusion worse confounded. An apology for the sudden indisposition of Mr. Holland was made, and the public informed that Mr. De Camp had "kindly undertaken to go on for the part."

TWO ACCIDENTS.

AT one time there were two actors of the name of Palmer—John Palmer, nicknamed "Plausible Jack," and another, Isaac Palmer, who, being less celebrated than his namesake, was styled in the play-bills Mr. I. Palmer. A day or two after the sudden death of "Plausible Jack" on the Liverpool stage, an actor, on leaving the green-room after a rehearsal, meeting a friend in the street, was asked if there was any news in the theatrical world. "Yes," was the reply, "most melancholy news: John Palmer is dead, and another Palmer has had an eye knocked out." It may be proper to add that the initial "I" to the name of Palmer the second had been immediately omitted in the play-bills on the death of his namesake, because he was then the only Mr. Palmer.

A DEED OF DREADFUL NOTE.

PAUL BEDFORD, among many good anecdotes in his *Reminiscences,* has the following:—On one of his provincial tours with manager Yates, the *répertoire* included a farce, entitled *Deeds of Dreadful Note.* A dummy was used in this piece; it was called "the victim," and, being life-size, used to travel with the troupe deposited in a capacious bag, which entirely hid it from the vulgar gaze. On leaving Newcastle for York, in the hurry of packing the bag was mislaid, and the only remedy was to put "the victim" into a potato-sack, which just reached to the neck of the figure, leaving the head exposed to view. In that state it was deposited in the luggage van with the rest of the theatrical belongings. The company had to change trains at North Allerton, and as the York train was about to start, it was discovered that the "victim" was missing. Tom Lyon at once rushed to the luggage van, and recovered the lost one. He threw the sack across his manly shoulders, and trotted along the platform, to the great disgust of all the passengers, who thought he carried a dead body; for the head of the "victim" hung on Lyon's back, and at every step the agile bearer took, it wobbled up and down in a ghastly manner. Arrived at York, the actors took up their abode at the Royal Hotel, and soon were quietly sitting down to their dinner, when a waiter entered in consternation, and whispered that a police inspector wanted to see the gentlemen who had just arrived. The myrmidon of the law made his appearance, and informed them that it was his painful duty to arrest them all as a gang of body-snatchers, a party of police being in waiting outside for that purpose. Roars of laughter greeted this communication; the victim in the sack was introduced to the police, and the character of the company redeemed. The inspector left, highly amused, and making all sorts of apologies; but the affair was rumoured through the cathedral town, and the victim became the most attractive star of the whole party.

ALL THE DIFFERENCE.

A CERTAIN actor was playing *Richard the Third* at Wells. Disapprobation of his performance was soon manifested in very palpable hisses, and by the end of the third act the endemic pervaded the whole audience. The acting certainly was bad, but the ill-nature of the audience was worse. Suddenly the poor, persecuted player, dropping his character, advanced to the front of the stage, and thus addressed his judges: "Ladies and gentleman, Mr. Kean is playing this part in London, at a salary of £30 per night. I receive but 15*s.* a week; and if it isn't good enough for the money, may the Lord above give you a better humanity." This well-timed reproof, delivered with much point and feeling, won instantly all hearts to his favour.

A FALLING STAR.

IN 1823, Barnard, an actor in the Drury Lane company essayed a benefit at the Croydon Theatre, on which occasion Elliston volunteered his services. Elliston had taken up his quarters at the Crown Inn, and the accommodation at the theatre being but indifferent, he equipped himself at his inn for the part he had to play. The approach to the theatre was by a rough and dirty lane; six o'clock was at hand, and no conveyance could be obtained; it rained, moreover, steadily. Elliston, dressed for Belcour in *The West Indian*, was presently to appear on the stage. There was no choice; throwing over his shoulders a thick woollen blanket, he got the ostler to be his beast of burden. Jumping on the man's shoulders, his whitney tightly round him, Elliston turned his "conveyance" up the lane, and, holding an umbrella over the two heads, commenced his journey to the playhouse. The exhibition was sufficiently grotesque: Belcour's silk stockings peeping from beneath the dirty blanket, his head surmounted by a huge cocked hat, could not fail to excite the native merriment of the country bumpkins who were loitering about the place; but Elliston felt that he was in for it, and would have run the gauntlet gallantly. Joe, the ostler, less patient, and additionally roused by a projectile, which hit him full in the face, deliberately flopped our hero into the mud, and scampered after the retreating rioters. Poor Belcour was now up to his ankles in the mud, and the moisture having sucked off one of his shoes in the attempt to escape, the result might have been fatal to *The West Indian*, had he not been rescued by one more humane than his fellows, and carried on to the theatre, where he at last was safely deposited.

THE STATUE OF PYGMALION.

THE conduct of Mademoiselle Raucourt, the once celebrated tragedian, of the Théâtre Français, was so indecorous, that the otherwise rather indulgent audiences of that day could not overlook her vagaries. In 1774, she had incurred public disapprobation to such an extent, that she was hissed the whole time she was impersonating Hermione in Racine's *Andromaque*, a part in which she had once been pronounced insurpassable, and which she acted then as well as ever. A curious incident procured her once more the favour of the public. It was of the same nature as that which obtained for Phryne of old the verdict of the Heliasts' tribunal. Rousseau's *Pygmalion* was to be produced, and, in order to justify the sculptor's mad passion for his work, a very exquisite statue was requisite. No greater perfection of female forms could be found than Mademoiselle Raucourt presented, and that lady had, moreover, no objection on the score of delicacy against the somewhat *léger* costume in which she had to appear. The effect she produced on the spectators when the curtain rose may be better imagined than described. There stood the matchless beauty, robed in little else but her innocence, and a ray of light as fierce as ever beat on a throne. La Harpe exclaimed, in his squeaking voice, that it was the head of Venus with the limbs of Dian. Many were the poets who sang her charms. Dorat proclaimed her more beautiful than Dido, but less chaste than Penelope. He might have added less thrifty also, for Raucourt, lavish as were the sums squandered upon her, was always over head and ears in debt. At last she had to fly from Paris to escape from her creditors. This occurrence gave the name to a new bonnet, to which there was no back, and which looked like a basket without a bottom. Now, as everybody knows, *panier percé* is synonymous for a person deeply in debt, and so the new-fashioned backless bonnet came to be called *la Raucourt*.

ABOUT BILL-STICKING.

THERE was an old lady named Wall, who had been an actress in a subordinate situation for many seasons in the Haymarket Theatre, and for whom George Colman, from early associations, had a kind consideration. In due time the old lady died. Somebody from the theatre went to break the intelligence to Colman, who, on hearing it, inquired "whether there had been any bills stuck up?" The messenger replied in the negative, and ventured to ask Mr. Colman why he had put that question. Colman answered, "They generally paste bills on a *dead wall*, don't they?"

ROMAN CITIZENS.

EDWIN FORREST'S legs were a theme of great admiration to the world at large, and of no little pride to himself. As he was playing Virginius in Baltimore, Forrest, in the costume of the Roman General, was standing at the wings, with his usual scornful smile, gazing at the actors and supernumeraries standing on the stage. The lower limbs of the actors, for the most part being plentifully padded, presented a respectable appearance; but the poor supers, being, as is usually the case in American theatres, mere overgrown boys, and having no pads, their limbs were ridiculous, and the tights with which they were covered being "a world too wide for their shrunk shanks," their appearance roused the ire of Mr. Forrest. The manager passing at the time, Forrest called his attention to the supers, and said, "Mr. Ford, for heaven's sake, *what* are those?" "Those," replied the manager, "are Roman citizens, Mr. Forrest." "Roman citizens!" exclaimed Forrest. "Ye gods!

did Romans have legs like those?" The air of utter disgust attending the words was indescribable, and Forrest stalked on the stage as if he could devour the Roman citizens, bony as they were.

ANN OLDFIELD.

THE position occupied by Mrs. Oldfield in society may be ranked among the most curious phenomena in the social history of the eighteenth century. Many actresses have played quite as well and better, many have lived purer lives, yet none have made their way into Vanity Fair with the same success as Mrs. Oldfield. Although leading a by no means irreproachable life, this comedian, "in the tea-cup days" of Queen Anne and the first two Georges, was invited to the houses of ladies of fashion as much distinguished for spotless reputation as for elevated rank. Her irregularities seem merely to have been considered "pretty Fanny's ways." Even the royal family did not disdain to see Mrs. Oldfield at their levees, and George II., when Prince of Wales, took pleasure in conversing with her. She was to be seen on the terrace of Windsor Castle, walking with duchesses and countesses and the wives of English barons. The whole gay troupe might be heard calling one another by their Christian names, and treated the pet actress on the most intimate terms of equality.

For many years Mrs. Oldfield lived with Arthur Mainwaring, the friend of Marlborough and Godolphin. After Mainwaring's death, in 1712, the Hon. Brigadier Churchill became her protector. "I hear you and the general are married," said Queen Caroline to her one day. "Madame," she replied, "the general keeps his own secrets." Mrs. Oldfield died at her house in Grosvenor Street, on the 23rd of October, 1730. On the next day she lay in state in the Jerusalem Chamber, Westminster, and, perhaps in anticipation of this "last appearance in public," had ordered the funeral attire satirized by Pope—

"Odious! in woollen! 'twould a saint provoke!
Were the last words that poor Narcissa spoke.
No! let a charming chintz and Brussels lace
Wrap my cold limbs, and shade my lifeless face.
One would not, sure, be frightful when one's dead;
And, Betty, give this cheek a little red."

"As the nicety of dress was her delight when living," says Egerton, her biographer, "she was as nicely dressed after her decease, being by Mrs. Saunders' (a friend and fellow-actress) direction thus laid in her coffin: she had on a very fine Brussels lace head, a Holland shift, with tucker and double ruffles of the same lace, a pair of new kid gloves, and her body wrapped up in a winding sheet." Late in the same night she was interred in Westminster Abbey, the supporters of her pall being the Lords Delawar and Harvey, Mr. Cary, Mr. Hedges of Finchley, Mr. Donnington, and Captain Elliot. Her tomb is at the west-end of the south aisle, near the monuments of Secretary Craggs and of Congreve, adjoining which is the room in which the Consistory or Spiritual Court used to sit. As both these gentlemen, as well as Oldfield, had been noted for amours not recognized by the Church, a witling is said to have pencilled the following ungrammatical epigram on the actress's tomb:—

"If penance in the Bishop's Court be feared,
Congreve and Craggs and Oldfield will be scared
To find that at the Resurrection Day,
They've all so near the Consistory lay."

Mrs. Oldfield had one son by Mainwaring and one by General Churchill. The latter, Colonel Churchill, married a natural daughter of the Earl of Orford, and their daughter married, in 1777, Charles Sloane, first Earl of Cadogan. Their two daughters married two brothers of the Duke of Wellington, so that Lord Cowley, late ambassador at Paris, and Lord Alfred Paget are the great great grand-children of Ann Oldfield. In the Cadogan family the Oldfield blood was increased by the marriage of Henry, Ann's grandson, in 1836, with his cousin Mary, daughter of Gerald and Emily Wellesley.

LEMAITRE'S FREAKS.

FRÉDÉRIC LEMAITRE was a singularly gifted actor, but afflicted with a certain something offensive to good taste. A note of vulgarity was observable in the man, partly owing to his daring animal spirits, but still more to an innate vulgarity of nature. He was a great favourite of the audiences of the Porte St. Martin, but, like a spoiled child, too often he abused their favour. Once he made a bet that he would take his wig off on the stage. He did so, and nothing was said. This success emboldened him; a second time he took off his head-gear, and wiped his forehead with it. Still no notice was taken of this singularity. Surprised at so much magnanimity, Lemaitre took it off a third time, and used it as a handkerchief. Then a terrible storm arose; a chorus of groans, hisses, the usual hurricanes of theatrical disapprobation, and the insulted audience roaring for the actor to make apologies. He resisted, the play was interrupted; and, in accordance with French modes of doing, the offending actor was sent to jail, where he remained for thirty-nine days, to do penance for his disgraceful jest. After that his peace with the public was soon made; his remedy was efficacious, he played if possible better than ever. A score of circumstances of this kind may be found in Lemaitre's life. Once, in the drama of *Cardillac*, he actually flung his wig to the pit. This breach of good manners was also punished with imprisonment.

DOCTOR KENT.

JOHN KEMBLE used to relate many whimsical anecdotes of provincial actors whom he knew in the early part of his life. He once "forgathered" with an actor who, being about to perform the character of Kent in *King Lear*, had dressed himself like a doctor, with a large grizzly wig, having a walking-stick which he held up to his nose, and a box under his arm. Being asked why he dressed the Earl of Kent in that manner, he replied, "People mistake the character. He was not an earl; he was a doctor. Does not Kent say, when the king draws his sword on him for speaking in favour of Cordelia, 'Do kill thy *physician*, Lear;' and when the king tells him to take his hated '*trunk* from his dominions,' and Kent says, 'Now to new climes my old *trunk* I'll bear,' what could he mean but his *medicine chest* to practice in another country?" This notion, in Whinstone's *English Dramatic Poets*, is attributed to Hall, who was a famous actor of Queen Anne's time, and the original Lockit in the *Beggar's Opera*.

ACTING WITH SPIRIT.

HURST was an actor quite of the ordinary stamp, and finding his salary not adequate to support the rank to which he aspired, he became a brandy merchant. While he was performing one of the characters in *The Rehearsal* soon after he had assumed this business, Garrick, who in representing Bayes generally introduced some opportune or personal joke, thus addressed Hurst, "Sir," said he, "you are an actor and, I understand, a brandy merchant. Now, sir, let me advise you to put less spirit in your liquor and more in your acting, and you will preserve the health of your friends, and the approbation of the public." This sally was well received, and, as Garrick intended, augmented the number of Hurst's customers.

A TEMULENT PLAY.

A SINGULAR occurrence took place at the Theatre Royal, Drury Lane, in 1693. A comedy entitled *The Wary Widow, or Sir Noisy Parrot*, written by Henry Higden, was produced. "It was condemned on its first representation owing to the extraordinary circumstance that the author had introduced so much drinking of punch into his play, that the performers got drunk during the acting of it, and were unable to go through their parts. On which account, and the treatment the audience gave them by hisses and catcalls, the house was obliged to be dismissed at the end of the third act." So says Reid's *Biographia Dramatica.* Higden's comedy was subsequently printed, and is now a scarce book, but there is a copy in the British Museum. The play, which is by no means bad, is ushered in by several complimentary verses, some of them by the well-known Tom Brown, and a prologue by Sir Charles Sedley. In the lengthy preface by the author, though he is sufficiently out of humour, no mention is made of the above untoward circumstance. The fall of the piece is solely attributed to malevolence. "The theatre was by faction transformed into a bear-garden, hissing, mimicking, ridiculing, and catcalling ; the actors could not support themselves against so strong a current." The Bacchanalian scenes in the play were not above the ordinary. In the second act, "colour'd water, prepared to look as wine," plays a part ; and one of the scenes in the third act is laid at the Rose Tavern, Covent Garden. There a vigorous drinking bout took place, at the end of which the stage direction has "Sir Noisy lets fall his glass and sinks in the chair." In this scene the punch probably was too strong, and led to the catastrophe.

HOW TO GET A PLAY ACTED.

WHEN Mallet had finished his tragedy of *Elvira* he cast about in what manner he could best prevail upon Garrick to put it on the stage. He knew that his two former plays, *Eurydice* and *Britannia*, had been no great success ; manœuvring, therefore, was necessary. One day he called upon Garrick, with *Elvira* in his pocket. After some conversation, Garrick inquired on what studies Mallet was engaged just then. "Why, 'pon my word," replied he, "I am eternally fatigued with preparing and arranging materials for the life of the great Duke of Marlborough. All my days and nights are occupied in that bright and interesting period of the British annals. But, hark you, my friend, do you know that I have found a pretty snug niche in it for you?" "Heh! how's that? A niche for me!" exclaimed Garrick, delighted. "How on earth could you bring me into the history of John Churchill, Duke of Marlborough?" "That's my business, my dear friend," was the answer; "but I tell you I have done it." "Well, faith, Mallet," rejoined David, "you have the art of surprising your friends in the most unexpected and polite manner. But why won't you, now, who are so well qualified, write something for the stage. You should really. *Interpone tuis*—ha! you know; for I am sure the theatre is a mere matter of diversion, of pleasure to you." "Why, faith," rejoined Mallet, "to tell you the truth, I have, whenever I could rob the duke of an hour or so, employed myself in adapting Lamotte's *Inez de Castro* to the English stage, and here it is." The manager embraced *Elvira* with rapture, and brought it out with all expedition.

A SMALL AUDIENCE.

WHILE Stephen Kemble was manager of a theatre at Portsmouth, which was only open twice or thrice a week, a sailor applied to him on one of the nights when there was no performance, entreating him to open that evening. He was informed that as the town had not been apprised on the occasion, the manager could not risk the expense. "What will it cost," inquired the sailor, "to open the house to-night? for to-morrow I leave the country, and God knows if I shall ever see a play again." Kemble told him that it would be five guineas(!). "Well," said Jack, "I will give it upon this condition, that you will let nobody into the house but myself." He was then asked what play he would choose, and fixed upon *Richard III.* The house was immediately lighted, the rest of the performers attended, and Jack took his station in the front row of the pit.

The play was performed throughout; the sailor was very attentive, sometimes laughing and applauding, but frequently on the *look-out* lest some other auditor might intrude. After the conclusion, he retired perfectly satisfied, and cordially thanked the manager for his ready compliance.

A GHASTLY STUDY.

WHEN the Cato-Street conspirators were to be executed, Kean sat up all night in a room opposite the debtor's door of the Old Bailey to catch a full view of the proceedings. The next morning he watched the sickening performance with the greatest attention, and as he was going on the stage in the evening, to act in a part in which he had to die, he observed, "I mean to die like Thistlewood to-night; I'll imitate every muscle of that man's countenance."

"SCHOOL FOR SCANDAL."

VANDENHOFF, in his *Dramatic Reminiscences*, gives a bit of a conversation between Mrs. Glover, Mrs. Orger, and Mrs. Humby, which, for epigrammatic *finesse*, would figure well in Sheridan's witty comedy. The ladies were discussing the marriage between Madame Vestris and Charles Mathews. "They say," remarked Mrs. Humby, with a quaint air of assumed simplicity, "that before accepting him, Vestris made a full confession of all the indiscretions of her life. What touching confidence!" "What needless trouble!" said Mrs. Orger. "What a wonderful memory!" exclaimed Mrs. Glover, capping the exclamations of her sisters triumphantly.

FEMALE DUELLISTS.

IN former times, when duels were the order of the day in France, the actresses occasionally showed themselves quite as pugnacious as the sterner sex. In 1649, Mademoiselle Beaupré, one of the first women who appeared on the Parisian stage, considering herself insulted by a sister comedian, Catherine des Urlis of the Palais Royal, sent her a challenge. The pair fought with stage swords behind the scenes; Catherine received a wound in the neck, and would have been killed by her infuriated antagonist had they not been parted.

A few years later Mademoiselle Maupin, a singer of the Parisian stage and a notorious adventuress, the heroine of one of Theophile Gauthier's novels, had nearly as many duels as Paul de Cassagnac. In one of her encounters she faced three men, and came off victorious. On another occasion, Dumesnil, an opera singer, having insulted her, she sent him a challenge. The singer declined the honour, whereupon La Maupin, assuming male attire, lay in wait for him in the Place des Victoires, and on his refusing to draw, soundly caned him.*

In the last century a meeting was appointed between two rival ladies of the Opera in Paris, Mademoiselle Beaumesnil, a singer, and Mademoiselle Theodore, a celebrated dancer. With great propriety, the ladies had chosen the Porte *Maillot* as the arena of their fight. They arrived at the trysting-place, attired in riding habits, accompanied by their seconds, four in number,

* This latter mode of avenging an insult, the reader will remember, was also adopted by Lydia Thompson, on the body of an American critic who had spoken disparagingly of the "B. B. B." or Blonde Troupe. Another celebrity in this line was the mother of Avonia and Melinda Jones, two well-known American actresses, who was known in the West as "the man flogger," from having cowhided more actors and editors than any other representative of the weaker sex.

all members of the same theatrical company. The weapons this time were pistols; but just as the ladies had measured their ground, Rey, the thorough bass singer, made his appearance as the *Deus ex Machina.* His presence and his eloquence being unable to allay the fierce passions of the amazons, the considerate bass singer bethought himself to lay the pistols on the wet grass. The consequence was that when the inexorable beauties fired at each other, the primings being wet, both hung fire. No supply of powder had apparently been brought to reload the weapons, and the scene ended, stage fashion, with embraces all round.

In 1820, two female dancers, quarrelling in the greenroom about the gold collar of a dog presented to them by a Swedish count, determined to settle the question at once. They adjourned behind the scenes, and had a vigorous set to with swords. Fortunately, the weapons used were those employed for stage duels, and harmlessly blunted, so that the combatants could prog each other to their hearts' content without a drop of their precious blood being spilt.

A CHEMICAL JOKE.

TAYLOR, the dramatist, was as inveterate a punster as Theodore Hook. Going into the greenroom of the Haymarket Theatre on one occasion, he was requested by Colman, the manager, to subscribe a small sum to a distressed chemist, who had lived in Panton Street, and was well known to the theatrical company. "A broken chemist, is he?" said Taylor. "Well, there's half-a-crown for the *exhausted receiver.*"

THE GREAT THIRSTLAND.

THE two first operas of Michael Balfe—*The Siege of Rochelle* and *The Maid of Artois*—were produced at Drury Lane in 1835-6. The gifted and ill-fated Madame Malibran sustained the principal part in *The Maid of Artois* a few months before her premature death. In Bunn's *History of the Stage* we are told an amusing anecdote of the famous vocalist in this character. She was supposed in the last act to be perishing with thirst in the desert; the scene was long and exhausting, the lady in delicate health. She therefore proposed to Bunn that he should somehow convey a pint of porter to her in the desert, promising him in that case an *encore* to the finale. "So," says Bunn, "I arranged that behind the pile of drifted sand, on which she sinks exhausted, a small aperture should be made in the stage, and through that aperture a pewter pint of porter was conveyed to the parched lips of this rare child of song, which so revived her, after the terrible exertion of the scene, that she electrified the audience, and had strength to repeat the finale."

LOGICAL.

N one of Dryden's plays there was a line which the actress endeavoured to speak in as moving and affecting a tone as she could—

> "My wound is great, because it is so small."

Then she paused, and looked very distressed. The Duke of Buckingham, who was in one of the boxes, rose immediately from his seat, and added in a loud tone, parodying the manner of the actress—

> "Then 'twould be greater, were it none at all,"

which had such an effect on the audience, who before were not very well pleased with the play, that they hissed the poor woman off the stage, and the piece fell.

HIS LAST JOKE.

ELLISTON, within a few hours of his death, objected to take some medicine, and, in order to induce him to do so, he was told he should have some brandy and water afterwards. A faint smile stole over his face, and the old roguish light gleamed for a moment in his glazing eye, as he murmured, "Bribery and *corruption*." They were almost the last intelligible words he uttered.

LISTON'S PUFF.

THE following advertisement from Liston, the comic actor, appeared in the newspapers in June, 1817, on the approach of his benefit. It is a good satire on shopkeepers' puffing :—

"*Mr. Liston to the Editor.*

"Sir, my benefit takes place this evening, at Covent Garden Theatre, and, I doubt not, will be splendidly attended. Several parties in the first circle of fashion were made, the moment it was announced. I shall perform Fogrum in *The Slave*, and Leporello in *The Libertine;* and in the delineations of those *arduous* characters I shall display much feeling and discrimination, together with great taste in my dresses and elegance in my manner. The audience will be delighted with my exertions, and testify by rapturous applause, their most decided approbation.

"When we consider, in addition to my professional merits, the loveliness of my person and fascinations of my face,* which are only equalled by the amiability of my private character,

* The reader will remember that Liston was as ugly as sin is said to be. "There is one face of Farley, one face of Knight, one—but what a one it is !—of Liston," says Charles Lamb.

having never 'pinched my children, nor kicked my wife out of bed,' there is no doubt but this puff will not be inserted in vain.

"I am, sir, your obedient servant,

"J. LISTON.

"*June* 10, 1817."

OPPORTUNE ADVICE.

IN 1713 a troupe of strolling actors were murdering *Cato* one night at Windsor. The ancient Roman senators met with little respect from the audience, and poor King Juba was so truly an object of ridicule, that when, hearing Marcia's confession of love for him, he cried out in a transport of joy, "What do I *hear?*" Lord Malpas, wilfully mistaking the inquiry, answered from the pit, "Upon my word, sir, I don't know. I think you had better be gone." This opportune advice put an end to the play.

FORTUNATE POOR.

A CERTAIN member of what Kitty Clive emphatically used to call the "damaged quality," in other words a scion of a noble French family, *déclassé* through misconduct, took it into his head to make Mademoiselle Dejazet pay "smart money." For this purpose he assailed the celebrated actress in a vile newspaper, but which was extensively read in all the minor *cafés* of the Boulevard. Though far above such foul attacks, Dejazet was annoyed at these proceedings, and applied personally at the office of the paper in question. This was what the damaged one desired. He now changed his tactics, protested that he had only resorted to the traducements as a means to obtain an interview with the charming actress, and, after some preliminaries, ended in offering her his hand and heart. Dejazet declined the honour, when the lovesick swain exclaimed, "Take compassion; do me the charity of one kiss, at least." "*Non pas, non pas*," replied the actress, "*jai mes pauvres*."

NAÏVETÉ.

DIGNUM, was once impersonating one of the dumb nobles in Shakespeare's *Henry the Eighth*. On hearing the words in praise of Cardinal Wolsey's learning, "Witness those *twins*, Ipswich and Oxford," colleges which the cardinal had founded, Dignum whispered to his brother nobles on the stage, that he never knew the cardinal had been married, and asked if the twins were his illegitimate offspring.

THE DOG-STAR.

IN 1803 Reynolds, the dramatist, produced a musical after-piece in Drury Lane, entitled *The Caravan; or, the Driver and his Dog*. There was some pretty music in it. It had a great run, and brought much money to the treasury, but the chief attraction of the piece was a dog called Carlo. One day Sheridan went to see the performance of this wonderful dog. As he entered the greenroom, Dignum, who played the principal part in the piece, said to him, with a woebegone countenance, "Sir, there is no guarding against illness; it is truly lamentable to stop the run of a successful piece like this, but really——" "Really what?" cried Sheridan, interrupting him. "I am so unwell," continued Dignum, "that I cannot go on longer than to-night." "You!" exclaimed Sheridan. "My good fellow, you terrified me; I thought you were going to say *the dog* was taken ill."

POLITE TO THE END.

THE late Signor Giulini, being much applauded in the *Trovatore* one night as Manrico, quitted the dungeon in which he was confined, came forward to the public, bowed, and then, not to cheat the executioner, went calmly back to prison to meet his fate.

AN ECCENTRIC ACTRESS.

A CURIOUS type of an actress occurs in Tate Wilkinson's *Wandering Patentee*, an amusing though very oddly written book. On Tuesday, March 20, 1794, Tate made the acquaintance of an extraordinary "stage princess" named Hannah Brand. He describes her as "very sensible, but too learned," and asserts that she considered that the only bar to her success was the envy of the Kembles and Mrs. Siddons. "She values herself on not holding up her train, as her constant use of large drawing-rooms, and a frequent habit of brilliant assemblies," she said, "prevent such trifles ever to occur as necessary." Fielding's works she thought not worth reading; the Latin authors, "in their original purity of language," were this tremendous lady's only relaxation. "No sensible person ever sat to see a farce; it is only a loss of time and degrading to taste," she observed. Her mode of expressing herself would be thought exaggerated in a comedy. When Wilkinson inquired what play she would prefer to have acted for her benefit, she replied, "Why, sir, should I strike the anvil of my brain when there is nothing to hammer out?" She sent Wilkinson one morning a note somewhat incorrectly penned, which the waggish manager pointed out to her. Hannah, "puffing out her chest with infinite majesty," answered, "Mr. Wil-kin-son, had I wrote that note to Mrs. Wil-kin-son, I had peradventure not been so precisely exact as to grammatical points; but when I consider that I was addressing a classical gentleman, I judged it obviously necessary to be careful of any unguarded slip. If you would attentively peruse the note, you will quickly perceive that the line alluded to was appertaining to the *plural*, not the *singular* number." Wilkinson burst out laughing, and assured her that the gods had made him neither learned nor classical. "Well," said Hannah, "it is wonderful not to converse with the ancients—the Italian, French, Latin, Greek authors, all which I can read, perfectly understand, and speak fluently." Immediately after this, she pronounced a word without being able to say whether it was Greek or Latin, and quoted a line in each language to ascertain to which it belonged. Nor was she much more definite in her English, for she would say on the stage *u*state for estate, and *arch*angel, and make hundreds of errors of that description.

Her theatrical dresses were elegant, but all their effect was lost, because the classic dame wore old-fashioned stays, up to her throat, at a time when low-bodied dresses were all the rage. "Hannah Brand," says Wilkinson, "would not unveil her charms even to the chaste Diana; therefore she, with well-bound bone, forbade all access. Troy was not more impregnable within its walls, bulwarks, and gates of brass than was the fearless Hannah." Her first appearance as the gay Lady Townly "met with rude remarks of disgustful behaviour, and that from ladies." Her presence at the playhouse as a spectator in a box was thus described: "She was accoutred in an old-fashioned jacket with deep flaps, with a tremendous long bosom-frill, over which the right hand was extended, and in this fixed attitude she continued, pensively superior, from the beginning of the evening's entertainment to the finale." She never went to the theatre or returned home otherwise than in a chair, so afraid was she of the insulter—man. Her dresses always were very good, her linen of the finest quality, all was rich enough for the royal drawing-room; but they were of eccentric fashions, and either in the street or the room, she wanted only a spear and a shield to have awed the wondering beholders with her grand and portly bearing.

Hannah Brand finally gravitated into her real vocation, and ended her days as the mistress of a "respectable seminary for French education" at Norwich.

INCLEDON'S "VAMPING."

INCLEDON had always a very bad memory for "study," and, to use a theatrical term, could never "vamp," which means that an actor substitutes his own words when the author's are forgotten. One night, whilst playing a lover, in the midst of a passionate address to his mistress he "stuck." In vain the lady hemm'd and ha'd, the prompter whispered, his agitation only increased. All came to a standstill till Incledon suddenly observed to the lady that love having taken away his language, perhaps she would permit him to express what he felt in a favourite air. He then broke into "Black-eyed Susan," and whilst singing one verse recollected the author. A thunder of applause greeted this effusion, after which Incledon proceeded with spirit in his part as written in the book. Incledon availed himself so often of this resource that it became a remark in the greenroom, whenever he was heard singing on the stage, "Is he singing the music, or recollecting the words?"

A WELL-SPREAD BOARD.

LAST winter, when the sandwich-men of the Royalty Theatre used to perambulate the streets of London with a Mephistophelian red cap and feather, and a red-hot poker in their hands, to announce the play of *Pluto*, a well-known actor, walking one morning with a friend down the Strand, came upon this melancholy string of human beings. "I pity those poor beggars," the friend said, "dressed up like that, and condemned to trudge the streets all day for eighteenpence." "Eighteenpence and their *board*," the actor replied.

"AND THEREBY HANGS A TAIL."

MRS. INCHBALD, a very pleasing actress, a most agreeable woman, and a charming writer, waited one morning with a new play on Mr. Harris, the chief proprietor of Covent Garden Theatre. That gentleman, not accustomed to find the virtue of some of his fair performers impregnable, suddenly became violently enamoured of the handsome authoress, and signified his devotion in a rather rough fashion. Those were the days when queues were worn, and Mrs. Inchbald seizing the inflammable manager by his caudal appendage with one hand, with the other hand lustily rang the bell, till assistance appeared. Ever afterwards, when speaking of this love *rencontre*, she used whimsically to stammer out, with that peculiar impediment in her speech, "How f—ortunate for me he did not w—ear a w—ig." To which apparently just remark, a certain punning brother dramatist one day replied, "I beg your pardon, Mrs. Inchbald; had your aggressor worn a *tie-wig*, you would have been wholly saved from his amorous attacks, because

> "Love, light as air, at sight of human *tyes*
> Spreads his light wings, and in a moment flies."

ECCENTRIC SPEECH.

MR. BLISSETT, the Bath comedian, like many other children of Thespis, was an oddity in private as well as in public life. Among other whimsicalities he had framed for his own use a brief number of original words, well known and understood by the accustomed ear of his intimates. Though those words were few, one serving many purposes, they were mixed up with Mr. Blissett's general phraseology and employed in every affair of life, whether serious or comic. After a long life spent in Bath, Blissett, in 1803, was tempted by Colman to appear at the Haymarket, to take the lengthy part of Vigil in *Love laughs at Locksmiths.* Visions of dreary days of study and waste of midnight oil flitted fearfully before Blissett's imagination, and he at once resolved to decline the honour. Walking deliberately up to the table where Colman sat, and looking into his merry face with his own as serious as nature would allow it to appear, he thus intended to express his meaning: "Mr. Colman, your farce is excellent, and the part you have assigned me is a very good one; but, at my time of life, I had no intention of coming up to London to study new characters, and I would rather resign my engagement than attempt to force such a number of lengths * into my head, which would rob me both of my rest and health." This is what Blissett *meant* to say, but owing to his inveterate habit of using a phraseology of his own, he delivered himself as follows:—"Your farce, Mr. Colman, is a real *kappips*, but I am too old a *Foozle* to set about such an *innimungoozlum*, good as it is; and I would give up my engagement sooner than *innimollidato* over an *innikappips*, which would keep me *foozling* day and night, and rob me of my rest for a fortnight to come."

Colman, quite mystified, turned round to Elliston for a solution to his old friend's jargon, which was freely translated, and the weighty matter transferred to younger, though not abler, heads.

PEACE OR WAR.

DURING the performance of a play not calculated to add greatly to the treasury of the proprietors, Reynolds, its author, entered the theatre with a friend, who, perceiving a very thin audience, delicately accounted for it by observing that the badness of the house must be owing to the *war*. "No," replied the author, shaking his head; "I suspect it is rather owing to the *piece*."

* A length is forty-two lines, cues included.

A THEATRICAL *TOUR DE FORCE.*

FARLEY on one occasion acted an important part at Covent Garden and also at the Haymarket on the same night, the two plays being the first pieces at both houses. At Covent Garden the curtain rose at 6.30, at the Haymarket at 7 o'clock. At the former, he was cast into one of Macbeth's witches; and at the latter, in the part of Sir Philip Modelove, in *A Bold Stroke for a Wife.* Having gone through the mystery of the first scene at Covent Garden, Farley reached the Haymarket in time to equip himself for the baronet, who does not make his appearance until the second act of the play. This act concluded, Farley returned to the witchery at Covent Garden, which being perpetrated, he again mounted his broom, and sped through the air a second time to the Haymarket, where he reappeared as Sir Philip Modelove, who does not make his second entry until the fifth act of the comedy.

The dovetailing of this remarkable night's performance was accomplished by means of a hackney coach, furnished with a dresser, the necessary habiliments, and a pair of candles. The metamorphose from the witch to the old beau, and *vice versâ*, was accomplished during the journey from one theatre to the other, the blinds being drawn up. As bad luck would have it, in one of these journeys the hackney in turning the corner of Whitcomb Street was upset, and actor, dresser, candles, and the rest were deposited into the highway. Notwithstanding this misadventure, Farley reached Covent Garden still in time, by means of another coach.

LITERARY PROPERTY.

AMONG other occasional trifles to which Sheridan condescended for the advantage of Drury Lane, when he was proprietor of that theatre, was the pantomime *Robinson Crusoe*, of which he is understood to have been the author. There was a practical joke in this pantomime—where in pulling off a man's boot, the leg was pulled off with it—which drollery Delpini, the famous clown, laid claim to as his own, and publicly complained of Sheridan's having stolen it from him. Sheridan said it was claimed as literary property "*in usum Delpini*," alluding to the famous edition of the classics.

PUFF *À LA FRANÇAISE.*

HALF a century ago, when Mademoiselle Georges, the great tragedian of the Théâtre Français, was starring it in the provinces, the manager of the theatre at Angers sent round the following circular to the chief patrons of the drama in that district :—

"Mademoiselle Georges, the first tragedian of France, and of the two theatres of the capital, having condescended to consent to appear on the stage to which I endeavour to draw the honourable public, I venture to hope that you will deign to encourage my efforts by a tribute of admiration in favour of the most beautiful woman in Europe, such a woman as has not her equal, in all the pomp of her brilliancy—the pupil of Talma and of Mademoiselle Raucourt, and, above all, of beneficent and generous nature. In coming to see Mademoiselle Georges, you will see at once Nature, Talma, and Raucourt. In the first part of *Semiramis* she will appear with one hundred thousand crowns' worth of diamonds ; all the ornaments which she wears in that tragedy are real precious stones."

A STAGE VETERAN.

IN 1720, Peg Fryer gave a representation on the stage of Lincoln's Inn Fields. She was then aged eighty-five, and, according to the playbills, had never acted since the days of Charles II. The programme promised entertainments of dancing by Mrs. Fryer, particularly The "Bashful

Maid" and the "Irish Trot," but when the moment of dancing came she affected to be utterly exhausted. She made her obeisance to the audience, and was about to retire, when the orchestra struck up the "Irish Trot," and the lively old woman danced her promised jig with the nimbleness and vivacity of five and twenty, laughing at the surprise of the audience, and receiving unbounded applause. After this final adieu from the stage she kept a tavern and ordinary in Tottenham Court Road, and we are told that her house was continually thronged with company, who went out of curiosity to converse with this extraordinary old woman.

A SOPORIFIC.

FOOTE was envious of Colman the elder's success at the Haymarket; he could not bear to see anybody succeed but himself. One morning he came hopping upon the stage, during the rehearsal of *The Spanish Barber*. The performers were busy in a scene of that now forgotten piece when one servant is under the influence of a sleeping draught, and another of a sneezing-powder. "Well," said Foote drily to Colman, "how do you go on?" "Pretty well," was the answer; "but I can't teach one of those fellows to gape as he ought to do." "Can't you?" exclaimed Foote, "read him your last comedy, *The Man of Business*, and he'll yawn for a month."

HIGH-HANDED DISAPPROVAL.

ONE night in March, 1733, a curious affair occurred at the Haymarket Theatre. On that occasion a pantomime was represented entitled *Love Runs all Dangers*. Among the jokes uttered, one of the actors made a hint at Sir Robert Walpole's intended Excise Act. Sir Robert happened to be present, and at the end demanded of the prompter if the words were in the book. Being assured they were not, he went behind the scenes and gave the actor a sound thrashing. Fancy Mr. Gladstone making a descent on the stage of Drury Lane, and giving, say, Mr. Arthur Roberts a beating!

A LOST ILLUSION.

WHEN MACKLIN attempted his last return to the stage, with the weight of a century on his shoulders, he walked about the stage during rehearsal, flapping rather ostentatiously his original part of Shylock, which was covered with a bill of his first performance of that character in Ireland. The lady who played Nerissa was at that time courted by Frank Aiken, who, by means of a good wig, sound teeth, and a slim figure, contrived to sink nearly twenty years of his age without suspicion. On Macklin's bill Frank's name appeared for Bassanio, and Mrs. ——, reading Macklin's precious relic of antiquity, naturally fixed her eyes on her lover's name. Then glancing at the date of the bill, some five and thirty years back, exclaimed, with a mixture of surprise and disbelief, "Mr. Aiken, Mr. Macklin? February the 8th, 1745—not Mr. Francis Aiken?" Macklin comprehended her. Glaring with his large eyes, he gave a savagely exulting chuckle, and replied, "Yes, Marm; that's your Frank!"

NO SEATS.

DR. JOHNSON, bear as he was, could be polite when he liked. In the last year of his life, he sent Windham to Mrs. Siddons, to beg that she would do him the honour of taking tea with him at Bolt Court. Such compliments are always welcome to the artist, and the tragedian, with her brother and Windham, repaired up the narrow stairs to the doctor's apartments. All the chairs in the room were littered with books and papers, so that Mrs. Siddons was kept standing a few moments. Dr. Johnson's tact furnished him with a compliment that seems almost elegant. "Madam," said he, gallantly, "you who so often occasion a want of seats to other people will the more readily excuse the want of one yourself." Johnson's admiration was rewarded with a chair always ready for him at the wing of the stage, he being at that time too deaf to hear her in the pit or boxes.

ORIGIN OF "PAUL PRY."

IT has often been repeated that *Paul Pry* was drawn from a familiar figure of the time, the eccentric Tom Hill, editor of the *Dramatic Mirror*. Mr. John Poole, the author of the delightful comedy, expressly contradicted this, in a little biographical sketch of himself which he addressed to one of the magazines of the period. "The idea of the character of Paul Pry was suggested," he says, "by the following anecdote, related to me several years ago by a beloved friend :—'An idle old lady, living in a narrow street, had passed so much of her time in watching the affairs of her neighbours, that she at length knew the sound of each particular knocker within hearing, and could tell to which house it belonged. It happened that she fell ill, and was for several days confined to her bed. Unable to observe in person what was going on outside, she stationed her maid at the window, as her substitute for the performance of that task. But Betty soon grew weary of the occupation ; she became careless in her reports, impatient and tetchy when reprimanded for her negligence. "Betty, what *are* you thinking about ? Don't you hear a double knock at No. 9 ? Who is it ?" "The first-floor lodger, ma'am." "Betty ! Betty ! I declare I must give you warning ! Why don't you tell me what that knock is at No. 24 ?"—"Why, Lord, ma'am, it is only the baker with pies." "*Pies !* Betty ? What *can* they want with pies at No. 24 ? They had pies yesterday !'" Of this very point I have availed myself. Let me add that Paul Pry was never intended as the representative of any one individual, but of a class. Like the melancholy of Jacques, he 'is compounded of many simples;' and I could mention five or six who were unconscious contributors to the character. That it should have been so often, though erroneously, supposed to have been drawn after some particular person is perhaps complimentary to the general truth of the delineation. With respect to the play generally, I may say that it is original; it is original in structure, plot, character, and dialogue—such as they are. The only imitation I am aware of is to be found in part of the business in which Mrs. Subtle is engaged: whilst writing those scenes, I had strongly in my recollection Collin d'Harleville's *Vieux Célibataire*. But even the little I have adopted is considerably altered and modified, by the necessity of adapting it to the exigencies of a different plot."

PREMEDITATED JOKES.

FORMERLY it was the custom for some actors, at the end of the first piece, to give out the performance of the following evening. It was a too often repeated trick of Liston to have his joke on that occasion. No sooner had the man who was to communicate the name of the play for the ensuing day, uttered the words "Ladies and gentlemen, to-morrow evening this comedy will be repeated," or "the play of *Hamlet* will be performed," than Liston would walk on from the opposite side, face the actor giving out the play, start back as if taken by surprise, and exclaim, "Prodigious!" "My conscience!" "York, you're wanted," or any other phrase which during the evening had occurred in his part. This of course would cause a laugh from the supposed victim of the jest, but it was not generally known that the whole affair was premeditated and got up in the greenroom.

A SHORT PART.

WHEN Sheridan's *Glorious First of June* was produced, Storace and Kelly gave it some new songs, but the music was chiefly old. Kelly was to represent the character of Frederick, and as he was much employed in composing the music, he begged Sheridan, who wrote a good many of the speeches for it, to make as short a part for him and with as little speaking in it as possible. Sheridan assured him he would. In the scene in which Kelly came on to sing a song, "When in War on the Ocean We meet the Proud Foe," there was a cottage in the distance, at which—the stage-direction said—Frederick was to look earnestly for a minute or two, and the line he then had to speak was this: "There stands my Louisa's cottage; she must be either in it or out of it." The song began immediately, and not another word was there in the whole part. This sublime and solitary speech produced a loud laugh from the audience.

AIDING AND ABETTING A SUICIDE.

MRS. DANCER, the tragedian, was shortsighted. One night, at Crow Street Theatre, acting Calista in *The Fair Penitent*, as she was about to stab herself she dropped the dagger. The faithful attendant endeavoured to push it towards her with her foot, but, this failing, was obliged to pick it up, and very civilly handed it to her mistress, to put an end to herself—a somewhat awkward effect, as it took away the probability of the scene, yet completed the necessary catastrophe.

A DUET WITH A GOAT.

EVERYBODY has heard the "Baa baa! glou glou," duet in the *Mascotte*, but it has fallen to the share of few playgoers to hear a duet between a man and a goat. An instance of such a performance is related, in Belton's *Reminiscences*, to have taken place circa 1835. Usher, a well-known clown at that time, announced a great entertainment in a field, when a pig, a gown, and a guinea were to be raffled for, with ground and lofty tumbling, comic songs, tight-rope dancing by Miss Usher (afterwards Mrs. Alfred Wigan), to conclude with a duet between Mr. Usher, the clown, and a goat. And the way it was effected was thus: a rude kind of piano was brought forward, then the goat was introduced on his hind legs by Usher, and, after some ludicrous tricks, he was led to the piano. The clown then imparted some advice to the quadruped concerning due regard to the notes, the band struck up the then popular ballad of *No*, and Usher began as if playing. "When you was a young one, and wanted some wittles, oh, what did you say to me?" The goat replied, "*baah!*" and so the duet went on, until, mounting *cresendo*, it actually reached a scream. The way the goat was induced to sing would not have met with the approbation of the Society for the Prevention of Cruelty to Animals. A wire had been passed round his tail, and was pulled by Usher, hard and harder, until the poor goat actually screamed with agony. This caused peals of laughter, and the whole entertainment was a success.

DICKENS AND THE STAGE.

IT is recorded in Forster's *Life of Dickens* that when the amiable novelist was about twenty years old, he applied to Mr. Bartlett, the then manager of Covent Garden, for an engagement at that theatre, and that a day was fixed for him to make trial of his powers. When the day came, Dickens was laid up with a bad cold, and could not appear; his trial was therefore postponed to the next season. In the mean time, he had made himself famous by his pen, and so he took to literature instead. That he would have made his mark on the stage there can be little doubt, for his amateur acting in later years was of the highest order. Still, we cannot call that a "bad cold" to which we owe *Pickwick*, *Nickleby*, *Oliver Twist*, and the rest of his immortal works.

INTERNAL WAR IN AN ELEPHANT.

IN 1862, the pantomime *Harlequin Blue Beard* was produced at Drury Lane Theatre. The hero of the piece, in the character of a pasha, rode in procession on a large elephant. This specimen of natural history had not been borrowed from the Zoological Gardens, but issued from that wonderful laboratory—the stage machinist's workshop. The body was of basketwork, the legs canvas, the feet and head modelled, the tusks wood, the trunk and tail wirework—all covered with painted canvas. To give this creature life and motion, a man was placed in each of the legs. On one occasion the internal structure of the near hind leg had been drinking, and entered his leg in a very quarrelsome disposition, talking of fighting the off fore leg for some affront. The march commenced; the elephant moved, but evidently badly lame in the near hind leg, which dragged along in a shaky and sleepy manner. In vain did the other legs remonstrate, the near hind leg would not stir. In an unfortunate moment of over-zealousness, off hind leg kicks the irritable near hind, which retaliates, and is heard to swear from his cavernous inclosure that "he'll punch his blooming 'ead." Fore legs join in the fray, and a general kicking ensues. Blue Beard's position on the undulating mass was anything but pleasant, and ends in a fall. Wild yells of laughter from the audience greet the catastrophe, in the midst of which the elephant topples over, and the four legs conglomerate in a free fight. Here was burlesque with a vengeance It could go no further, so the manager wisely discharged the legs, and in the future substituted a palanquin for the elephant.

DAMNING THE PUBLIC.

A MRS. MONTAGUE, in the last century, had been cast to play the Queen in a version of *Henry the Second*, which was put up for a fellow-actress's benefit at Hull. With most unprofessional disobligingness, Mrs. Montague refused to study the part, and when the night came proposed to read it. This the audience would not have, and, in spite of her grand tragedy airs, called to her to go off the stage. Whereupon the angry lady elegantly exclaimed, as she threw her book which she was not allowed to use into the pit, "Well, then, curse you all!" and made her way off the stage. Two years afterwards, she offered the insulted public her apologies, and was forgiven—as a lady ought to be when she says that she is sorry for her faults, but it was certainly carrying the privileges of her sex to their fullest extent.

"THOUGH LOST TO SIGHT, TO MEMORY DEAR."

IT is told of "Old Barry," formerly prompter in the Dublin Theatre, that he was usually very inattentive, and did not at all follow the piece. One night an actor "stuck," and looked anxiously towards Barry at the wing for the "word." Barry was of course engaged in some other business at the time; his thoughts were far away, and he took not the slightest notice of the appeal. The actor at last called out in despair, "Barry, give me the word, will you?" To which Barry, with the imperturbability of a prompter and the exquisite unconsciousness of an Irishman, replied, loud enough for the audience to hear, "What word, my boy?" and, coolly wetting his thumb, began turning over the leaves to get up with the unfortunate defaulter.

THE MISERIES OF A THRONE.

ELLISTON, in his younger days, once took Buxton in his circuit. The theatre there, at that time, was one of those wretched little buildings resembling nearly the Globe of Shakespeare's days, open to the sky, and devoid of every theatrical appointment. The play acted was Tobin's *Honeymoon*, in which he took his favourite part of the Duke of Aranza. All went on amazingly well, considering the circumstances, until the scene with the "mock Duke" in the fourth act. Here Jacques is discovered sitting in a large armchair, which, to give it dignity, had been covered over with an old curtain. On rising from his seat, the hilt of the Duke's sword most inopportunely got entangled in one of the sundry holes of the loose coverlid, which, on the actor walking towards the front of the stage, "like a wounded snake dragged its slow length along." This certainly provoked something more than a smile; but it so happened that the chair in question had been borrowed for the occasion from a neighbouring inn, and being originally fashioned for the incidental purposes of the sick-room, its available conversion was so palpably disclosed to the whole body of spectators, that the people absolutely screamed with merriment—in fact, they laughed for a whole week afterwards.

THE TWO DROMIOS.

WHEN Foote was acting in Dublin, he introduced into one of his pieces, called *The Orators*, the character of George Faulkner, the well-known printer, whose manner and dress he so closely imitated that the poor fellow could not appear in public without meeting with scoffs and jeers from the boys in the streets. Enraged at the ridicule thus brought upon him, Faulkner one evening treated to the seats of the gods all the devils of his printing-office, for the express purpose of their hissing and hooting Foote off the stage. Faulkner placed himself in the pit, to enjoy the actor's degradation, but when the objectionable scene came on, the unfortunate printer was exceedingly chagrined to find that, so far from a groan or a hiss being heard, his gallery friends joined in the general laughter. The next morning he arraigned his inky conclave, inveighed against them for having neglected his injunctions; and, on demanding the reason of their treachery, was lacerated ten times deeper by the simplicity of their answer. "Arrah, master," said the spokesman, "do we not know you? 'Twas your own sweet self was on the stage, and shower light upon us if we go to the playhouse to hiss our worthy master." Failing in this experiment, Faulkner commenced an action against Foote, and got a verdict of damages to the tune of £300. This drove Foote back to England, where he resumed his mimicry, and consoled himself by humorously taking off the lawyers on his trial, and the judges who had condemned him.

EATING ON THE STAGE.

A CIRCUMSTANCE not generally known is communicated by Kelly, on the occasion of his taking a part in the farce *A House to be Sold*. "There was a supper scene," he says, "in which I was obliged to eat part of a fowl. Bannister told me at rehearsal—what I then would hardly believe—that it was very difficult to eat and swallow food on the stage. But, strange as it may appear, I found it a fact, for I could not get down a morsel. My embarrassment was a great source of fun to Bannister and Suett, who were both gifted with the accomodating talent of stage-feeding: whoever saw poor Suett as the Lawyer in *No Song, No Supper*, tucking in his boiled leg of lamb, or in *The Siege of Belgrade*, will be little disposed to question my testimony to this fact."

PATRIOTISM.

AN Italian gentleman at Paris, the firmest article of whose creed was that none but Italians could possibly sing well, refused to admit that Mademoiselle Nillson, whom he had never heard, could be at all equal to the singers of Italy. With great difficulty, he was induced to hear her. After listening for five minutes, he rose to depart. "But do stay," said his friend; "you will be convinced presently." "I know it," said the Italian, "and therefore I go."

HER DYING SPEECH.

THE public once took exception at Mrs. Farrel's impersonation of Zaïra, the heroine of *The Mourning Bride*, especially in the dying scene. The moribund thereupon rose from the spot chosen to give up her breath, and, advancing towards the foot-lights, said, "Ladies and Gentlemen, I am very sorry to have incurred your displeasure, but, having accepted the part only to oblige a friend, I hope you will kindly excuse me." After this little dying speech, she returned to the spot, assumed once more a recumbent position, finished dying, and the attendants covered her with a black veil.

GAPING WONDER.

CERVETTO, the violoncello-player, who formed part of Garrick's orchestra, once ventured to yawn noiselessly but portentously while the great actor was delivering one of his most pathetic passages. The house gave way to laughter. After the play, Garrick lectured the musician on the rudeness of his behaviour; but his wrath was appeased by Cervetto's absurd excuse, that he invariably yawned when he felt "the greatest rapture," and to this emotion the passage so admirably delivered by his manager had justified him in yielding. Garrick accepted the explanation, perhaps rather on account of its originality than of its truthfulness.

STAR-DUST.

MISS FARRAN, in 1797, exchanged the buskin for a countess' coronet, by marrying the Earl of Derby. It is said that Lord Derby, subsequently to the marriage, applied in the greenroom to Sheridan for the arrears of Lady Derby's salary, averring that he would not leave the room until it was paid. "My dear lord," said Sheridan, "this is too bad. You have taken from us the brightest star in our little world, and now you quarrel with us for a little dust which she has left behind her."

"GOOSE," OR "TO CALL AZOR."

HISSING, in English stage-language called "goose," is described by French actors as *Appeler Azor*, to "call the dog Azor." The origin of this cant term is as follows:—Between 1733 and 1736, there was an inferior tragedian attached to the Théâtre Français named Achille Fleury. The public did not relish him, and could bear him still less, because in those days Quinault Dufresne graced the boards. Fleury's father was a soldier in the guard; he, moreover, kept a tavern, and fondly believed in his son's genius. Annoyed at the reception Achille daily met at his entrance on the stage, the old soldier resolved to put a stop to what he considered a spiteful combination. With this laudable intention, he one evening donned his uniform, went to the theatre, accompanied by his dog—a splendid animal named Tarquinius—which he held by a string, and sat down behind the scenes. That evening Achille appeared in *Iphigenia in Aulis*, and was received by the public in their usual manner. The actor, accustomed to this treatment, calmly played on; but the father jumped to his feet, burning with rage. He completely forgot the dog, and the faithful animal, seeing his young master, immediately ran up to him, wagging his tail, licking his hands, and, in his canine fashion, expressed his joy at their unexpected meeting. The spectators, still more incensed at Fleury on account of this breach of etiquette, hissed twice as much; and father Fleury's rage reached such a pitch that he drew his sword, when Gaussin, a leading comedian, held him back, smilingly observing, "My dear sir, they see your dog; don't you perceive, it is Tarquinius they are calling." The poor man was willing to believe this, especially when his son, to get rid of the dog, called to his sire, at the top of his voice, "Whistle, father; do whistle." Thus "hissing" came to be named "to call Tarquinius;" but this dog-name in course of time being considered too classical, Azor, a favourite name of the French poodle, was substituted for the appellation of the proud Roman king.*

A TRAGEDY QUEEN.

WHEN the eccentric actress and dramatist, Hannah Brand, brought out her tragedy of *Agmunda*, in 1794, she was so jealous of this invaluable treasure being purloined that she would not suffer the manuscript to remain in the prompter's hands. She wrote out a copy herself, entirely omitting her own part, as a safeguard against literary pirates. Finding, at the end of one act, that an altar requisite in the drama, was too far back, she exclaimed, "If the theatre were to fall in one momentous crash, I would not begin

* This anecdote loses much of its point in English, as people do not "hiss" to call a dog, the French verb *siffler* being used in both these senses. Another Parisian circumlocution for "hissing" is *il y a des bossus*, "there are hunchbacks." This phrase arose when the play *Les Aventures de Mayeux*, which related the misfortunes of a hunchback, was condemned by the public. The author of the piece was behind the scenes, and exclaimed, "I expected as much; it is a cabal. There are at least a dozen hunchbacks in the house, who have come on purpose to damn my piece."

unless that altar was brought more to the front!" At the end of the fourth act, she told the prompter, with the most dignified solemnity, that she would not proceed "unless he first assured her that she might depend upon two flourishes of the trumpets, previous to her entrance." *Agmunda*, under the title *Huniades, or The Siege of Belgrade*, had been acted in 1792 at the Haymarket, by the Drury Lane company, without success. Miss Brand altered the piece, omitting Huniades, the principal character. Under its new name, *Agmunda*, it was condemned at the Haymarket in 1794.

SWEARING ON SHAKESPEARE.

WHEN Woodward was manager of Crow Street Theatre, Dublin, the mob one morning beset the Parliament House, in order to prevent the members from passing an unpopular bill. Such of the senators as were supposed to belong to the court party were treated with the grossest insults, and some of the ringleaders, thinking it necessary to make the representatives swear that they would not pass the bill, surrounded Mr. Woodward's door, opposite the Parliament House, in College Green, and called repeatedly upon his family to throw them a Bible out of the window. Mrs. Woodward was greatly alarmed at the request, as it happened at that time that she had no such book in her possession. In the midst of her agitation, her husband, with great presence of mind, snatched up a folio edition of Shakespeare, which, tossing out of the dining-room window, he told the insurgents they were welcome to. Upon this they gave him three cheers, and the ignorant rabble administered their oath to several of the Irish members of the House of Commons upon the works of our immortal bard.

BORROWED LIGHTS.

A WHIMSICAL accident occurred one night when Richard Winstone acted the character of the crooked-backed tyrant in Shakespeare's *Richard the Third*, at the Jacob's Well Theatre, at Bristol. The stage at that time was lighted with tallow candles, stuck round four hoops, suspended from the roof by ropes. In the fifth act, when Richard rushes on the stage exclaiming, "A horse, a horse! my kingdom for a horse!" Winstone flourished his sword so valiantly over his head, that the weapon coming in contact with the rope by which one of the hoops of candles was suspended, cut it through, and the blazing circle fell round the neck of Richard and lodged there, greatly to his discomfiture and to the amusement of the audience. The amazed Catesby of the evening, instead of helping his royal master to a horse, had enough to do to extricate him from this unexpected crown of glory.

INDEFINITELY POSTPONED.

ELLISTON had the proper worship for true genius, the proper contempt for pseudo-genius, and he perhaps never gave a better proof of his discernment than one evening when, on entering the greenroom, he was accosted in the most supercilious manner by a performer dressed for the character of Rob Roy, a part the histrio thought derogatory to his reputation, with "Pray, Mr. Elliston, when do we act Shakespeare?" The manager pithily replied, "*When you can.*"

COLLABORATION.

CO-OPERATION in the production of vaudevilles is one of the institutions of the stage in Paris. Two, three, four authors clubbing their wit and puns together, is quite an ordinary thing; such combinations may be seen on the playbills any day. But sometimes the collaboration assumes almost the character of a limited liabilities company. Thus the short-lived Théâtre des Troubadours, about half a century ago, produced a vaudeville of one act, *Monsieur de Bièvre ou l'Esprit*, at which eleven authors collaborated, yet it was no illustration of its title. The names of the guilty ones were communicated to the public in a couplet, sung or recited by the manager. All of them were men of mark in the walks of literature, and some of them in course of time became academicians, others deputies, dramatists, poets. The same society, with the addition of two new members, produced another piece, entitled *Christophe Morin, ou Que je suis faché d'être riche*; and the names of the two new members, as well as the retirement of one of the former collaborators, was duly announced to the public in a song—

> " Citoyens, les auteurs de *Christephe Morin*
> Ont pour *Bièvre* deja mis l'œuvre à la main ;
> Ajoutez à leurs noms, sur les noms déja lus,
> Alexandre de moins, Léger, Mautort de plus."

But how to "add a name less" (*ajoutez Alexandre de moins*) the public were not informed.

In 1811, when Laujon, a playwright and member of the poetical "Caveau," died, his brother poets thought fit to embalm his memory in a vaudeville, with the title *Laujon de retour à l'ancien Caveau.* All the members of the said "Caveau," to the number of twenty-four, contributed to the construction of this comedy in one act. More recently, on the 12th of July, 1853, the Théâtre des Délassements produced *Les moutons de Panurge*, the joint work of eight and twenty authors, including Paul de Kock, Dumanoir, Henry Monnier, Samson of the Théâtre Français, and Potier the comedian. But the greatest mass of collaborating genius was brought to bear upon a revue-vaudeville in one act, entitled *La Tour de Babel.* This child of many fathers was produced at the Théâtre des Variétés, on the 24th of June, 1834, and could boast not less than thirty-six authors, among whom were many celebrities. Adolphe Adam, the compositor, had contributed the music for some of the songs ; and the couplets, jokes, puns, and witticisms had been hatched in the brains of Dumas, Annicet Bourgeois, Dumanoir, Dennery, and many other tip-top dramatists of the day, whose names are less familiar on this side of the Channel.

NO SHAMMING.

SAMUEL SANDFORD usually played the parts of stage-villain, for, being of a low stature and slightly hunch-backed, he was scarcely fit to enact amiable characters. Once a new play was brought upon the stage, in which Sandford happened to perform the part of an honest statesman. The pit, after they had sat three or four acts in quiet expectation that the well-dissembled honesty of Sandford—for such they thought it—would soon be discovered, at last, finding out that nothing of the kind did happen, and that Sandford remained an honest man to the end of the play, condemned the piece, as if the author had imposed upon them the most incredible absurdity. A passage in the *Tatler*, February 16, 1709, concerning this excellent actor, gives a curious view of the scenes represented in those days : "When poor Sandford was upon the stage, I have seen him groaning upon a wheel ; stuck with daggers ; impaled alive ; calling his executioners, with a dying voice, cruel dogs and villains ;—and all this to please his judicious spectators, who were wonderfully delighted with seeing a man in torment so well acted."

A STAR SNUFFED.

BERTINI, the manager of the theatre of Brescia, was once compelled to engage a star, which the nobility of the place insisted upon should appear. This expensive luminary never performed anywhere without stipulating beyond his salary all his travelling expenses, and having during his stay apartments for himself and a table provided for six persons. In pursuance of such an engagement, he arrived at Brescia, and invited three friends to dine with him. They came, and the great man ordered his servants to let the manager know that he was ready for dinner, and desired it might be served. The servant returned and said that there was no dinner prepared. The infuriated performer went to the manager, and inquired why his dinner had not been prepared in proper time. "Sir," was the answer, "you gave no orders about providing dinners." "How, sir!" exclaimed the star. "Is it not set down in my articles, that you are to provide a table for six persons?" "Undoubtedly, sir, such is my agreement; and if you will walk into the dining-room, you will see I have fulfilled it to the letter. There is your *table*, sir, and a handsomer piece of furniture, I flatter myself, you never saw." No arguments could persuade the manager. "I know nothing about dinner," he said. "The words of the agreement are, that I am to provide a *table for six persons*, and I have even gone beyond my bargain, for this one will seat *eight*. As he was ready to try the issue in a court of law, the star had to submit, or to pay a forfeit. He chose the former alternative.

OIL ON TROUBLED WATERS.

ONE day, just before the *Christmas Tale* made its appearance, Garrick went into the painting-room, and, seeing as he imagined a prodigious quantity of gold strewn about the floor, began to abuse the man who was grinding the colours, and afterwards to bawl out lustily for French the scene-painter. The artist, seeing Roscius in a great fury, asked what was the matter. "The matter, sir! why, zounds, Mr. Thing, don't you—bless my soul!—see that the ground is all strewn with gold?" French replied that it was Dutch metal, rubbed off in gilding the scene, and not worth twopence. "Well," rejoined Garrick, "twopence! and pray, why the devil should I lose twopence? Do you consider what twopence a day comes to, sir?" "Well, sir, it is nothing out of your pocket," objected French. "Yes, sir; but—a—your—you—are a damned curious sort of a—hey! how is it nothing out of my pocket?" "Why, you know, sir, I have to find these things out of my salary." "Oh—a—hey—your salary!" rejoined Garrick, "why, a then, demme if I care twopence about it."

A MURDEROUS PIECE.

IN a play of Morand, the dramatist, entitled *Megara*, nearly all the characters were slain, only one survived. At the end of the piece the sole survivor was called before the curtain by the audience, to furnish a true return of all the casualties.

"TAKEN FROM LIFE."

MORAND, author of *L'Esprit de Divorce*, was present at the first representation of that play. The pit loudly expressing disapprobation at the extravagance and improbability of some traits in the principal characters, he exclaimed, "Gentlemen, I hear it remarked that the principal characters in my play are exaggerated. Allow me to assure you that they are taken from life, and that I have toned them down considerably in order to present them on the stage." This led to questions, and the fact of the author's unhappy life with his wife and mother-in-law were then elicited. When the same piece was announced for the next evening, somebody in the pit called out, "With M. Morand's compliment." This so incensed the dramatist that he flung his hat into the pit, exclaiming, "Whoever it is that wants to see Morand, can see him on returning this hat." The poet was arrested for this unbecoming behaviour, and forbidden to enter a playhouse for two months.

"PERSONAL."

SOME particulars concerning Ned Shuter's birth having been incorrectly stated in the *Theatrical Biography*, Shuter sent the following protest :—

"Ned Shuter to the Printer, greeting : Whereas in a quotation from a book entitled *Theatrical Biography* there is a circumstantial account of my family, I beg, for the credit of your book, and to avoid an imposition upon the public, in a matter which so much concerns them to be acquainted with, that you will correct a mistake the writer of those memoirs has made. For whereas the said writer does, with great confidence, assert that my father was a chairman, and my mother sold oysters, and that I, Ned Shuter, was born in a cellar; now, though I will acknowledge that my father was a chairman, though I have no objection to own that my mother sold oysters in the winter and cucumbers in the summer, yet I do solemnly aver that I was *not* born in a cellar, but in a front room, up two pair of stairs, at one Mr. Merit's, an eminent chimney sweeper's, in Vine Street, St. Giles's. Having thus discharged my conscience by rectifying any mistakes the public might fall into on so important a subject, I remain, with much gratitude, their obedient servant,

"NED SHUTER."

UPHILL WORK.

CHARLES MATHEWS used to tell a good story in support of the truth of the remark anent a Scotchman, a joke, and a surgical operation. When "starring" in Edinburgh, his landlord, who seldom attended any other public meeting save the "kirk," asked Mathews if he would oblige him with "a pass for the playhoose." This favour being readily granted, the "guid mon" donned his cheerful black suit, and witnessed Mathews's two great performances, Sir Charles

Coldstream in *Used Up*, and Plumper in *Cool as a Cucumber*, both downright "side-splitters." Meeting his landlord on the stairs as he proceeded to his own room after the performance, Mathews was cordially greeted by that gentleman, of whom he then inquired how he had enjoyed the entertainment. "Aweel," said the Northerner, "it pleased me vara much, ye ken, and I conseeder you played unco' naturally; but, heigh, mon, I'd a hard matter to keep frae laughing."

MADAME CELESTE.

THE late Madame Celeste made her first appearance at Drury Lane in the ballet of *La Bayadère* in 1830. This lady may fairly be ranked among the wonders of her age, for it was only in October, 1874, that she took her farewell of the stage, in the part of the Indian huntress Miami in Buckstone's drama of *The Green Bushes*, with all the vigour and pathos and much of the freshness of her youth. During those four and forty years, generations of great actresses had arisen, shone as stars for a score of years, and passed away into oblivion, marriage, or death. But Celeste still survived and flourished—half a century after her *début*, bidding defiance alike to old time and new fashions, as if warranted, like Tennyson's "brook," to "go on for ever." This once highly popular actress expired in Paris, on February 12th, 1882.

MARKS OF LOVE.

HERE is a pleasant *entrefilet* from Chetwood's short biography of Wilks, the comedian: "There was an actress for whom Wilks conceived so ardent an attachment that he fell ill, until she promised to favour his addresses. But such violent attachments have too often but violent endings. The lover soon cooled, but they had still to act together in tender characters, such as Jaffier and Belvidera in *Venice Preserved*, when the lady took the opportunity of leaving on his face visible marks of her jealous resentment. This, however painful to him, was sport to the audience."

THE DEPTH OF CONSECRATION.

WHEN Molière died, the Archbishop of Paris would not allow his body to be buried in consecrated ground. Louis XIV., being informed of this, sent for Archbishop Harlay, and expostulated with him, but the prelate remained inflexible. The king, finding him unwilling to comply with his wishes, inquired how many feet deep the holy ground reached. "About eight feet, I should say," replied his eminence, taken by surprise. "Well, then," exclaimed the king, "since I cannot remove your scruples, let the grave be made twelve feet deep, that is four feet below your consecrated ground, and let him be buried there." The archbishop was obliged to give in. Such the legend. The historical fact is, that on its being shown that Molière had received the sacrament on the preceding Easter, the archbishop was pleased to permit that the glory of France should be inhumed but without any pomp, with two priests only, and without any church solemnities.

VALUABLE NOTES.

STORACE when a boy was studying music under his father, who once gave him a bravura song of Bastardini to copy. The boy was astonished that fifty guineas should be paid for singing a song. He counted the notes in it, and calculated the amount of each note at 4*s*. 10*d*. He valued one of the divisions running up and down at £13 11*s*. It was a whimsical thing for a boy to do, but perfectly in character; his passion for calculation was beyond all belief.

MAKING SURE.

THE night when Counsellor MacNally's *Robin Hood* was brought out at Covent Garden Theatre, a young Irish friend of the composer, on his first visit to London, was seated in the second row in the boxes. In the front row were two gentlemen, who at the close of the first act warmly commended "Mrs. Cowley" as the composer of the opera. On hearing this, the Irishman got up, and, tapping one of them on the shoulder, said, "Sir, *you* say that this opera was written by Mrs. Cowley; now *I* say it was not. This opera was written by Leonard MacNally, Esq., Barrister-at-Law, of No. 5, Pump Court, in the Temple. Do you take my word for it, sir?" "Most certainly," replied the astonished gentleman; "and I feel very much obliged to you for the information." At the end of the second act, the Irishman got up and again accosted the same gentleman. "Sir," said he, "upon your honour as a gentleman, are you in your own mind perfectly satisfied that Leonard MacNally, Esq., Barrister-at-Law, etc., etc., has actually written this opera, and not Mrs. Cowley?" "Most perfectly persuaded of it, sir," replied the other, bowing. "Then, sir," replied the Irishman, bowing, "I wish you good night." But just as he was leaving the box, he turned to the gentleman whom he had been addressing, and said, "Pray, sir, permit me to ask, is your friend here convinced that this opera was written by Leonard MacNally, Esq., etc., etc.?" "Decidedly, sir," was the reply; "we are both fully convinced of the correctness of your statement." "Oh, then, if that is the case, I have nothing more to say," observed the Hibernian, "except that if you had not both assured me you were so, neither of you would be sitting quite so easy on your seats as you do now." After this observation he withdrew, and did not return again to the box.

THE PARSON'S NIGHTCAP.

MR. GEORGE HARVEST, minister of Thames Ditton, was a great character. One evening, Lady Onslow took him to the theatre, to see Garrick play some favourite character. In order that he might hear and see well, her ladyship procured front seats in the boxes. Harvest, knowing he was to sleep in town, brought his nightcap in his pocket. It was a striped woollen one, and had been worn since it was last washed for at least half a year. As Harvest pulled out his handkerchief the cap came out with it, and fell into the pit. The person on whom it fell tossed it from him, the next did the same, and the *casque-à-mèche* was for some time tossed all over the pit. At last, Harvest, afraid of losing his property, rose up, and after hemming two or three times to clear his pipes, made the following address:—"Gentlemen, when you have sufficiently amused yourself with that cap, please to restore it to me, who am its rightful owner," at the same time bowing to the pit, and placing his right hand on his breast. A gentleman, struck with his appeal, handed up the cap on the end of a walking-stick, like the head of a traitor stuck on the point of a lance, and the rightful owner, after shaking it, gravely returned it into the capacious pocket of his coat.

"*REVENONS À NOS MOUTONS.*"

THIS well-worn quotation is taken from the old French play, *L'Avocat Pathelin*, the oldest extant play in the French language, and still one of the stock-pieces of the Comédie Française. The titular part of maître Pathelin, whenever the piece is played at that theatre, is very properly taken by M. Got, the oldest associate of the Français. This amusing comedy was written some time in the fifteenth century. The name of the author is uncertain: some attribute it to François

Villon, others, with more probability, to Pierre Blanchet. Saturated in situation and language with Gallic salt, it was the most popular farce of the century, and doubtless received additions on all sides. Both Molière and La Fontaine admired its frank gaiety. But after their death comedy stiffened, and the frantic farce was metamorphosed into a mild three-act comedy by Brueys and Palaprat, which held the stage for nearly two centuries, till 1872, when Mr. Edouard Fournier brought out a revision of the original text, far more easy and idiomatic than the washed-out comedy whose usurpation it ended.

The popularity of the old farce did not limit itself to France. It was imitated by Reuchlin in Germany, soon after its appearance, and one of its most amusing scenes is to be found in the *Townley Mysteries*. In the last century, it served as a basis for *The Village Lawyer*, a two-act farce, brought out by Garrick at Drury Lane Theatre, with a rather more lasting success than most of Garrick's productions obtained. It was played by Mr. Jeffreson in New York within the last twenty years. A perversion of *The Village Lawyer*, under the name of *The Mutton Trial*, is frequently represented on the other side of the Atlantic in so-called *Ethiopian Sketches*.

The phrase "Revenons à nos moutons" is introduced in the original piece on the occasion of a woollendraper pleading against his shepherd, concerning some sheep the latter had stolen from him. The draper continually digresses from the point, to speak about a piece of cloth of which his antagonist's attorney had likewise robbed him. From these digressions he is constantly recalled by the judge, with the words "Revenons à nos moutons."

STAGE AND AUDIENCE.

THE late Mrs. Rousby, playing one night at the Queen's Theatre—now the Universities Co-operative Store in Long Acre, was greatly annoyed by some talkers in a private box. The actress stopped twice in the middle of a speech, as a hint for the occupants of the box, but finding they did not take it, Mrs. Rousby at last came to the foot-lights in a rage, and said, "Ladies and gentlemen, when those persons in the third box from the stage have finished their conversation, I will go on with my part." A roar of applause followed, in the midst of which the offenders quitted the theatre. In a like manner, John Kemble, when excruciated in one of his great parts by the perpetual squealing of a baby, advanced to the foot-lights and observed, in his most tragic tones, "Ladies and Gentlemen, unless the play is stopped, that poor child cannot possibly go on."

"BY ORDER."

HERR SCHRÖDER, a performer of great ability and an ardent lover of Shakespeare, in 1776 brought *Othello* in German on the stage at Hamburg. It was not a success, however; the close of the tragedy was so much objected to, that the Hamburg senate commanded the *dénouement* to be altered, and ordered that *Othello* should end happily. It was found that the murder of the unhappy Desdemona worked the audience up to such a pitch of excitement, that ladies fainted by the score, and had to be carried out of the theatre.

A BEARDED POLLY.

FORMERLY, the *Beggar's Opera* was sometimes travestied, the men's parts being played by women, and *vice versâ*. The first time that Mazzanti, a celebrated soprano singer, went to an opera in London, the performance happened to be the above travesty at the Haymarket Theatre, which he mistook for the opera-house opposite. The part of Polly upon that occasion was represented by the elder Bannister, who gave her tender airs with all the power of his deep, sonorous, bass voice. The Italian's astonishment and horror were unspeakable, when he saw the part of a young woman acted by an old man; for he had not been informed, nor did he even guess at the time, that he was witnessing a burlesque. On the contrary, he thought that it had been so intended by the author, and was always so acted. A few nights after, he was invited to see the tragedy of *Isabella* at Drury Lane. "No, no," said he, "I will not go to your theatres, to see heroines acted by old bass singers with beards." Nor could he for a long time be prevailed upon to attend any of our theatrical exhibitions, in consequence of his early disgust.

TIERCE AND *CARTE*.

DOUGLAS JERROLD, being a very nervous man, usually suffered torments of apprehension on the first representation of any of his pieces. A brother dramatist—remarkable for his successful specimens of "fair adaptation" or imitation from the French—on one such occasion sought to rally the trembling scribe by stating that he himself never felt any nervousness on the first production of his own pieces. "Oh, my boy," said Douglas, "but then you are always so sure of success! Your pieces have all been tried before."

A VESTED RIGHT.

DR. FISHER, an eminent violin-player in his day, married a daughter of the famous William Powell, and, in right of his wife, had a sixteenth share of the Covent Garden Theatre. Coming one evening into the green-room, he observed that an actress had torn her petticoat, which formed part of the stage property, for which offence he soundly abused her. The actress, unaquainted with Fisher's authority, asked him what right he had to speak to her in that manner. To which he answered, with great pomposity, "All the right in the world, madam. I have to look after my property; for know, madam, the sixteenth part of the petticoat you have destroyed belongs to me, and is mine to all intents and purposes, madam!"

EGO ET REX MEUS.

IN 1824, when the question of erecting a monument to Shakespeare in his native town was discussed, George IV. took a lively interest in the matter. Considering that the leading people in both the patent theatres should be consulted, he directed Sir Charles Long, Sir George Beaumont, and Sir Francis Freeling to ascertain Elliston's sentiments on the subject. As soon as these distinguished individuals—who had come direct from, and were returning to, the palace—had delivered themselves of their mission, Elliston loftily replied, "Very well, gentlemen; leave the papers with me, and I *will talk over the business with his Majesty.*"

ABSENT ON LEAVE.

QUIN was once at an auction of pictures, when old General Guise came into the room. "There's General Guise," said somebody to Quin; "how very ill he looks!" "Guise, sir!" says Quin; "you're mistaken. He has been dead these two years." "Nay, but," says the other, "believe your eyes: there he is." At this Quin put on his spectacles, and, after viewing him from head to foot for some time, exclaimed, "Why, yes, sir, I'm right enough. He has been dead these two years, 'tis quite evident, and has now only gotten a day-rule to see the pictures."

MEMORY WORN OUT.

THE *Beggar's Opera* had a run such as never had been witnessed before in London, or perhaps in the world. "Nothing stopped its progress through the course of a whole season," says a theatrical writer, in the beginning of the present century, admiringly. We have seen other phenomena of that kind, but it was wonderful for those days. When Walker, the original Macheath, was performing his part on the seventy-second night, he happened to be a little imperfect, which Rich observing, called out to him on his return from the stage, "Holloa, mister, I think your memory ought to be pretty good by this time." "And so it is," said Walker; "but, zounds! sir, my memory cannot last for ever."

AN UNEXPECTED ADMIRER.

AT a representation of *King Lear*, whilst Garrick, in the last act, was melting in tears over the dead body of Cordelia, his face all at once assumed an expression of merriment quite foreign to the part he was playing. At the same time, Edgar and the officers were seen to make unsuccessful attempts to repress laughter; even Cordelia reopened her eyes, and burst out in an uncontrollable fit of merriment. The audience thought that all of them had gone mad. Was—

> "This the promised end?
> Or image of that horror?"

But soon the innocent cause of this merry conclusion became apparent. On the front seat of the pit sat a stout butcher, accompanied by his bulldog. Leaning far back in his seat, the man had placed the dog between his legs, and the animal, seeing the bustle on the boards, stood erect on his hind legs, leaning his paws on the railing which divided the stage from the pit. It was a very hot evening, and the butcher, in order to wipe his head, had taken off his wig and placed it on the head of his bulldog. In this posture, and with this attire, the dog stood looking earnestly and fixedly at the actors, and had caught Garrick's eye. The scene proved so irresistible, that Lear forgot his sorrows and laughed outright; and, instead of ending with a dead march, the tragedy concluded with roars of merriment.

NO DECEPTION.

THERE was a scene in the comedy *Tragaldabas*, in which Frédéric Lemaitre had to drink a bottle of champagne; but, as dramatic companies can scarcely afford to treat their members nightly to a bottle of Aï, it was customary to substitute some other sparkling beverage. One evening, Lemaitre put the glass to his lips, and, making a horrible grimace, exclaimed, "Call the manager; tell him I want to speak to him." General commotion, in the midst of which the manager makes his appearance. "Come forward," said Frédéric, gravely. "What do you mean by this untimely hoax, sir? Do you think I feel inclined to be your accomplice in deceiving the public?" "*I!*" exclaimed the dumbfounded manager. "*You*, sir; *you*." Then turning to the pit, Frédéric added, "Gentlemen, you think that I am drinking champagne, but it is nothing of the kind; it is simply Seltzer water!" The public, amused at the actor's impudence, loudly cheered and applauded his sally; whilst the manager exclaimed, "It is a mistake, Mr. Frédéric—a pure mistake, on my honour. You shall have a bottle of champagne directly." And whilst waiting for his real champagne, Frédéric whiled the time away by making a speech to the pit, concerning Seltzer water and the general want of honesty in managers.

SWORD AND GOWN.

AMONG the portraits of queens of the theatre painted by Sir Joshua Reynolds is that of Mrs. Baddeley, an actress more celebrated for her beauty and gallantry than for her wit and professional skill. Her picture represents the most voluptuous of faces, with large, melting dark eyes and full, rosy lips. The beauty is caressing a cat; the cat plays with a tress of soft hair which has fallen over the white shoulder.

In 1772, when the Pantheon in Oxford Street was opened, it was whispered that the managers had determined to exclude all "women of slight character." The young bloods of the period, Lord Palmerston, Lord Carlisle, Lord March, and Sir Charles Bunbury, were, however, no partisans of the Pantheon Catos. They vowed that, whoever was excluded from the Pantheon, Sophia Baddeley should be let in. Twenty gentlemen, headed by Mr. Hanger (afterwards Lord Coleraine) and Mr. Conway, son of the Earl of Hertford, met at Almack's, and bound themselves to escort her and stand by her chair. When she was set down under the portico—the same we still see, for it escaped the fire of 1792—her escort had swelled to nearly fifty gentlemen. The constables allowed Mrs. Baddeley's companion, a Mrs. Steele, to pass; but when she herself followed, they crossed their staves, and civilly but resolutely said their orders were to admit no players. On this the gallant escort drew, compelled the constables to give way at the sword's point, and, raising their chivalrous blades, protected Mrs. Baddeley as she passed proudly into the rotunda, blazing with lights, and surrounded between its ranges of pillars with all the gods and goddesses of the Olympus. But the difficulty was not yet at an end. The enraged gentlemen refused to sheath their swords, or to allow the music to proceed, till the managers came forward and humbly apologized to Mrs. Baddeley and her escort. It is related by Mrs. Baddeley's biographer, that when the managers had apologized, the Duchess of Argyle and the Duchess of Ancaster stepped forward and expressed the pleasure it gave them to receive such an ornament to their assembly as Mrs. Baddeley. A few days later, an advertisement appeared in the morning papers, stating, that "as it was not convenient for ladies always to carry the certificate of their marriages about them, the subscribers were resolved, in opposition to the managers, to protect the ladies to whom they gave their tickets."

A LONG JOURNEY.

GARRICK was accused of being parsimonious, and throughout his life a certain thriftiness which characterized him was made the subject of much joking. One day, when he and Foote were leaving their usual haunt, the Bedford Coffee-house, in Covent Garden, Foote dropped a guinea, and exclaimed, as he looked for it, "Why, where on earth has it gone to?" "Gone to the devil!" replied Garrick, continuing the search. "Well said, David!" was the quick and smart reply of Foote; "let you alone for making a guinea go further than any one else in the world."

A CONVERTED BEAU.

IN 1703, *Tunbridge Walks; or, The Yeoman of Kent*, written by Thomas Baker, the son of a London attorney, was acted at Drury Lane. It is stated in Baker's *Biographia Dramatica*, that the character of Maiden in this play was the origin of all the Beau Fribbles, Mizens, and the rest of the effeminate beau-species which have figured in so many subsequent plays. This character was said to have been drawn without exaggeration from the author's former self, as a warning to other beaus, after he had felt the wickedness of his ways. There is a curious spice of the "Old Adam" in the pleasure with which this picture of his former weaknesses was drawn, and placed before the public in a form by no means unattractive to the eyes of those it was to convert.

BUSKIN OR SOCK.

JOHNNY M'CREE, an eccentric, good-humoured Scotchman, once applied to Garrick to introduce a production of his on the stage. Johnny had four acts of a tragedy ready, but was dissuaded by Garrick from finishing it, the comedian telling him that his talent did not lie in that way. So Johnny abandoned his tragedy, and set about writing a comedy. When this was finished, he showed it to Garrick, who found it, if possible, even more exceptionable than his first attempt, and of course could not be pursuaded to bring it forward on the stage. This surprised poor Johnny, who feelingly remonstrated, "Nae, now, David, did na you tell me that my talents did na lie in tragedy?" "Yes," replied Garrick; "but I did not tell you that they lay in comedy." "Then," exclaimed Johnny, justly puzzled, "gin they dinna lie there, then where the deil doo they lie, mon?"

RICHESSE OBLIGE.

WHEN Macklin was in Dublin, on one of his theatrical trips, Reddish, a vain, conceited fellow belonging to the same company, and who gave himself out for a gentleman of easy fortune, was playing a character where, in reading a book, it was necessary on the approach of another person to throw it aside. Reddish, however, threw the book into a rivulet, supposed to be at the bottom of the garden. On a gentleman asking Macklin, "Is it usual for actors to throw away their books thus?" "Why no, sir," replied Macklin, "not for an actor; but a gentleman of easy fortune can afford it."

A SLIPPERY CUSTOMER.

AS Dicky Suett was entering the stage door at Covent Garden Theatre, one pouring wet night, he was tapped on the shoulder by a dun, who had been laying in wait for him, saying, " I believe your name is Suett, sir?" "Oh no!" replied Dicky, escaping from the clutches of his aggressor ; " I'm *dripping*." Dripping happened to be the name of another actor in the same company.

CONJUGAL LOVE.

INCLEDON and Mathews were travelling on the outside of a stage-coach, soon after the death of Incledon's first wife, to whom he had been very much attached. A very consumptive-looking man was also a passenger, and Incledon's heart was touched by the sickly look of the poor fellow. He entered into conversation with him, inquired about his health, and learned that he was going home to his friends to be nursed. When the coach reached its destination, Incledon addressed the invalid for the last time, and said, " My good man, we're going to leave you. It's my opinion, my poor fellow, that you're *bespoke;* you're now, I take it, as good as ready money to the undertaker. In fact, you're *booked*, so there is a seven-shilling piece for you ; and when you go to heaven, and see my dear sainted Jane, pray tell her you saw me, and that I'm well." The invalid stared, took the money with a humble bow, but made no reply to this extraordinary address, which he doubtless supposed to come from a lunatic.

A FOND WISH.

A MR. FAULKNER had been engaged at the Haymarket Theatre from a provincial theatre, and appeared in a tragedy without producing any sensation ; in fact, Colman, the then manager, was disappointed with this new acquisition, who had to deliver the following line, which he spoke in a cadaveral, nasal tone :—"Ah ! where is my honour now ?" Colman, who was behind the scenes, took a leisurely pinch of snuff, and muttered, "I wish your honour was back at Newcastle again, with all my heart."

"LES FOURBERIES DE SCAPIN."

ONE day when Elliston, then manager of the Manchester Theatre, was in London, beating up recruits, he happened to meet the American Roscius, John Howard Payne, an old friend. "My dear fellow, come down to us," said Elliston ; "see us ! hear us ! mark us ! observe—a—how we do the thing at our good theatre at Manchester. Ha! ha !" Payne promised he would run down, but protested against playing, as he had forgotten all his old parts. The morning after his arrival, Payne went to the rehearsal of *Richard the Third.* Elliston at that time, among other sins, used to murder the third Richard. That morning, however, being busy, as he said, he invited Payne to rehearse for him. "Perhaps you will *play* Richard, too," he added, in his chuckling tone of comedy. But this Payne assured him was totally out of the question. With much prompting, the American got through the part, and at the conclusion, seeing Elliston at his elbow, he observed, "You perceive how utterly ridiculous it would have been, had I accepted your invitation to play the part." Elliston assumed a look of horrible amazement. "My dear fellow, are you in earnest ? I am *sure* you are not. You are all over the town by this time in large letters : 'For this night only the part of Richard by the celebrated American Roscius, Mr. John Howard Payne.' You must play for us to night." There was no help for it. Payne had to study all day, and at night gave as much of the part as he could recollect. When he could not recollect, he spouted "something like Shakespeare." The audience seemed to consider this "vamping" better than the original, for Payne roared it twice as loud as the legitimate text, and it elicited thunders of applause.

A PROFESSIONAL EPITAPH.

THOMAS JACKSON, of the Norwich company, lies buried in the churchyard of St. Peter's Mancroff, Norwich, with the following curious epitaph inscribed on his tombstone:—"Sacred to the Memory of Thomas Jackson, Comedian, who was engaged December 21, 1741, *to play a comic cast of characters in this great theatre*, the World, for many of which he was *prompted* by nature to excel. The *season* being ended, his *benefit* over, the *charges* all paid, and his *account* closed, he made his *exit* in the *Tragedy* of "Death," on the 17th of March, 1798, in the full assurance of being *called* once more to *rehearsal;* when he hopes to find his *forfeits* all cleared, his *cast* of *parts* bettered, and his *situation* made agreeable by Him who paid the great *stock*-debt for the love He bore to *performers* in general."

BLACK ON WHITE.

WHEN Colman the younger's affairs with the Haymarket Theatre were in great embarrassment, some one lamented that he could not be relieved from ultimate responsibility by a bankruptcy, he not being a trader. "You are mistaken," said the witty author; "I am a paper-stainer."

FUEL.

IS it because money keeps the pot boiling that an actor's salary in French is called *feu*, and in English *coal?* Let philologists decide. Like most theatrical cant terms, it is of old standing—witness the following pun made by James Spiller, the famous comedian. It was at a time when the public gave but very little encouragement to the Lincoln's Inn Theatre, in consequence of which the proprietor was frequently unable to pay his actors. One Saturday morning when they met as usual at rehearsal, with hopes of receiving at least some part of their pay, Bullock, a brother comedian, said to Spiller, with a sorrowful countenance, "Faith, Jimmy, there is no *coal* again this morning." "Why," replied Spiller, "if there is no coal, we'll have to burn *Wood*," which was the name of the manager.

A DELICATE HINT.

CAPTAIN HARWOOD, the manager of the Dundalk Theatre, was a navy officer on half pay. A gentleman living in the suburbs of Drogheda used frequently to invite him to dine. Christmas being near, this gentleman considered a good dinner on the day that comes but once a year would be desirable, and accordingly he told his friend, the manager, that he would present to the company a quarter of an ox. "I suppose," said he, "they can eat?" "Yes, by my faith," replied Harwood, "they can eat, indeed; but it would do your heart good to see them *drink*."

A FALSE ALARM.

WHEN the dramatic version of Sue's *Mysteries of Paris* had its run at the Porte Saint Martin, at Paris, the close of the last act was one evening unceremoniously cut short by the sudden fall of the curtain. The audience stared at each other, suggested the probability of an accident behind the scenes, or even of fire, and ended by shouting with one accord for the stage-manager. Scarcely had that functionary appeared and made his three customary bows, when he was assailed by cries from all parts of the house, loudly demanding an explanation. "Gentlemen," he commenced. "Is the fire out?" interrupted one of the deities. "*Plait-il?*" inquired the manager, utterly taken aback by the question. "The fire! the fire! Is it extinguished?" anxiously asked a hundred voices. "Gentlemen, there is no fire that I know of. I was about to say that the curtain had been inadvertently let down half a minute too soon, and that Mr. Frédéric Lemaitre" (who played Jacques Ferrand, the wicked notary) "was consequently prevented from having the honour of exclaiming, as he has done every evening since the first performance of the piece, '*Mon Dieu! Mon Dieu!! Mon Dieu!!!*'" With these words, uttered with the most perfect gravity, and a conscientious attempt to imitate the actor's tone, the worthy stage-manager made his parting bow, and retired amid uncontrollable bursts of laughter—a *dénouement* to the lugubrious drama certainly never contemplated by its author.

TOO TOOTLE.

WHEN Mrs. Bellamy played in the Dublin Theatre, she became such a favourite with the public that she was greeted with the most endearing expressions. These she accepted graciously, until one of her admirers, Mr. St. Leger, was so carried away by his admiration, that he kissed her as she passed him on quitting the stage. The offended actress gave him such a box on the ear, that it tingled for the rest of the night. Lord Chesterfield rose in his box to applaud her; and at the end of the act, Major Macartney was sent by the viceroy to insist upon Mr. St. Leger making a public apology.

SALTS AND SENNA.

MR. VANDENHOFF relates, in his amusing *Dramatic Reminiscences*, that rehearsing one day the play of *Hamlet* at a small theatre in Lancashire, a Polonius, in the second act, after telling him that the actors were arrived, proceeded to describe them in this manner:

"The best actors in the world, my lord, for tragedy, comedy, history, pastoral, pastorical comical, historical pastoral, scene individable, or poem unlimited. *Plautus is too heavy, and senna is too light.*" Polonius was very indignant when Mr. Vandenhoff mildly suggested the incorrectness of the reading, and inquired from him, if Shakespeare had not rather written : "*Seneca cannot be too heavy, nor Plautus too light.*" "Oh, fudge!" replied he; "I know what senna is, as well as you; as for Plautus, I don't know what that is, nor I don't care. But I have spoken it so for twenty-five years, and I ain't a-going to change it now." Accordingly at night, when he came to the passage, he walked deliberately up to Hamlet, looked him full in the face, and, in a very emphatic tone, said—

"Plautus *is* too heavy, and senna *is* too light."

"I could only wish him a good dose of it," says Mr. Vandenhoff, "by way of clearing his thick head. But it passed with the audience; apparently no one noticed. Perhaps he had read it so to them for twenty odd years, and they were used to it; who knows?"

THE RULING PASSION.

WHEN Macready was performing in Mobile, U.S.A., in 1844, his manner at rehearsal displeased one of the actors, a native American of the pure western type. This person, who was cast for the part of Claudius in *Hamlet*, resolved to "pay off" the Britisher for many supposed offences, and thus he carried out his purpose. When in the last scene Hamlet stabbed the usurper, he reeled forward, and after a most spasmodic finish, he stretched himself out precisely in the place Hamlet required for his own death. Macready, much annoyed, whispered, "Die further up the stage, sir." The monarch lay insensible. Upon which, in a louder voice, Hamlet growled again, "Die further up the stage, sir." Hereon the Claudius, sitting up, observed, "I b'leeve I'm King here, and I'll die where I please!" The tragedy concluded shortly after that.

"GAMMER GURTON'S NEEDLE."

DR. JOHN STILL, a Vice-Chancellor of the University of Cambridge and Bishop of Bath and Wells, was the author of the above play. It is impossible to settle the date of the first appearance of this comedy with accuracy. Malone was of opinion, and with reason, that it was acted at Christ's College, Cambridge, in 1566, when Still was in his twenty-third year. The story of this play, which is written in metre and extends into five regular acts, is very silly. The whole plot relates merely to the loss of a needle, with which an old woman was mending a countryman's breeches; this needle is afterwards found by its incommodating the person upon whose apparel it had been employed. The characters are all rustics with the exception of Diccon the Bedlam (*i.e.* Dick the Fool), Dr. Rab, and the Bailey. The dialogue is usually in the broadest provincial dialect. Now and then it has flashes of humour, but of the coarsest kind; whilst some points which are pleasant in the outset, are rendered absurd by being carried to extremes. Thus the description of Hodge, trying to light a candle by the cat's eyes in the dark, and endeavouring to blow them into a flame, is laughable enough, until he is made to give the alarm of fire, because the animal ran away into the hayloft. This was just beyond the bound, though still a pleasant exaggeration. The best thing in it, however, is the drinking-song which opens the second act.

Dr. Still afterwards became Rector of Hadleigh, in the county of Suffolk, and was appointed Bishop of Bath and Wells in 1607. In December, 1592, when he was at the head of the University of Cambridge, he received a command from London, that a comedy in English should be got up there for the amusement of the queen, as, in consequence of the prevalence of the plague, her own actors could not play before her at Christmas. A request was made by Dr. Still and six other learned gentlemen that the play should be in Latin, as "more beseeming the students;" and, though it is not known what play was produced on this occasion, there is reason to suppose that the request was granted.

IRISH PUFFING.

KEMBLE and Lewis, happening to be in Dublin at the same time, were both engaged by the manager of the theatre in Smock Alley for one night's performance, in Leon and the Copper Captain. The announcement of their appearance was coupled with the following delectable passage :—"They never performed together in the same piece, and in all *human probability* they never will again. This evening is, the *summit* of the manager's *climax*. He has constantly gone higher and higher in his endeavours to delight the public, beyond this it is not in *nature* to go."

MACKLIN AND SHUTER.

DURING the rehearsal of *Macbeth* by Macklin, when he was in the seventy-fifth year of his age, he was so prolix and tedious in his own part, as well as in his instructions to the other actors, that Shuter exclaimed, "the case was very hard, for the time has been, that when the brains were out the man would die, and there an end." Macklin, overhearing him, good naturedly replied, "Ah, Ned; and the time was, that when liquor was in wit was out, but it is not so with thee." Shuter rejoined, in the words of Shakespeare, "Now, now thou art a man again."

A THEATRICAL LEGEND.

TWO of the greatest French painters, Ingres and Gérôme, have depicted a scene representing Louis XIV. breakfasting with Molière. The great comedian was an hereditary *valet-de-chambre* of the king, and according to the legend, some of the other valets objected to his company on account of his being an actor. To rebuke them, the king one morning ordered in a repast always kept ready during the night against his royal hunger, and commanding Molière to sit down, his Majesty himself helped him to the wing of a chicken, in the presence of the discomforted courtiers. This pretty story does not occur in any of the thousand and one memoirs and collections of letters of that period. Saint Simon declares distinctly that, except in the army, the king never ate with any man, not even with the princes of the blood, excepting only at the feasts he gave at their weddings. Such a remarkable fact, therefore, as his Majesty's inviting a *valet-de-chambre*, dramatist and actor, to his table would have been far too great an event to be passed by in silence. It was first made public in 1823, in the Memoirs of Madame Campan, who asserted that she had it from her father, who heard it from an old physician-in-ordinary to Louis XIV. But, in the absence of all further corroboration, the second-hand authority of an anonymous physician can go for nothing, and the whole affair may be dismissed as a legend.

A BAD CONSCIENCE.

THE production of Poole's comedy of *The Patrician and the Parvenu* at Drury Lane, gave rise to a humorous equivoque. The worthy author was at that time in difficulties, as many persons have been before and after him. At a particular moment, in a particular scene, a horn had to be blown, and the player in the orchestra, not exactly "suiting the action to the word," was ordered to be in attendance at the end of the last rehearsal to settle the point. As Poole was crossing the stage, he saw dodging about a man more than six feet high, wrapped up in a thick, shaggy "upper benjamin," with his chin sunk into the folds of a Belcher handkerchief, his hat cocked on one side, and each of his hands dipped into their respective side coat-pockets. His eyes at once caught the fellow's look, and his ear took alarm at hearing him say to a diminutive and familiar little wag, the call-boy, "Can you tell me if Mr. Poole is anywhere about here?" The author shot off like an arrow, and had nearly reached the door, when the skirts of his coat were pulled by the call-boy, who vociferated, "Don't you be afraid, sir; it's only the feller as blows the horn, vants to know ven it's to come in."

BLISSET'S READING.

ONE night when Blisset was having his benefit at Bath, he was playing Rueful in *The Natural Son.* At the moment he was, in that character, about to make the disclosure of his birth, a party of ladies and gentlemen entered one of the boxes, and commenced talking so loudly that the actors could no longer be heard. Blisset stared at them for an instant, indignantly and disconcerted; then taking Blushenly, his interlocutor, by the arm, he said, "Come along, you can't hear me here, and I'll tell you all about it in the next room;" with which he went off, and gave vent to his vexation.

EX UNGUE LEONEM.

FOX, the Brighton manager, was a very odd character. He was a kind of *Caleb Quotem* in real life. He could combine twenty occupations, without being clever in one—a pretty general characteristic of country managers in those days. He was actor, fiddler, painter, machinist, and tailor, besides check-taker and bill-sticker on occasions. But he prided himself more especially on his talents as a painter, had executed all his own scenery, and accomplished in person the embellishment of the house. Sheridan was down at Brighton one summer, and Fox, desirous of showing him some civility, took him all over the theatre and exhibited its beauties. "There, Mr. Sheridan," said he, "I constructed this stage, I built and painted those boxes, and I painted all those scenes." "Did you, indeed?" said Sheridan, surveying them rapidly. "Well, I should not have known you were a Fox by your *brush*."

DIAGNOSTICS.

JOHN EDWIN, the actor, frequently disobeyed the injunction which the King of Denmark lays down to the queen, "Gertrude, do not drink." When in his cups, he used to forget all about his engagements, and a brother actor had to apologize for the defaulter's absence. One evening, Lewis went forward with the usual formula—that it was with the greatest regret that he had to inform the house Mr. Edwin was prevented from appearing that evening, in consequence of a sudden indisposition. "*Gradual* indisposition, you mean, Mr. Lewis," corrected a wit in the pit; "for I saw him ten minutes ago, getting drunk in the Piazza Coffee-house."

A THIMBLE EMEUTE.

IN 1805, Dowton, an actor of Covent Garden Theatre, chose for his benefit Foote's burlesque, *The Tailors; or, a Tragedy for Warm Weather*, in which the fraternity of the thimble were not treated with the respect their importance in all ages appears to have enjoyed. Like the footmen some years before, on the representation of *High Life Below Stairs*, they resolved to vindicate the dignity of their order. An angry battalion of tailors occupied—as well they might—the *dress*-boxes, another operative line threaded the pit, whilst not a few were prepared for backing the suit in the galleries. Dowton had advertised *The Tailors*, but they were resolved on *Measure for Measure*. Being well assured that the first blow is half the battle, Dowton, on his appearance, was assailed by no less a missile than a pair of tremendous shears, large enough to cut the thread of his existence had they touched him. This pretty strong demonstration of hostility caused the immediate interference of the constables, and in three minutes the uproar was at its best. The tailors, it is true, were three to one, but recollecting how many go to a man, it is not surprising they were soon overpowered. Some of the ringleaders, or foremen, were handed over to Mr. Aaron Graham, the chief police magistrate; but that gentleman being one of the committee of management at Drury Lane Theatre, the whole party were sent about their business, with the exception of the desperate little mechanic who had thrown the shears.

NOTHING LIKE LEATHER.

VICTORIEN SARDOU, before he obtained fame and wealth, lived at a shoemaker's in the Faubourg St. Dénis, where he earned his living by carrying and stowing away huge rolls of leather and other merchandise belonging to the owner of the shop. There seemed to be "nothing like leather" at that time for the hapless dramatist, inasmuch as another kindly Crispin, who dwelt in the Rue de la Seine, supplied him for ten years with boots on credit, having such a prophetic belief in his genius that he never troubled him for the money. Needless almost to add that the custom is still continued, though on rather more ready-money principles than in days of yore; and when the old bootmaker visits the successful playwright, at his chateau at Marly, he slaps his thighs, and exclaims, "Ah! if you had not been properly shod, you would never have arrived at fortune, for how could you have walked from theatre to theatre with your first plays?"

JUDGING BY APPEARANCES.

ANDREW JACKSON ALLEN, better known as "Dummy Allen," a subordinate New York actor, was very deaf. This infirmity rendered him very annoying to those with whom he played, who not unfrequently took an unkind revenge on his misfortune by misleading him with an inaudible movement of the lips during the performance, to which he thought he must reply, his speeches being often very *mal-à-propos*. On one occasion, when an actor's lips seemed moving beyond the cue, by which he was to reply, Allen exclaimed aloud, "What is all this? Are you going to do all the talking? Stop, or I'll go off the stage." The audience roared with laughter.

CAUTIOUS APPROVAL.

MRS. SIDDONS' first reception in Edinburgh, on May 22, 1784, in *Belvidera*, was very cool. "I own," she says, "I was surprised, and not a little mortified, at that profound silence, which was a contrast to the burst of applause I had been accustomed to hear in London. Not a hand moved to the end of the scene." She felt as if she had been speaking to stones. At last she gathered herself up for one passage, and threw all her powers into it; then paused, and looked steadily at the audience, when in the hushed silence a voice was heard, exclaiming, "Come, that's no' bad!" This produced roars of laughter, and the wished-for burst of applause.

SLEEPING PARTNERS.

M. MAZÈRE receives a certain share in the profits of the opera *Le Serment, ou les Faux Monnayeurs*, every time that piece is represented, and yet he has not written one note of the music, nor one word of the text. His share in the work was simply that he once told Scribe, the playwright, the anecdote of the Marshal Turenne and the coiners, which forms the subject of this piece, adding that "something might be done for the stage with it." Scribe replied, "I have heard the anecdote before, but I have never thought of that. We will see, however." No more was said about it, but a long time after, the opera *Le Serment* was produced. As soon as M. Mazère heard that the rehearsals were proceeding, he wrote to Scribe: "I claim my share of collaboration in the opera now under rehearsal, but I will not be named. I have taken no part in the composition of the piece in question, but *I might have done so*, for I told you the anecdote which forms the subject," etc. He obtained what he asked, and, moreover, the opera is always announced on the bills as the work of "M. Scribe et * * *." Surely delicacy can go no further. In a similar manner, Scribe himself used to receive a certain share every time the *Favorita* was played, to which, however, he had contributed nothing, the libretto having been written by Alphonse Royer. It was a compensation because Donizetti, after entrusting him with the libretto of *Le Duc d'Albe*, had taken back the score to make use of it in the *Favorita*.

A HANDSOME OFFER.

THE following is told by John Bernard, in his *Retrospections of the Stage*, and as the story relates to his own wife, we must believe it to be true. When the troupe to which he belonged was at Plymouth, "Mrs. Bernard on her benefit night received an unexpected compliment. We were playing *The Chances*, in which my wife enacted the Second Constantia, and when, repeating the soliloquy upon her escape from Antonio, she exclaimed, 'Well, I'm glad I've got rid of that old fellow, however; and now, if any handsome young man would take a fancy to me and make me an honest woman, I'd make him the best wife in the universe,' a middy in the slips, who had never seen a play before, and took a deep interest in the scene, immediately started up, and leaning over the box, in a manner which made him conspicuous to the whole house, clapped his hands and cried out, 'I'll have you, ma'am! I'll have you, demme if I don't! I have three years' pay to receive, besides prize-money.'"

DEATHS ON THE STAGE.

IN the annals of the stage there are a few instances of performers who expired whilst performing some actors part. What makes these sudden deaths still more striking, is the fact that in some instances the last words they uttered had some reference to the uncertainty of life. The first instance on record is that of one Paterson, an actor long attached to the Norwich company. This gentleman, in October, 1752, was performing the Duke in *Measure for Measure*, which he played in a masterly style. Moody was the Claudio, and in the third act, when the Duke, disguised as the Friar, was preparing Claudio for execution next morning, Paterson had no sooner spoken these words—

> "Reason thus with life :
> If I do loose thee, I do loose a thing
> That none but fools would keep ; a breath thou art,"

than he dropped in Moody's arms, and died instantly. He was interred at Bury St. Edmunds, and on his tombstone his last words, as above, are engraved.

A gentleman of the name of Bond, with a number of friends, got up Voltaire's *Zaïre*, translated into English, at the music-room in Villiers Street, York Buildings, Strand, and chose the part of Lusignan for himself. His acting was considered marvellous, and he so far yielded himself up to the force and impetuosity of his imagination, that on the discovery of his daughter he fainted away. The house rung with applause, but finding that he continued a long time in that situation, the audience began to be uneasy and apprehensive. The representatives of Chatillon and Nerestan placed him on a chair. He then faintly spoke, extended his arms to embrace his children, who were present among the audience, raised his eyes to heaven, and closed them for ever.

John Palmer, familiarly known as "Plausible Jack Palmer,"

an excellent general actor who opened the Royalty Theatre at the East end of London, terminated his life on the Liverpool stage in 1798. On the morning of the day on which he was to have performed *The Stranger*, he received the distressing intelligence of the death of his second son. The play in consequence of this was deferred, and he in vain endeavoured to calm the agitation of his mind. When, a few days afterwards, the performance took place, its success was so marked that a second representation was called for, which took place on August 2, 1793. In the fourth act, Baron Steinfort obtains an interview with the "Stranger," whom he discovers to be his old friend. He prevails on him to relate the cause of his seclusion from the world. In this relation Palmer was visibly much agitated, and at the moment when he mentioned his wife and children, the memory of his own loss rushed no doubt upon him, and after some vain attempts to speak, he fell lifeless on the stage. The audience supposed for the moment that his fall was nothing more than a studied addition to the part, but on seeing him carried away from the stage, the truth dawned upon them. Medical assistance was at once procured, but every means of resuscitation proved unavailing: death had been instantaneous.

In June, 1817, when the tragedy of *Jane Shore* was performed at the Leeds Theatre, Cummings, a veteran actor who had held an elevated rank on the stage for nearly half a century, played the part of Dumont. He had just repeated the benedictory words—

> "Be witness for me, ye celestial hosts.
> Such mercy and such pardon as my soul
> Accords to thee, and begs of heaven to show thee,
> May such befall me at my latest hour,"

when he fell down on the stage and instantly expired. For some time Cummings had laboured under that alarming malady designated by the name of ossification of the heart; and to this circumstance, added to the strength of his feelings in the mimic scene, his death is to be attributed.

The latest instance on record of sudden death before the foot-lights is that of Mr. Jordans, a respectable, painstaking actor. His appalling end, less than ten years ago, is too well remembered to bear repetition.

THE THREE COMMANDMENTS.

ALFRED BUNN, formerly manager of Drury Lane Theatre, was delivering a lecture on "the Drama," in the New Hall, Leicester, many years since, before a crowded audience, when the following anecdote elicited much applause. He said, "A wealthy old gentleman, who had a great veneration for the works of Shakespeare, had erected in the centre of his library a costly cabinet for the exclusive reception of what he believed to be one of the first copies of the immortal poet's work ever printed. Outside this cabinet were three brass plates, with the following inscriptions:—'To authors: Thou shalt not steal;' 'To critics: Thou shalt not bear false witness;' 'To actors: Thou shalt do no murder.'"

PROFESSIONAL JEALOUSY.

THE Pantheon Theatre was burned on January 14, 1792. Sheridan, then manager of Drury Lane, and Michael Kelly, the stage manager, were looking at the conflagration. Sheridan remarked that the flames were reaching the top of the building, and that it did not seem possible that they could be extinguished. An Irish fireman standing by, overhearing Sheridan make this remark, whispered to him, "For the love of heaven, Mr. Sheridan, don't be unasy, sir! By the powers, it will soon be down; sure, they won't have a blessed drop of water in five minutes." Pat said this in the natural warmth of heart, for he imagined that the ruin of the rival theatre could not but be gratifying to the proprietor of Drury Lane.

A RESUSCITATION.

IN Rowe's play of *The Fair Penitent* a curious scene was once witnessed. The "haughty, gallant, gay Lothario," after having been slain at the end of the fourth act by Altamont, lies dead, raised on a bier, covered with black by the property-man, and his face whitened by the barber. But, as Lothario does not come to life again, the part of corpse is usually taken by a double, which in general is the actor's dresser. The original Lothario was George Powell, a clever actor, admired by Steele and Addison, but a riotous, rollicking, quarrelsome fellow. On the occasion in question, Warren, Powell's dresser, had claimed the right of lying in state by proxy for his master, and of performing the dead part of Lothario to the best advantage, though Powell was ignorant of the matter. The fifth act began, and through the "soft music" which accompanied it, Powell, impatient to go home, was heard behind the scenes angrily calling for Warren, at that moment employed in the doleful duty of personating his master's corpse. The unfortunate dresser, extended on the bier, heard Lothario storming, yet for some time dramatic propriety overcame his fear. Trembling he lay, anxiously waiting for the curtain to descend. At length he could sustain it no longer, for he heard Powell vowing that he would "break every bone in his skin" if he did not come instantly, and the dresser knew that his master was a man likely to keep such a promise. So without a word of reply he jumped off, with all his sables about him, which unfortunately being tied fast to the handles of the bier, dragged that furniture of woe after him. The audience burst out in laughter, which frightened poor Warren so much that, with the bier at his tail, he threw down Calista (Mrs. Barry), and overwhelmed her with the table, lamp, book, skull, and other bones, and fled from the stage as fast as his charnel-house trappings would allow him. Thus for once the sombre tragedy of *The Fair Penitent* was permitted a mirthful conclusion.

ADAM AND EVE.

AMONG the many operatic libretti sent in to the celebrated French composer, Adam, at different periods of his professional career, in the hope that their perusal might inspire him with a burning desire to set them to music, was one—the work of a youthful poet unknown to fame—bearing the attractive title of *Eve*. Having looked over the text, which proved to be utterly devoid of literary or dramatic merit, Adam promptly forwarded it to the author, with the following happily turned note :—

"VERY MUCH HONOURED SIR,—To my lively regret, I find it quite impossible to avail myself of the accompanying libretto, with an offer of which your great goodness has prompted you to favour me. For, believe me, should Adam allow himself to be tempted by this particular Eve, the public would most assuredly undertake, with surprising spontaneity, the part of the Serpent—at least, as far as hissing is concerned. Disastrous precedent warns us against a revival of so sinister a combination; wherefore I hasten to return your remarkable production, with every assurance of my perfect consideration.—ADAM."

"A NEW WAY TO PAY OLD DEBTS."

MR. ROBERT MITCHELL, who supplied Sheridan with coals, had a heavy demand against him, long outstanding, and for which he was determined not to wait any longer. He went to Sheridan's house, accused him of having treated him shamefully, and swore he would not leave the house without his money. As the amount was several hundreds, and Sheridan had not as many shillings, compliance was more easily demanded than obtained. Sheridan made most eloquent appeals, and finally asked "if half would do to-day, and a bill for the remainder." "Not a farthing less than my whole bill, Mr. Sheridan," was the reply; "as I said before, I dare not show my face at home without it." After a pause, and apparently much moved, the dramatist replied, "Then, would to heaven I could assist you! I cannot—but" (and here he took a deep dip into his pocket), "one thing I can, I will, I ought to do. There" (taking Mitchell's hand, shaking it, and putting something in it) "there—never let it be said that while Sheridan had a guinea in his pocket, he refused it to his friend *Bob* Mitchell." Sheridan heaved with emotion, Mitchell stood aghast for a minute or two; then carefully tucked up the guinea in a corner of his leather breeches pocket, forgot his wrongs, and with the affectionate *Bob* ringing in his ears, he bolted out of the house, and to the latest hour of his life was fond of displaying "the last guinea his friend Sheridan had in the world!" This is perhaps the greatest feat Sheridan ever did, except when he softened an attorney.

BAD COMPANY.

BOMAN, an actor of the Bettertonian school, in his youth was famous for his voice. One night he was appointed to sing some part in a concert at Nell Gwynn's apartments. Only the king, the Duke of York, and a few courtiers of the highest rank were present at this entertainment. Boman sang his best, and when the performance was concluded, Charles expressed himself highly pleased, and warmly praised the musicians. "Then, sir," said Nell Gwynne, "to show you don't speak like a courtier, I hope you will make the performers a handsome present." The king replied that he had no money about him, and asked his brother if he had any. To which the duke replied, "I believe, sir, not above a guinea or two." Upon which Nelly, turning laughingly to the other gentlemen, and making use of the king's favourite expletion, observed, "Odds fish! what company am I got into!"

CHRISTIAN DUTIES.

IN the last century a French actor named Béjart, having inherited a fortune, bought what is called in France a *terre seigneuriale*, corresponding more or less to our manor. The first Sunday after he had taken up his abode in the *chateau*, he went to church. It was the curate's duty to offer prayers for the new lord of the manor, but here a difficulty arose, for all players were excommunicated by the Church. There was no help for it, however, and the mode in which the curate fulfilled his task was as follows:—"My dear brethren," he said, "let us pray for the conversion of M. Béjart, a sinner, comedian, and lord of this manor."

MATHEWS' *DÉBUT*.

IN 1835, Charles Mathews the second made his first bow to a London public at the Olympic, then under the management of Madame Vestris, as George Rattleton in *The Humpbacked Lover*, after little more than a fortnight's preparation. This was followed by a little piece, written for the occasion by Leman Rede, *The Old and the Young Stager*. Liston, who, it was said, had delayed his own farewell to the stage that he might introduce the son of his old friend to the public, took the part of the Old Stager; young Mathews played Tom Topple the Tiger, and showed himself the true son of his father—a chip of the old block. The dialogue was of the punning kind then much in vogue; the hits, many and good, were conveyed in stage-coach phraseology, with an occasional sprinkle of St. Giles's Greek, but applicable to the stage that goes without wheels, past and present. All that bore reference to the sun which had forever set, and that which had just risen, was eagerly seized by the audience and applauded to the echo. Liston spoke a serious poetic address very beautifully, and in the tag of the piece drew tears. "Tim," he said, "let me give you some advice. You are entering a new line of life, a stranger to the road. *I* know it well. It has its errors and its accidents, but you reach the inn at last; and, I believe, there's not one here need be asked twice to remember the *coachman*." Here Liston was enthusiastically cheered. He then led Mathews forward, and proceeded thus: "Passengers, we leave you here. As he carries on the stage, be his guard. He's my boy, and if he don't always handle the whip like an old hand, make allowances, *for the sake of his father*."

A PLEDGE OF FRIENDSHIP.

MATHEWS was always well dressed, and carried a handsome umbrella. Munden was miserly, generally meanly dressed, and carried an old gingham "Paul Pry." After Munden had left the stage, Mathews met him one day in Covent Garden. "Ah, Munden," said Mathews, "you must let me have something of yours as a remembrance." "Certainly, my boy," replied Munden; "we'll exchange umbrellas." Mathews was so taken aback, that Munden quietly walked off with his new umbrella.

SOMETHING IN THAT.

THERE was some humour in the retort of a country actor of the name of Knipe to the famous Barry, who was impatient of the incompetency of the players engaged with him. "Do not speak your speech, sir, in that drawling way," said Barry, in his energetic manner. "Look at me, sir! speak it in this way, 'To ransom home revolted Mortimer!' that is the way to speak it, sir." To which the actor immediately replied, "I know that, sir, that *is* the way; but you'll please to remember you get £100 a week for speaking it in *your* way, and I only get thirty shillings for *mine.* Give me £100, and I'll speak it in your way; but I'm not going to do for thirty shillings what you get paid £100 for."

STAGE FEVERS.

WANLEY, in his *Wonders of the Little World*, has a curious anecdote of a singular epidemic which about the year 200 B.C. prevailed in the present province of Roumelia. "In the reign of Lysimachus, king of Thrace," says he, "the people were infected by a strange disease. First, a violent and burning fever seized them. Upon the seventh day after, they bled at the nose very copiously, or others of them fell into an exceeding sweat. But a ridiculous affection was left upon their minds, for they all fell *to acting of tragedy*, thundering out iambics, especially the *Andromeda* of Euripides and the part of *Perseus* therein, so that the city was full of pallid, attenuated actors. This dotage lasted till the winter, when the sharp frost put an end to it. The secret of the malady was this: Archilaus, a famous tragedian, had in the summer represented *Andromeda*, and while in the theatre the people were first seized with fever, and thus the representations of the stage got dominion over their senses." In modern times, about 1744, when Garrick was playing in Dublin, a fever broke out which was called the Garrick fever. Some eighty years later a complimentary fever broke out in Edinburgh, when Mrs. Siddons was playing there. Sceptical doctors, however, attributed it to the heat from over-crowding at her performances.

SINGLE PART ACTORS.

IN the *Guardian*, Steele has given an amusing account of one William Peer, an actor who took his degree with Betterton, Kynaston, and Harris, whose memory has been preserved by playing only one part. But this single part was such a *pièce de résistance* in his career, that it sufficed to establish his solid fame. The character was that of the actor in *Hamlet.* No one could like him repeat the lines—

> "For us and for our tragedy
> Here stooping to your clemency,
> We beg your hearing patiently."

"His whole action in life," says the essayist, "depended on his speaking these three lines, which he did better than any man else in the world."

On one occasion when Elliston acted *The Three Singers*, the person who was to have played the part of Renaud was taken suddenly ill, during the very representation of the piece. Ward, the leader of the band, laying down his fiddle, volunteered to finish the character. This offer being received by the public with rounds of applause, he jumped on the stage, and went through the business with admirable art. Owing to his success on this remarkable occasion, Ward determined to hang up his fiddle and turn actor. He made several attempts in other characters, but signally failed in them all. Renaud, however, stuck to him like a plaster.

A very similar occurrence took place once at Covent Garden Theatre. Braham was taken ill during the first act of *The Cabinet*, when Woodham, a trumpeter in the orchestra, took up the part of Orlando, and went through it with remarkable effect. He also, on this success, turned his attention to the stage, but failed in all subsequent attempts.

THE AUTHOR AND THE MANAGER.

THE "iron tongue of midnight" had tolled twelve as Elliston was stepping into his carriage from the stage door of Drury Lane Theatre, when a stranger suddenly sprang forward from an obscure corner of the hall, and, presenting his card, demanded an instant audience from the fleeting manager. "I am the author," the stranger said, "of a tragedy,

John Sobieski, forwarded many months ago to this theatre. I have called, sir, fourteen times at this door, and——" "Just step into my carriage, and we will talk the matter over," replied Elliston. The author obeyed; Elliston followed, and the carriage drove on, but not a word was spoken. Within twenty minutes it drew up in Hadlow Street, Burton Crescent, at the residence of James Wallack, where Elliston begged to be excused for a short time. Out stepped the manager, leaving *Sobieski* tenant of the vehicle. The fact was, Elliston was engaged to sup with Wallack, and during that agreeable occupation forgot all about his friend in the coach. About three o'clock in the morning the manager took his departure, after the best manner he was able. Some faint recollection of *John Sobieski* now dawned upon his mind, and not feeling in a mood for discussion, Elliston desired his coachman to take his seat inside *vis-à-vis* the patient Pole, and, mounting the box, gathered up the reins and drove home. What passed between John the coachman and John the Pole, deponent sayeth not; but in due time, when the party reached Elliston's stables, the gallant manager gravely descended from the box and walked home. In the forenoon of that same day the enraged dramatist received his missing tragedy, accompanied by a penitent letter and a free admission to Drury Lane for the season.

A STAGE STORM.

HUNDER on the stage was formerly produced by rolling cannon-balls. In his prologue to *Every Man in his Humour*, Ben Jonson promises that

> "No nimble squib is seen to make afeard
> The gentlewoman; nor rolled bullet heard
> To say it thunders."

Dr. Reynardson, in 1713, in his poem of *The Stage*, noticing the incongruous articles to be seen in the dressing-room of the theatre, mentions—

"Hard by a quart of bottled lightning lies;
A bowl of double use and monstrous size,
Now rolls on high and rumbles in its speed,
Now drowns the weaker crack of mustard seed;
So the true thunder," etc.

In the first quarter of the present century, one Lee, manager of the Edinburgh Theatre, with a view to improving the thunder of his stage, ventured to return to the ancient system of representing a storm. His enterprise was attended with results at once ludicrous and disastrous. He fastened ledges here and there along the back of his stage, and obtaining a number of nine-pound cannon-balls, placed these in a wheelbarrow, which a carpenter was instructed to wheel to and fro over the ledges. The play was *Lear*. The jolting of the heavy barrow, as it was trundled along its uneven path over the hollow stage, and the rumbling and reverberations thus produced, counterfeited most effectually the tempest in the third act. Unfortunately, however, while the King was braving in the front of the scene "the pitiless storm" raging at the back, the carpenter missed his footing, tripped over one of the ledges, and fell down, wheelbarrow, cannon-balls, and all. The stage slanting forward as usual, the cannon-balls came rolling rapidly and noisily down towards the front, gathering force as they advanced; and overcoming the feeble resistance offered by the scene, struck it down, passed over its prostrate form, and made their way towards the footlights and the fiddlers, amidst the amusement and wonder of the audience, and the amazement and alarm of the Lear of that night. As the nine-pounders advanced towards him, and rolled about in all directions, he was compelled to display an activity in avoiding them singularly inappropriate to the age and condition of the character he was personating. He was even said to resemble a dancer achieving the terpsichorean feat known as the egg hornpipe. Presently, too, the musicians became alarmed for the safety of themselves and their instruments, and deemed it advisable to scale the spiked partition which divided them

P

from the pit; for the cannon-balls were upon them, smashing the lamps, and thundering into the orchestra. Meantime, exposed to the full gaze of the house, lay prone beside his empty barrow the carpenter, the innocent invoker of the storm he had been unable to allay or direct, not at all hurt, but exceedingly frightened and bewildered. After this unlucky experiment, the manager abandoned his wheelbarrow and cannon-balls, and reverted to more received methods of producing stage storms.

MATHEWS AND METAL.

CHARLES MATHEWS, while performing at the Lyceum in a little comedy entitled *My Heart's Idol*, was so unfortunate as to receive a wound in the hand while fighting a duel with Mr. George Vining, who impersonated one of the characters in the same play. It was Mathews' misfortune to have been obliged, twice in his life, to compose with his creditors, and in allusion to these misadventures and the above accident the following epigram went the round of the papers:—

"Poor Charley's misfortune the public deplore.
Metallic advances he never could stand;
The *tin* always slipped through his fingers before,
And now the *steel* goes through the middle of his hand."

STALLS AND PIT.

IN the early years of the Restoration, the pit was a favourite place with the "young gallants." Pepys records his sitting there with the Duke of Buckingham, Lord Buckhurst, Sir Charles Sedley, and Etheredge the poet and play-writer. But a few years later, the same chronicler observes anent the pit in the Duke of York's playhouse: "Here a mighty company of citizens, 'prentices, and others; and it makes me observe, that when I first began to be able to bestow a play on myself, I do not remember that I saw so many by half of the ordinary 'prentices and mean people in the pit at two shillings and sixpence a piece as now." Before this tide of vulgarity, the fashion retired to the boxes, and for many years the whole ground-floor of the house was left in undisturbed possession of the "groundlings." In course of time, however, true lovers of the stage began to venture the contact with "the sinful sixpenny mechanics," as the public of the pit are called in an old play. The journal of the Right Honourable William Windham, at one time Colonial Secretary, tells us of his frequent visits to the pit of Covent Garden, where, on one occasion, he records that he "sat by Miss Kemble, Steevens, Mrs. Burke, and Miss Palmer." At Mrs. Siddons' representations, Boaden describes the seven first rows of the pit as crowded with "ladies and gentlemen of the first fashion." Hazlit and Charles Lamb were both faithful patrons of the pit, and so were most of the critics and literary gentlemen of that day.

It was not till 1829 that stalls were introduced, the opera-house in the Haymarket taking the lead in this movement. Dissatisfaction was openly expressed by the *habitués* of the pit, when the best seats were thus taken away from them. But although the overture was hissed—the opera being Rossini's *Donna del Lago*—no serious disturbance took place, and the audience either paid the increased price or was content to sit on the back seats. The example of the opera manager was presently followed by all other theatrical establishments, and high-priced stalls became the rule everywhere. The introduction of stalls has brought another advantage; for, once retained, they are reserved during the whole evening. Such was not the case in former days: those who retained seats in the dress circle were obliged to occupy them before the first act, or they were forfeited.

RESTLESS ZEAL.

DAVID MORRIS, at one time proprietor of the Haymarket Theatre, was a great character, and prided himself especially on his managerial abilities. Faithfully fulfilling all his own obligations, he expected, justly enough, equal rectitude on the part of others. Observing one morning, at the rehearsal of some music, that one of the band was quiescent, he lent over from the pit, in which he was standing, and touched him on the shoulder. "Why are you not playing, sir?" "I have twelve bars rest, sir," answered the musician. "Rest! don't talk to me about rest, sir! Don't you get your salary, sir? I pay you to play, and not to rest, sir! Rest when you've done your work, and not in the middle of it."

SARAH BERNHARDT'S DRESSES.

ALTHOUGH it must be admitted that this celebrated actress is dressed more gorgeously than the lilies, who are said to have surpassed Solomon's wardrobe, yet this splendid attire is not altogether from choice. Not many years ago, Mesdames Bernhardt, Fargueil, and Desclées made public protest against the *pièces à robes*, in which they were required to dress like empresses, at their own expense. They traced the ruinous custom to the period when the Imperial Court was at Compiègne, and when the actresses "invited" to play to the august company there, were required, by the inexorable rule of the court, to obey the sumptuary laws which regulated costume. Every lady was invited for three days; each day she was to wear three different dresses, and no dress was to be worn a second time. Count Bacciochi, the grand chamberlain, kept a sharp eye on the ladies of the drama. Histrionic queens and countesses were bound to be attired as genuinely as the historical dignitaries themselves. The story they represented might be a romance, the outward and visible signs were to be all reality. The awful grand chamberlain is said even once to have refused to admit an actress to the court stage at Compiègne, for the crime of wearing mock pearls when she was playing the part of a duchess. Owing to these regulations, the ladies had to be possessed of very extensive wardrobes, and as the same dresses were not permitted to be seen a second time at Compiègne, they wore them on the stage of the Théâtre Français. Thus the eye of the public became accustomed to a luxury, which has ended in becoming a necessity.

ADJOURNED FOR A BALLET.

WE are wont to see the House of Commons annually adjourned for the Derby day, but it will scarcely be believed in our day that that august senate once adjourned in order that the *patres conscripti* might be present at the benefit of a dancer at the Haymarket Theatre. Such, however, was the case, as will be seen by the following extract of a letter from Horace Walpole to Mr. Mason, dated February 19, 1781. "They have put off the second reading of Burke's Bill because Wednesday was a fast day, and Thursday Vestris' benefit. Religion has had its day, and the French dancer his." The abovenamed Vestris was he who in his meridian French called himself *le Diou de la Danse.** In London he carried all before him, but at Paris he had a young and powerful rival in Duport, whence the French pun, "Vestris a fait naufrage en approchant Du port. His son was also a popular dancer, but is better known to posterity as the happy man who gave his name to Bartolozzi's pretty daughter, the notorious Madame Vestris.

* "There are only two great men in the world," he used to say, "I and the King of Prussia," *i.e.* Frederick the Great.

AN INSANE HAMLET.

SAMUEL REDDISH—Horse Reddish Foote called him—the second husband of Mrs. Canning, the mother of the eminent statesman, George Canning, distinguished himself in some of Shakespeare's characters, but ended his days in a lunatic asylum. His insanity arose from an unlucky occurrence at Covent Garden Theatre on the first night of his engagement. He appeared in the part of Hamlet, and in the fencing scene between him and Laertes, Whitfield, who performed the latter character, made so clumsy a lunge that he struck off the bag-wig of Hamlet, and exposed his bald pate to the laughter of the audience. "In conversing with him in Bedlam," says Mr. Taylor, the correspondent of the *Sun* newspaper, in his *Records*, "I soothed him by telling him that I was present at the scene, and that, though the accident had a visible effect, the audience knew the fault was wholly to be ascribed to the awkwardness of his competitor. The mortification, however, made so strong an impression on his mind that he never appeared on the stage again, and, I heard, ended his days in the asylum at York."

KEMBLE A COMIC.

JOHN KEMBLE certainly believed that he possessed comic talents, and, as far as a strong sense of humour and a disposition to enjoy jocularity could tend to excite such a suspicion, he might yield to this self-deception. George Colman, being asked his opinion of Kemble's Don Felix, replied that it displayed "too much of the Don, and too little of the Felix." Reynolds describes Kemble, at a supper-party, contributing a jovial hunting-song to the entertainment, sung with extraordinary gravity, and introduced by the remark that it was a favourite with one of the first comic singers of the day, Mrs. Siddons. He had no voice, so the performance must have been a curious one.

AN ACTOR HANGED.

"AH! ye who think the actor's life is passed in idleness and dissipation, hear this truthful confession, and blush that you should ever malign a profession that in the heavy criminal calendar is unknown. *No actor yet was ever hanged!* What other profession, trade, or even creed, can say this?" So writes Mr. Belton, with amiable enthusiasm, in his entertaining *Reminiscences.* It is a pity to disturb so kindly a conviction, but *veritas prevalebit.* There are one or two examples of actors who have fully *deserved* hanging, and there is at least one instance of a comedian who, in this respect, obtained his deserts. Mathew Coppinger, an actor of the end of the seventeenth century, was a man of considerable abilities. He was the author of a volume of "*Poems, Songs, and Love-verses, upon Several Occasions,*" 1682, which he dedicated to the Duchess of Portsmouth; but all that can be said of them is that they are exactly what might have been written by such a man to such a woman. Coppinger one night, after personating a mock judge on the stage, took the road in the character of a real highwayman. The consequence was, that a few days afterwards the unfortunate actor found himself before a real judge, receiving the terrible sentence of death. The town was filled with pity and dismay; for a paltry watch and seven pounds in money, the amusing Coppinger was to lose his witty life! Petitions poured in from every quarter, expressing much the same sentiments as those of ancient Pistol:

"Let gallows gape for dog; let man go free,
And let not hemp his windpipe suffocate."

But in vain. In due course, Mat made his final bow at Tyburn. A stave of an old ballad tells us that

> "Mat did not go dead, like a sluggard in bed,
> But boldly in his shoes died of a noose,
> That he found under Tyburn tree."

A POPULAR MAYOR.

DURING the management of Thomas Sheridan in Dublin there was an actor named Sparks, who was famous for his Lord Mayors in *Richard the Third* and *The Beggar's Bush*. On one occasion he had to recite some blank verses, but being too indolent to learn them by heart, he turned them into drollery. Sheridan, who was the Richard of the night, objecting to jokes being mixed in his serious scenes, addressed Sparks the next morning in these words: "Mr. Sparks, you are an excellent comedian; in most of the parts you undertake you are unrivalled. But, sir, I hope you will pardon me for what I have done; I have taken the liberty to set down Mr. Pakenham for the Lord Mayor in to-morrow's bills. You know, my dear sir, that the extraordinary good humour your very appearance throws the whole audience into, without any sinister design in you, so totally disconcerts the gravity and proper attention that should attach to so interesting a scene of the play, wherein you are concerned, that my feelings are discomposed for the whole evening after." "Very well," replied Sparks, "mighty well, Mr. Sheridan; I thank you, sir, for many holidays I am likely to enjoy during this suspension from my civic office." No sooner, however, at the next performance, did the new Lord Mayor make his appearance than the gallery began to shout, "off! off!" accompanied with volleys of potatoes and other missiles, and Richard had to promise that the Lord Mayor should be reinstalled. "Psha! Psha!" said Sparks, when Sheridan with many apologies once more solicited his presence; "my dear sir, you did me no injury at all; but I was sure you would never have a big loaf till I was chosen your Lord Mayor again."

SHAKESPEARE AND THE STAR-SPANGLED BANNER.

THOMAS ALTHORPE COOPER, at one time a successful London actor, when "starring" in America, in 1802, was very imperfect in the text of some of the parts he acted. As, for instance, in *Othello*, when he had to use these words: "Yet I will not scar that whiter skin than snow, and smooth as monumental alabaster," he substituted: "I will not scar that beauteous form, as white as snow and hard as monumental alabaster." An actor of the name of Higgins, not to be outdone by the Britisher, on one occasion playing the Duke to Cooper's Moor, having to say, "Take up this tangled matter at the best," actually substituted, "Take up the star-spangled banner in the West." This is an actual fact. Higgins was a member of the old South Street Theatre Company. His extraordinary interpretation of the language of Shakespeare in the end was the cause of his leaving the theatre, when he took to selling lottery tickets and policies.

SENSATIONAL.

THE murder of Mr. Weare, at Watford, by Thurtell, on the 24th of October, 1823, startled all England by its almost unparalleled savageness. The incidents were dramatized and presented at the Surrey Theatre on the 17th of November, pending the trial of the ill-fated Thurtell. A vehicle was brought on the boards described as "the identical gig in which Weare was at the time murdered." Threatened with a criminal information the managers withdrew the piece after a few nights' representation.

A SUDDEN CALL.

C. B. PARSONS, a very bad actor, who sometimes played tragedy, was converted at Louisville, U.S., by a celebrated evangelist, named John N. Maffit. The actor was playing an engagement at the Louisville Theatre, and, if we may believe the report of the affair, the building was crowded to excess to witness his performance of Othello. Just before the curtain was to rise, the manager appeared and announced that there could be no performance that evening owing to the surprising conversion of the principal actor, who declined to act any longer, although "billed" and bound to do so. This statement was received with indignation, and several young fellows ran into Maffit's meeting, calling loudly for "Othello! Othello!" The preacher stopped his sermon, and the actor, who was present, walked into the centre of the church, and in the most emphatic manner possible exclaimed, "Othello's occupation's gone." He then began his first exhortation, saying that a change had come over the spirit of his dream; that he had fretted his brief hour upon the stage, and henceforth would frequent only the house of prayer and the temple of Zion; that he had left the sock and buskin for the sword and helmet of righteousness, and that instead of fighting Shakespeare's mimic battles any longer, he should hereafter fight only under the banner of the cross, and closed by exhorting his old friends to remain with him, and leave the playhouse to become the abode of the bats. Parsons was duly admitted to the Methodist Church, became a class preacher, and was licensed to hold forth. He was in great demand for a time, but he preached no better than he acted, and afterwards resumed his old profession, changing from one to the other occasionally, but finally dying a preacher in 1871.

MISS OR MISTRESS.

PRIOR to the reign of Charles II. both married and unmarried women were called Mistress. But in the reign of the Merry Monarch a fashion arose to abbreviate the word to designate the ladies of the stage. In Richard Flecknoe's "Epigrams of all sorts," published in 1669, there is one "To Mis. Davies on her Excellent Dancing."

> "Dear Mis., delight of all the nobler sort,
> Pride of the stage and darling of the Court," etc.

Evelyn's notice of this word is prior to the above instance, and he adds an unpleasant qualification. Under the 9th January, 1662, he has, "I saw acted the third part of *The Siege of Rhodes*. In this acted ye faire and famous comedian call'd Roxalana, from ye part she perform'd; and I think it was ye last, she being taken to be ye Earle of Oxford's *misse*, as at this time they began to call lewd women." Unmarried ladies not on the stage continued to be described as Mrs. long after this time. Pope, in his letters about 1719, mentions Mrs. Lepel and Mrs. Bellenden, maids of honour. The examples are innumerable, but perhaps the latest instance of this practice is the Duchess of Queensbury, addressing Patty Blount, in 1756, as "Mrs. Blount," though no doubt Patty was by that time certainly entitled to what may be called "brevet rank."

A RED INDIAN ACTOR.

TOWARDS the close of his second visit to America Edmund Kean made a tour through the northern parts of the States and visited Canada. There he fell in with the Red Indians, and was chosen a chief of the tribe. "Some time after," writes Dr. Francis in his "Old New York," I received at a late hour of the evening a call to wait upon an Indian chief named Alantenaida. I repaired to the hotel and was conducted upstairs to the folding-doors of the hall. I entered, aided by the feeble light of the moon, but at the remote end I soon perceived something like a forest of evergreens lighted up by the rays of many lamps, in the midst of which on a throne sat the chief in great state. A more terrific warrior I never beheld. Full dressed, with skins tagged loosely about his person, a broad collar of bearskin over his shoulders, his leggings with many stripes garnished with porcupine quills, his mocassins decorated with beads, his head decked with the war eagle's plumes, behind which flowed massive black locks of dishevelled horsehair, golden-coloured rings pendant from the nose and ears, streaks of yellow paint over the face, massive red daubings about the eyes, with various lines in streaks about the forehead. A broad belt surrounded his waist, with tomahawk ; his arms, with shining bracelets, stretched out with bow and arrow, as if ready for a mark. He descended from his throne and rapidly approached me. . . . . It was Kean. The Hurons had honoured him with admission into their tribe, and he could not now determine whether to seek his final earthly abode with them for real happiness, or return to London, and add to his fame by performing the Son of the Forest. He was wrought up to the highest pitch of enthusiasm at the Indian honour he had received, and declared that even "Old Drury had never conferred so proud a distinction on him as he had received from the Hurons." The next year, 1827, Colley Grattan, when his tragedy, *Ben Nazir, the Saracen*, was to be presented, visited Kean one morning at the Hummums Hotel. He found him sitting up in his bed, a buffalo skin wrapped around him, a huge hairy cap decked with many-coloured feathers on his head, a scalping knife in his belt, and a tomahawk in his hand. A tumbler of white wine negus stood at the bedside ; two shabby looking heroes stood by with similar potations within their reach, and a portrait painter was placed before an easel at the window, taking the likeness of the renowned Alantenaida, the name in which the chief most sincerely rejoiced.

A REVIVAL OF MACBETH.

HALF a century ago an actor named Klanert recruited a theatrical company, and gave some representations at Richmond, Surrey. An actor of small parts at Covent Garden, Klanert, on his own stage, became a genius of grand proportions, in his own opinion. Always letter-perfect himself, he imagined every one else ought to be so. On one occasion Edward Stirling was very imperfect when playing Malcolm to Klanert's Macbeth. He stuck in the speech—

> "My Thanes and kinsmen
> Henceforth be . . . be . . ."

"Go on, sir," said the dead tyrant lying at his feet. Stirling tried in vain to raise his Thanes and kinsmen to peerages. "*Will* you go on?" hissed the irate deceased. "I cannot," was the whispered reply. Up jumps the dead king, saying, "Then I'll speak for you, sir.

> "'Henceforth be earls;
> So thanks to all at once, and to each one
> Whom we invite to see us crown'd at Scone.'"

And calmly lying down, he died again, loudly applauded and laughed at. The following Saturday, Stirling and Klanert parted company.

AN ECHO IN THE PIT.

IN 1734 Voltaire brought out *Adelaide du Guesclin*. This drama had been performed before under the title of *Adelaide*, and having but a mediocre success on either of these occasions, it was afterwards produced under the title of *Duc de Foix*. One of the characters in this play was called Coucy, to whom another addresses the question, "Es-tu content, Coucy?" A man in the pit immediately gave the answer, "Coussi, coussi!" This is a provincial admission derived from the Italian "cosi, cosi," which signifies so, so; an expression particularly well adapted for the occasion, because in the Italian burlesques represented at that time in Paris, it was frequently used by Harlequin.

A WANDERING SPIRIT.

THE following anecdote may have been composed in cool blood, or it may be "based on fact," much "made up," corked and rouged *secundum artem.* But it is an amusing legend in any case, and may be found in Angelo's *Reminiscences*, who had it from Bannister. An Irish manager, who was a great snuff taker, and remarkably absent, played the character of King Henry in *Richard III.*, at his own theatre, in one of the provincial towns in Ireland. In the tent scene the ghost of King Henry takes precedence of the other ghosts, in his address to Richard, who is sleeping on the couch. The Irish ghost, who was certainly the plumpest ghost that ever waddled on the stage, was with great difficulty forced half-way up the trap, and appeared as the fat shadow of King Henry, whom he had murdered in the first act. He began—

"Oh thou, whose unrelenting thoughts
Not all the hideous terrors of thy guilt can shake,
Whose conscience with thy body ever sleeps—sleep on!
Now shall thy own devouring conscience gnaw thy heart," etc.

After this solemn address, the ghost remains some time without speaking. Seized with one of his fits of absence, the manager-ghost, interested in the receipts of the house, took this opportunity of counting the persons who composed the audience. Taking his snuff-box from his waistcoat pocket, totally forgetting the part he was representing, and absorbed in snuff and arithmetic, he said with inward satisfaction: "Sixteen pounds two in the boxes; three pounds ten in the pit; gallery, seventeen thirteens!" The prompter at this moment perceiving the spirit had quitted the flesh, bellowed out the words of the author, "The morning's dawn," sir, "the morning's dawn has summoned me away; Richard, awake, to guilty minds a terrible example." Seeing that the manager merely put up his snuff-box, unconscious of all, the prompter pulled his bell, and the fat ghost sank through the trap much quicker than the carpenter could wind him up.

VAIN DEVILS.

ABOUT the year 1766, when old Crawford was manager of Covent Garden Theatre, a dancer named Le Grand Perrot was engaged as first dancer and ballet-master. After a long and expensive preparation, the ballet *Orpheus* was announced, and in the scene where the matchless singer visits the lower regions, a number of devils had to appear. At the first performance, a general dissatisfaction arose among the female devils; all refused to dance in the worsted flame-coloured stockings provided for them, claiming silk ones, which showed the comely shape of their limbs to better advantage. Old Crawford persisted to oppose their demands, but the devils were equally resolute, and the audience was kept waiting, until the manager gave in and sent for silk stockings, upon which the audience were gratified with one of the most splendid ballets seen in London up to that time.

LAST APPEARANCE OF PEG WOFFINGTON.

THIS charming actress had held Shakespeare's "Rosalind" as her own for ten years, when, on the 3rd of May, 1757, she put on the dress for the last time. She was then at Covent Garden. Some prophetic feeling of ill came over her as she struggled against a fainting fit, while assuming the bridal dress in the last act. She had never disappointed an audience in her life; her indomitable courage carried her on to the stage, and the spectators might have taken her to be as radiant in health and spirit as she looked. She began the pretty saucy prologue, with her old saucy prettiness of manner; but when she had said, "If I were among you, I would kiss as many of you as had beards that pleased me," she paused, tried to articulate, but was unable. She had consciousness enough to know she was stricken, and to manifest her terror at the catastrophe by a wild shriek, as she tottered towards the stage door. On her way she fell paralysed into the arms of sympathising comrades, who bore her from the stage, to which she never returned.

COMPOSURE.

IN the last century, there was an actor named Legrand, attached to the Théâtre Français. Though he was not a *very* bad player, the pit was in the habit of hissing him, more in order to provoke the funny speeches he used to deliver on such occasions, than as an angry protest against his shortcomings. Legrand always remained perfectly calm, and generally responded with a joke. As he was a very plain looking man, he was especially hissed when impersonating some hero of tragedy. On one occasion he exclaimed, "Gentlemen, it would really be much easier for you to get accustomed to my face, than for me to change it." On another occasion, Racine's *Phèdre* was given, and all the performers who appeared in the two first acts were received with hisses. After the curtain fell on the second act, Legrand came forward to avert a still greater outburst. "Gentlemen," said he, "I have heard your disapprobations, and I am sorry that my comrades have incurred them. But what will you say when you know that it is I who am going to impersonate Theseus?" Again, one day that the best actors of the company were at Versailles, to play before the king, the residue played *Andronicus*, followed by a new after-piece, *The False Widow*. The tragedy was received with roars of laughter, to evoke which, Legrand, as *Paleologus*, had contributed his share. Between the two pieces, when he came to announce the play for the next day, he said, "Gentlemen, to-morrow we shall have the honour to represent *The Gamester* and *The Grumbler*, and allow me to hope that the little piece we are going to act now, will make you laugh as much as our tragedy has done."

REVOLVING ACTORS.

"SO late as 1780," says Lee Lewes, in his Memoirs, "I saw the play of *The Recruiting Officer* performed upon the open camp ground at Tenpenny Common, in Essex, by the order of the late Earl of Orford, for the amusement of himself, the Earl of Rochford, and the officers and privates of the Norfolk Militia, which Lord Orford commanded. His lordship, being afflicted with the gout, was led round the airy theatre on a pony, by a careful servant. The ridiculous distress of the actors was truly amusing; as his lordship, by his circular progression, obliged them in good manners and profound respect to their patrons, to wheel about continually, to show him a full front."

"THE DYING GLADIATOR."

ON the 29th of September, 1860, *The Last Days of Pompeii* was performed in the Gayty Theatre, Albany, U.S., when a very amusing incident occurred. It was in the amphitheatre scene in the third act, where a grand gladiatorial combat is fought in the presence of the emperor. Lydon had already slain one or two competitors, and their bodies had been carried from the stage. Enter Niger, the last and most formidable contestant. He was personated by C. B. Bishop, a man who weighed at least seventeen stone. Bishop was an adept at fencing, and the cutting and slashing were terrific, till at last, according to the business of the play, Lydon, himself mortally wounded, despatches Niger, who falls heavily on the stage. The emperor then cries out to his guards, "Bear hence the body!" The guards, four puny supers, awkward in manner and slim in the legs, advance to the big, prostrate form of Niger, and attempt to execute the mandate of the mighty monarch. They tug away, but cannot budge him an inch. After repeated efforts, they call, aside, for assistance, while the fat sides of Bishop shake with inward emotion. It so happened that nearly the whole force of the establishment was so disposed that no one, save the call-boy and the man at the curtain, was left to respond. The audience began to see the situation and burst into a roar. But the fun reached its climax when the colossal gladiator, dead as he was, got tired of waiting for a decent funeral, and compromised the matter by raising himself on all fours, and thus creeping off behind the scenes. Talk about a screaming farce; you might have heard the audience five miles off.

SHUTER'S IMPROMPTU.

SHUTER, the comedian, was so great a favourite with the audience that he could say anything he liked to them. One night there was a great and continued noise in the gallery, and general cries of "Throw him over! Throw him out!" which interrupted the play for some time. Shuter walked forward with great gravity, signifying by gesture that he wished to speak. The cries immediately changed to "Hear him! Hear him." A profound silence followed, when Shuter addressed the gallery as follows:—

"My good friends, how do you mean to end this pother?
Does he come this way, or does he go t'other?
You must determine: Let him go or stay,
Or we must give you nightcaps, not the play."

TAKING IT EASY.

WHEN Ross was manager of the Edinburgh Theatre, he once, through indolence, suffered a stocking weaver to attempt the part of Hastings in *Jane Shore.* The young man, who spoke the part in broad Scotch, no sooner had heard the hisses which greeted his performance, than he ran off the stage, went to the dressing-room, threw off his theatrical attire, and ran home as fast as he could. A messenger was immediately dispatched to Ross, who lived on the Castlehill, to desire him to come at once, and finish the part, which he had often played. Rather than quit his bottle he sent word to the prompter to cut out all Hastings' part, and begin with the following act. This was done, and passed almost unperceived.

THE LION'S SHARE.

JEMMY WHITE, the manager of a very primitive theatre in Nottingham, towards the end of the last century, was famous for his eccentricity. He played all the best parts in everything, as managers pretty generally do. When he enacted Othello, or Zanga in *The Revenge*, or Mungo in *The Padlock*, he uniformly coloured himself black from head to foot. This, he said, gave him a better idea of what a black man should be and feel. Jemmy dressed for his characters at home, walked through the streets to the theatre perfectly unconcerned, and, owing to the frequency of the sight, little noticed. It was a sharing company, and the following was Mr. White's manner of payment on Saturday nights at his treasury, where the assembled players were anxiously waiting. "There's so much for me, for acting and management," he would say, counting money. "Then there's so much for rent, oil, and candles. Then there's so much for scenery and dresses—a trifle for wear and tear. Then there's so much left for you. Take it, divide it among yourselves—mind, all fair—and thank God you've got it. Good night!" And thereupon the treasury closed, too frequently on the poor players' aching hearts for their miserable pittance after so much labour.

WALTER MONTGOMERY'S DEATH.

WALTER MONTGOMERY, the *protegé* of Charles Kean, the companion of Dickens, Douglas Jerrold, and Mark Lemon, was one of the handsomest men of his time. The circumstances attending his death are somewhat romantic. Whilst he was performing in America, a Mrs. Taylor fell desperately in love with him. This lady, under the name of Winetta Montague, had been one of the prettiest *danseuses* of the Boston Theatre, and at the age of sixteen married Mr. Arnold Taylor, a wealthy merchant of that city. She fled from her husband, and followed the brilliant and gifted Montgomery to Europe. Sailing in the same steamer with him, she told him her love but not her history, and the pair were married on their arrival in England in 1871. Four days after the wedding Montgomery ascertained that his newly made wife was a bigamist, and then he himself pleaded guilty to the soft impeachment of having also a wife and child living. Violent recriminations were the consequence of these discoveries, in the midst of which a pistol-shot was heard. People rushed into the room and found Montgomery dying, but whether he was murdered or a suicide is a question which has never been elicited. His wife, or rather Mrs. Taylor, attended his funeral, wearing her bridal wreath of *orange flower*, which she scattered in his grave. She returned to America and to the stage, describing herself as "from Drury Lane," and acted Hamlet dressed in Montgomery's clothes. After a series of discreditable adventures, she died, in great poverty, at New York, in 1877.

MINUTENESS OF DETAIL.

IN 1872 the comedy *Saratoga*, known to the London play-goers as *Brighton*, was performed at Albany, U.S. The arrangements were perfect and complete in every respect. The scenery and models were designed from sketches taken on the spot; the great dining-room at the Congress Hall was represented, even to the *monograms on the china;* the Congress spring was reproduced, and if it would have in the least added to the effect, genuine Saratoga water would have been dipped from it. Americans delight in these realistic touches. When Walter Montgomery played *As you like it*, in America, he was supported by Jem Mace, the pugilist, in the character of Charles the Wrestler.

TRAGIC BUSINESS.

IT is reported by Plutarch of the famous and wealthy player, Aesopus, that on one occasion he entered so completely into the part he was impersonating, that, whilst he was representing Atreus deliberating on the revenge of Thyestes, he smote one of the slaves who was hastily crossing the stage and laid him dead at his feet. But a more harrowing occurrence is said to have happened when a religious drama, *The Passion of our Saviour*, was acted in Sweden, in 1513. Lengis, the actor, had to pierce the side of the person on the cross, in the crucifixion scene, and in his enthusiasm he plunged his lance into him and killed him. The dead actor fell from the cross and fatally injured the Virgin Mary. The king, John II., shocked at such brutality, slew Lengis with his scimitar; when the audience, enraged at the death of their favourite actor, wound up this true tragedy by cutting off the head of his Majesty. This sequence of manslaughter puts one in mind of the concatenation of events attending the old woman's taking a pig to market.

SAINTED ACTORS.

THE stage cannot be considered badly represented in "the glorious army of Saints and Martyrs," for according to Baronius, the best authority on that subject, there are not less than three players among the rank and file of martyrs, besides one sainted actress. This person used to be "leading lady" on the stage of Antiochia, and did other less creditable things besides. She was known among play-goers as Margarita, on account of the profusion of pearls with which she used to deck her pretty person. At some period of her sinful life, she was taken in hand by Nonnus, bishop of Odessa, and this eloquent churchman managed to convince her of the wickedness of her ways. She was converted to Christianity, and was baptized with the name of Pelagia, in allusion to the sea of troubled waters in which she had so long fished with success. Renouncing the stage, its pomps and vanities, she distributed her property among the poor, assumed the garb of a male hermit, and ended her days as such on the Mount of Olives, in A.D. 451. In due time she was canonized, being honoured in the Church on the 8th of October. The actors were not quite so successful and never rose higher than the rank of martyrs. Genesius was a player in the time of the emperor Diocletian. He proclaimed his conversion to Christianity publicly on the stage, a piece of "gag" which so displeased the emperor, that he rewarded him with martyrdom, in A.D. 303. The incident of his confessing his faith on the stage has furnished the French dramatist, Rotrou, with the subject of a tragedy. A few years later, another actor, Ardaleon, was struck with the truth of Christianity whilst acting in a farce in which he ridiculed the Christians and their religion. For this he was martyred on the 18th of May, A.D. 310. Finally, in the reign of Julian the apostate, an actor named Porphyrius pretended to be a convert to Christianity in order that he might study the Christians and better be able to ridicule them on the stage. With that purpose he allowed himself to be baptized, but the holy water drove the arch-enemy out of him, and though "he came to scoff, he remained to pray." Julian was so incensed at this apostasy that he ordered him to be beheaded on the 17th of October, 362. Since that time no more names of players have been inscribed on the rolls of the hagiologists.

TOO OUTSPOKEN.

THE eccentric Francis Blisset was encored one evening in a comic song at Bristol, which he did not choose to repeat. Mr. C. Taylor, a member of the company, was sent to apologise, but nothing would do with the Bristolians but the song. Blisset swore he would not sing the song again, and told Taylor to say so. Taylor made every excuse he could invent, and being driven to the last extremity, said, "In fact, ladies and gentlemen, Mr. Blisset says,"—"That he will be d——d if he does," interrupted Blisset, popping out his head, adorned with an immense wig, at the prompter's door, in whose chair he had seated himself, to urge Taylor to comply. A great uproar ensued, which was not easily quelled, nor could Blisset appear in Bristol for near two years.

THE SOBER REALITY.

MRS. SIDDONS relates, after the first representation of *Macbeth*, "while standing up before my glass, and taking off my mantle, a diverting circumstance occurred, to chase away the feelings of this anxious night; for while I was repeating and endeavouring to call to mind the appropriate tone and action of the following words, "Here's the smell of blood still!" my dresser innocently exclaimed, "Dear me, ma'am, how very hysterical you are to-night; I protest and vow, ma'am, it was not blood, but rose pink and water; for I saw the property-man mix it up with my own eyes."

SHAKESPEARE ON THE BENCH.

EDWIN FORREST, the famous American actor, in his younger days was what the Americans call "one of the boys," and rather given to midnight merriment. As a consequence of one of these frolics, he on one occasion found quarters in the lock-up. Next morning he was brought before Squire John O. Cole, who discharged the actor, but just as he was leaving the office, the justice struck an attitude, and addressing Forrest in the words of Othello, exclaimed:

> "What's the matter
> That you unlace your reputation thus,
> And spend your rich opinion for the name
> Of a night brawler? Give me answer to it!"

This rebuke, so apt and timely, no doubt did the young man more good than a half-hour's sermon or ten days in jail.

"GOOSE."

THE technical phrase of "treating an actor with goose," was understood at a very early period of our stage history. Marston, in the introduction to his *What You Like*, 1607, says, "Monsieur Snuff, Monsieur Mew, and Cavaliere Blirt, are three of the most to be feared auditors," and farther on he asks if the poet's resolve shall be "struck through with the blirt of a goose's breath." The allusion to Monsieur Snuff, it may be observed, relates to the inconveniences the actors experienced from the consummation of the "titillating dust," by persons seated on the stage. Monsieur Mew is a circumlocution for "catcalls."

SHERIDAN'S SELF-DEFENCE.

SHERIDAN'S indolence was hardly to be credited. In the affair and duel between Mathews and himself at Bath, respecting Miss Linley, through the influence of his antagonist with certain newspapers, Sheridan's character was much injured by gross misrepresentations. He was strongly urged by a friend to defend himself against these attacks: "They are not yet sufficiently strong," said he, "for me to crush them, but from the rapid progress they are making, they will be very soon." "Then why not," said his friend, "do that yourself: abuse yourself, and then answer it." "A happy thought," said Sheridan; "I'll do it." He instantly sat down and wrote a letter abusing himself most cruelly. To his great delight, this appeared the following day in the paper. The abuse was now "sufficiently strong," but such was Sheridan's indolence, he could never find time to make the reply.

PROBABLY NOT.

IN Colman's time a certain aspirant for Thespian honours made his *début* at the Haymarket Theatre, in the character of Octavian in *The Mountaineers*. It was discovered very early in the performance that he had undertaken a task for which he was unqualified. Colman was in the greenroom and growing fidgety. When the new performer came to the line

"I shall weep soon, and then I shall be better,"

"I'll be d—d if you will," said Colman, "though you cry your eyes out!"

KEAN'S FIRST APPEARANCE.

EDMUND KEAN was a remarkably pretty child, on account of which Michael Kelly engaged him at the age of three, to represent Cupid in the opera of *Cymon*. Michael's style in relating this is incomparably more curious than the anecdote itself, and, if the latter part of this *little* paragraph be true, Edmund's gratitude must have commenced at the very tender age of three. "Before the piece was brought out, I had a number of children brought me, that I might choose a Cupid. One struck me, with a fine pair of black eyes, who seemed, by his looks and *little* gestures, most anxious to be chosen as the *little* god of love. I chose him, and *little* did I then imagine that my *little* Cupid would eventually become a great actor. The then *little* urchin was neither more nor less than—Edmund Kean. He has often told me that he, *ever after this period*, felt a regard for me, from the circumstances of my having preferred him to the other children. I consider *my* having been the means of *introducing this great genius to the stage* (! ! !) one of my most pleasurable recollections."

YORICK'S SKULL.

A HORSE stealer, named Fontaine, alias Lovett, being confined in Louisville jail, and unable to pay a lawyer, Junius Brutus Booth sent him one and defrayed the expenses. Notwithstanding the efforts made in his behalf Lovett was sentenced to be hanged. He bequeathed his head to Booth, with the request that "he would use it on the stage when playing Hamlet, and think when he held it in his hands of the gratitude his kindness had awakened." The skull was sent to Booth's residence while he was absent from the city, and his wife immediately returned it to the doctor to whom it had been entrusted for preparation and delivery. In 1857, the doctor who had retained the skull, sent it to Edwin Booth, the son of Junius, who on several occasions used it in the graveyard scene in *Hamlet*, and finally had it buried.

TRADE ASSISTANCE.

THERE was a curious troupe at Northampton in 1827: all the players but two were members of the same family, rejoicing in the name of Jackman. This gifted family wrote their own plays, acted the best parts, delivered the bills, painted the scenery; in fact, did everything and the rest. Jackman *père* played principal characters, and was a great favourite with the followers of St. Crispin, who form a considerable portion of the population of Northampton. One night the play was, very appropriately, *Jobson and Nell*, the principal characters of which are a cobbler and his wife. There is a scene in this comedy when Jobson beats his turbulent wife with his shoemaker's strap, an "effect" always approvingly applauded by the gods. On the night in question, cobbler Jobson had forgotten his strap, and Nell's tongue was going nineteen to the dozen. The situation was embarrassing, but an observant cordwainer in the gallery came to the rescue: "Here, Master Jackman," he called out, throwing his strap on the stage, "take mine, and lather her well with it."

"THAT IS THE QUESTION."

BARON, the elder, bred up under the eye of Molière, was an actor of extraordinary talent, and a dramatist of no mean quality. Being well paid, he lived in grand style and was something more than vain. His coachman and lackey having been one day ill-treated by the servants of the Marquis de Biron, he was determined to demand justice. Having met the Marquis, Baron preferred his complaint: "Monseigneur," said he, "vos gens ont battu les miens; je vous en demande justice." The marquis, nettled at the familiarity of *vos gens* and *les miens*, answered him drily : "Mon pauvre Baron, que veux-tu qui j'y fasse? Pourquoi as-tu des gens?"

A COMICAL JURY.

"OUR theatre was the scene of a terrible affair last night," wrote Mr. Buckstone in 1859, whilst acting in Mobile, U.S., "the murder of one of the performers, a Mr. Ewing, who was acting with us in *My Old Woman* the part of Cardinal Girouette. After the first act, a Miss Hamblin, who was performing Victor, the page, in the same piece, went into the dressing-room and stabbed the young man to the heart. Of course, we were obliged to dismiss the audience. A singular circumstance in connection with this occurrence is, that the woman was cleared by a jury, who were charged that "he *might* have died from a disease of the heart, with which he was afflicted, if he had not been stabbed."

KEAN'S VILLAINY.

ON the 25th of May, 1811, Edmund Kean signalised his first London benefit by a fine representation of his old character of Luke in Sir John Burgess's alteration of Massinger's *City Madam*, under a form entitled, *Riches; or, the Wife and Brother*. The soliloquy in the last act, in which the actor marked with fine and perfect gradations the increasing delirium of Luke in the contemplation of his ill-gotten wealth, was one of the most powerful effects ever witnessed on the stage. An old lady admired Kean's acting in Othello so much that she made no secret of her intention to bequeath him a large sum of money; but she was so appalled by the cold-blooded villainy and demoniacal ferocity of Luke, that, attributing the skill of the actor to the inherent possession of the fiendish attributes he so consummately embodied, her regard gave place to suspicion and distrust. In consequence of this, it was found upon her death, which took place shortly afterwards, that the sum originally intended for the actor, had been left to a distant relation, of whom she knew nothing but the name.

A PROVIDENT MANAGER.

LEE LEWES, the harlequin, joined Whiteley's company of strolling actors in 1760. Concerning this manager he relates the following anecdote. Like most "travelling companies," Whiteley's was a "sharing" concern, and it was customary in such societies to distribute the dividend as soon as the farce was concluded. On one occasion, whilst performing in Doncaster, the sharing had been very indifferent for several nights. However, a "bespoke play" filled the house one night, and eighteen shillings fell to the share of each performer. To one man, named Andrews, a poor sickly object, Whiteley gave only nine shillings. Andrews protested that no stoppage could be made from his pay, for he did not owe Whiteley anything. "True, my dear," replied the careful manager, "but you will very soon; you are in a bad state of health. Look at him, gentlemen; he wants to leave us without warning. You see he is in a consumption. Where did you get it? Not in my healthy company, but in the skin and bone troupe you came from. You'll die in a fortnight, my dear; and as we must bury you, I have stopped nine shillings towards your coffin."

A SNOW-BOUND EAGLE.

J. P. KEMBLE, whilst manager under Sheridan, frequently smarted at the fashion in which his authority was set at defiance, by which others below him were encouraged to do the same. One night he arrived, charged with his grievances, at one of the little supper-parties Mrs. Crouch used to give after the play was over. He expected to meet Sheridan there, and was not disappointed. At supper, Kemble looked unutterable things at Sheridan, occasionally emitted "a humming sound like that of a bee," and groaned in spirit, inwardly. A considerable time elapsed, and frequent repetitions of the same sound occurred. At last, "like a pillar of state," slowly uprose Kemble, and in these words addressed the astonished proprietor : "I am an eagle, whose wings have been bound down by frosts and snows, but now I shake my pinions, and cleave into the genial air unto which I am born." He then deliberately resumed his seat. There was something irresistibly ridiculous in this fashion of announcing a resignation, but Sheridan, with all the art of which he was master, soothed him, and the pair parted in perfect harmony. This scene might be accepted as an exaggeration, had it not been recorded by an eye-witness and intimate friend, Mr. Boaden.

THE STRENGTH OF IMAGINATION.

AT William's coffee-house, Bow-street, there was a public dinner on the Saturday, early in this century, when usually one of the leading actors of the day took the chair. Incledon, being president one day, found great fault with the port wine ; and though, by his order, it was repeatedly changed for a better sort, he continued dissatisfied, at the same time boasting what very fine wine he had in his cellar, bin No. 2, brandishing in his hand his "nectar key," as he called it. Munden, who sat next to him, adroitly managed, whilst Incledon was singing, to purloin the key from the singer's pocket. Leaving the room, he forwarded it to Mrs. Incledon, with a message to deliver to the bearer six bottles of the old port, bin No. 2. When the man returned, Mat Williams, the landlord, who was in the secret, brought up one of the bottles himself, and said he hoped the company would find it better, but that he had only six bottles of that wine. Incledon still persisted that it was worse than any of the former. This joke continued till the last bottle made its appearance, when a bumper was drunk to the president as donor of the last half dozen, more to his astonishment than delight, as may be imagined.

TO "PLAY" AND "TO BE."

TOWARDS the end of his professional career, Edwin Forrest was taking supper late one night with an old friend, who remarked to him, "Mr. Forrest, I never in my life saw you play Lear so well as you did to-night." Whereupon the veteran, rising slowly and laboriously from his chair, and stretching himself to his full height, replied, "Play Lear! What do you mean, sir? I don't play Lear. I play Hamlet, Richard, Shylock, Virginius, if you please; but, by Jupiter, sir, I *am* Lear!" At first sight such a remark looks like a joke. Yet nothing is more true; a great actor actually *is* for the time being the character he represents. "Whenever," says Mrs. Siddons, "I was called upon to personate the character of Constance, I never, from the beginning of the play to the end of my part in it, once suffered my dressing-room door to be closed, in order that my attention might be constantly fixed on those distressing events which, by this means, I could plainly hear going on upon the stage, the terrible effects of which progress were to be represented by me. Moreover, I never omitted to place myself, with Arthur in my hand, to hear the march, when, upon the reconciliation of England and France, they enter the gates of Angiers to ratify the contract of marriage between the Dauphin and the Lady Blanche; because the sickening sounds of that march would usually cause the bitter tears of rage, disappointment, betrayed confidence, baffled ambition, and, above all, the agonizing feelings of maternal affection to gush into my eyes. . . . If the character of the unfortunate queen ever were, or ever shall be portrayed, with its appropriate and solemn energy, it must be then, and then only, when the power I have so much insisted on, co-operating with a high degree of enthusiasm, *shall have transfused the mind of the actress into the person and situation* of the august and afflicted."

CIBBER'S FIRST APPEARANCE.

COLLEY CIBBER made his first appearance on the stage in a very subordinate part. After waiting impatiently for the prompter's notice, he, by good fortune, obtained the honour of carrying a message in some play to Betterton, one of the managers and one of the principal actors of that day. Arrived in the presence of the public Master Colley was so terrified that the scene was somewhat spoiled by him. On coming off Betterton asked angrily who the young fellow was that made such a fool of himself? The prompter replied "Master Colley." "Then forfeit him," rejoined Betterton. "Why, sir," said the prompter, "he has no salary." "No?" said the old man, "In that case put him down ten shillings a week and forfeit him five." To this good-natured adjustment of rewards and punishments, Cibber owed the first money he received from the dramatic treasury.

COOKE'S IMPUDENCE.

GEORGE FREDERICK COOKE'S popularity at one time far exceeded that of Kemble; but he became the very slave of intemperance, remaining at times for days together "on the drink." His habits of inebriety subjected him frequently to the signal disapprobation of his audience, upon whom he would sometimes retort with more vehemence than delicacy. On one occasion in Liverpool, when he was scarcely able to go through his part, the audience most justly manifested their indignation; he stopped, and addressed to them these insolent words: "How dare you hiss *me*, George Frederick Cooke, you contemptible money-grubbers. Your applause or your disapproval are utterly indifferent to me; but you shall never again have the honour of hissing me. Farewell, I banish you." Then, after a pause, with increasing passion and lofty contempt, "There is not one brick in your dirty town, but what is cemented with a fellow creature's blood," alluding to the African slave-trade then chiefly carried on in Liverpool ships. Strange to say this violent address so impressed the audience that the impudent orator was allowed to make his exit in peace.

HIS MAJESTY'S SERVANTS.

ACTORS were first known as "His Majesty's Servants" in 1605, up to which period they had been styled "The Servants of the Lord Chamberlain." As his Majesty's servants they were entitled to wear, and did wear, the royal livery of scarlet. The last actor who wore it was Baddeley, who gave the annual Twelfth Night cake to the greenroom of Drury Lane, and who created the part of "Moses" in the *School for Scandal.* A portrait of Baddeley, in his red waistcoat, used to be seen in poor old Paddy Green's collection at Evans's.

AN ACTOR-APOTHECAR.

ELLISTON, being at one time on a starring tour in the provinces, observed that at Cheltenham, then in full renown as a watering-place, and generally crowded with invalids, there was not one good chemist. He at once espied the way to make a fortune, and having purchased a large supply of drugs in Apothecar's Hall, opened a grand medicinal emporium, thinking no doubt that a knowledge of pharmacy would come by inspiration. He was, however, soon compelled to abandon this brilliant scheme, for it became evident that unless he could combine the business of an undertaker with that of a chemist, there was little prospect of his making a rapid fortune. About the same time that this began to dawn in Elliston's mind, there arose some unpleasant murmurs concerning coroner's inquests on some of his late customers, in consequence of which the promising chemist thought it advisable to throw over Æsculapius in favour of Thespis.

HERO WORSHIP.

MDLLE. DEJAZET was a great admirer of Napoleon, and had impersonated him in the play of *Bonaparte at Brienne.* One evening Volnys, a brother actor, entered the greenroom with a newspaper in his hand, and evident signs of emotion in his features. "What is the matter?" inquired Dejazet. Volnys read aloud a paragraph containing the information that Maria Louise, the wife of Napoleon I., had remarried. Dejazet would not believe it, took the paper, and having been convinced by reading the news herself, she exclaimed, "What a shame! . . . After having been Cæsar's wife! . . . Had I only once had the honour to touch the hand of that great man, I would never after in my life have washed my hands any more." When we consider that this applied to those small white hands of which Mademoiselle Dejazet was so proud, we may be certain that this asseveration was a particularly intense expression of admiration for her hero.

TRUTHFUL ACTING.

IT is said that one night when Garrick was performing Macbeth, and the murderer entered the banquet scene, Garrick looked at him with such an expressive countenance, and uttered in such an expressive manner, "There's blood upon thy face," that the actor forgot his part and rubbed his face saying, "Is there?" instead of "'Tis Banquo's then," thinking, as he afterwards acknowledged, that his nose was bleeding.

A DILATORY AUTHOR.

WE are told in the memoirs of Sheridan that his translation of *The Death of Rolla*, under the title of *Pizarro*, brought him £25,000 in five weeks. The production of this drama was a curious instance of Sheridan's inveterate habit of procrastination. On the first night's performance, at the time the house was overflowing, all that was written of the play was actually rehearsing, and, incredible as it may appear, until the end of the fourth act, neither Mrs. Siddons, nor Charles Kemble, nor Barrymore, had all their speeches for the fifth! Sheridan was upstairs in the prompter's room, where he was writing the last part of the play, while the earlier parts were acting. Every ten minutes he brought down, into the greenroom, as much of the dialogue as he had done piecemeal, abusing himself and his negligence, and making a thousand winning and soothing apologies, for having kept the performers so long in such painful suspense.

LIGHT OR HEAVY.

WHEN Sir Charles Sedley's comedy of *Bellamira* was performed the roof of the theatre fell in, by which, however, few people were hurt, except the author. This occasioned Sir Fleetwood Shepherd to say, "There was so much fire in the play, that it blew up the poet, house and all." "No," replied the good-natured author, "the play was so heavy, that it broke down the house, and buried the poor poet in his own rubbish."

WHEN THE WINE IS IN, THE WIT IS OUT.

THE following note in Chetwood's *General History of the Stage* affords an amusing picture of the Bohemian manners of a certain class of actors in a former period:—"William Phillips, the founder of the Capel Street Theatre,

Dublin, played with applause in a few low comic parts, but his great talent lay in mimics and harlequins. Being once arrested for debt in London, he first called for liquor in abundance, and treated all about him, to the no small joy of the bailiff. Phillips made him believe that he had six dozen of wine packed up which he would send for, to drink in the spunging-house, on payment of sixpence per bottle cork-money. The bailiff listened to the proposal with pleasure, and willingly went to order the wine to be sent. Accordingly, the following day a sturdy porter arrived, bent double under his heavy load. The turnkey told his master that the porter had brought a large hamper. 'Very well,' was the answer; 'then let nothing but the porter and the hamper out.' The porter performed his part very well; he came heavily in with an empty hamper, and walked lightly out with Phillips on his back. Harlequin was dishampered at an alehouse near the waterside, crossed the Thames, and made his way to Dublin, where soon after he became a shareholder in Smock Alley Theatre. The project of his escape had been contrived long before he was taken, and when concerting his scheme with the porter, though he was a Welshman by birth, he made the following taurine speech to his accomplice:—'Strike me plump,'—his usual oath—'if you are not as secret as *the sun at noonday*, I'll *broil* you and eat you *alive*, you dog!'"

THE BEGGAR'S OPERA IN FRENCH.

ADAM HALLAM, an actor in Rich's company, translated *The Beggar's Opera* into French, and carried it to Paris, in hopes of procuring a representation of it on the French stage, but the manager would not consent, unless he agreed that the hero of the piece should be hanged. Hallam, from respect for the memory of Gay, would not suffer the piece to be altered. It is related by Davies, in his *Miscellanies*, that this translation was subsequently represented at the Hay-market, with some success.

CRYING AND CRYING.

NED SHUTER used to give the cries of London on his annual benefit at the theatre. The day before one of these benefits, he followed through several streets a man whose cry of "Silver eels" was very peculiar, but who on that occasion was unaccountably silent. At last Shuter stopped him, told him he was Ned Shuter, and that he had followed him for half an hour in hopes to hear his usual cry. "Why, Master Shuter," replied the poor man, "my wife died this morning, and I *can't cry.*"

EFFRONTERY.

QUIN had considerable ascendancy over the audience, and occasionally took great liberties with them. Taylor relates, in his *Records*, that on one occasion when Quin was performing the part of Zanga, and a drunken man disturbed the pit, he came forward, saying, "Turn that fellow out, or by —— I won't go on." The man was accordingly turned out, and Quin resumed his part. This anecdote seems almost impossible, yet Taylor asserts that he had it from trustworthy authority.

THE FIRST LONDON THEATRE.

THE very first theatre ever built in London, stood in Shoreditch, for the previous playhouses had been merely temporary contrivances erected in the yards of the large inns, such as the Cross Keys, the Bull, the Pope's Head, etc. The earliest reference to this building, which was called *The* Theatre, is in an old book printed in 1576, and runs as follows :—

"Those who go to Paris Garden, Bell Savage, or *The Theatre*, to behold bear-baiting, interludes, or fence-play, must not account of any pleasant spectacle unless first they pay one penny at the gate, another at the entry of the scaffold, and a third for a quiet standing." This house, probably, was only a rude wooden erection, though it is noticed in a sermon preached at Paul's Cross, in 1578, as "the gorgeous playing place erected in the Fields." It stood in or near Holywell Lane, on the site of Holywell Priory, a Benedictine nunnery of St. John the Baptist. In 1598 this playhouse was taken down, and the timber of it was used for enlarging the Globe Theatre, on the Bankside. Hard by stood another early theatre, the Curtain, the site of which is still marked by Curtain Road.

In the days of Elizabeth and James, the players of distinction from "The Theatre" and "The Curtain," as well as those from the Blackfriars Theatre and Shakespeare's Globe, were fond of residing in this parish. Perhaps there is no church in London so intimately connected at any time with the stage as old St. Leonard's, Shoreditch. The parish register of that church, within a period of sixty years, records the interment of the following celebrated actors :—Richard Tarlton, the famous low comic and clown of Queen Elizabeth's time, 1528 ; James Burbage, 1596 ; and his more celebrated son Richard, 1619, the friend and companion of Shakespeare ; Gabriel Spenser, the player, who fell, in 1589, in a duel with Ben Jonson ; William Sly and Richard Cowley, two original performers in Shakespeare's plays ; Fortunatus Greene, the *un*fortunate offspring of Robert Greene, the poet and player, 1593. Another original performer in Shakespeare's plays, who lived in Holywell Street, was Nicholas Wilkinson, *alias* Tooley, whose name is recorded in gilt letters on the north side of the altar as a yearly benefactor of £6 10*s*., which sum is still distributed in bread annually to the poor inhabitants of the parish to whom it was bequeathed.

RETALIATION.

THERE was dignity in J. R. Kemble's rebuke to an aristocratic play-writer, the Hon. Mr. St. John, who had written one of the innumerable *Mary Queen of Scots* plays, and had an interview with the manager in the greenroom, when his play was refused. High words followed. "You are a person I cannot call out," said St. John contemptuously. "But you are a person I can *turn out*," was the ready reply, "and you shall leave this place at once." The offender had the good sense to return and offer his apologies.

GOODS THE "GODS" PROVIDED.

A *PROPOS* of the bombardment of Sarah Bernhardt at Odessa with a handful of pickled cucumbers, some one recently asked Laferrière whether it was true that in the good old days the "gods" at Montmartre used to pelt the actors with apples, crusts, Bologna sausages, etc. "Ay, my dear old boy," he replied; "and I mind me that many a time and oft we swallowed the insult with a certain pleasure!"

A MODERN ORPHEUS.

IT is related of Charles Bannister, that when returning to town from Epsom in a gig, accompanied by a friend, they found themselves penniless when they arrived at Kensington-gate, where the turnpike-man would not let them pass without paying the toll. Bannister, however, offered to sing him a song, and immediately struck up the "Tempest of War." His voice was heard afar, and "Bannister! Bannister!" was the cry. The gate was soon thronged, and he was loudly encored by the voters returning from Brentford. He complied with the request, and the turnpike-man declared him to be a "noble fellow," and that he would pay fifty tolls for him at any gate.

LOVERS OF LITERATURE.

CHARLES PORTER and James Hacket, two American actors, in their salad days made a theatrical tour. At New Brunswick they announced an entertainment consisting of readings and recitations, when on the first night the rising of the curtain was some time delayed, owing to the non-arrival of Porter. The audience showed signs of impatience, to allay which it became necessary that an apology should be made. Hacket, being unable to make a decent speech, was compelled to engage the services of the call-boy, a genuine specimen of that class, to make the necessary apology. He was told to say, "That in consequence of the non-arrival of Mr. Porter, Mr. Hacket would instead recite for them Young Norval's speech on the Grampian Hills." The call-boy, delighted at an opportunity to appear on the stage in any character, and paying little or no attention to what was told him, stepped boldly before the curtain. With the sound of the words just heard buzzing in his brain, he thus addressed the audience: "Ladies and gentlemen, Mr. Porter has not yet come." A pause. "Mr. Porter not being come, Mr. Hacket will appear as a steed and give you some novels, and account for himself being on the Campshire Hills." This communication was received with delight, and when Hacket appeared, he was hailed with deafening applause. Some looked for the fiery steed, others for the novels. Hacket commenced, "My name is Norval——" Some fellow shouted out, "D—n your name." "On the Grampian Hills my father feeds his flock." Here another voice yelled out, "Never mind your sheep, give us the novels." The cry became general, "The books! the books!" Hacket rushed off the stage, to find his friends in convulsive laughter. Porter, however, at that moment arrived, and "the books" were soon forgotten.

READING MADE EASY.

IN the season of 1784 *The Lord of the Manor* was substituted for the play which had been announced. Miss Farren was ill, and Mr. John Palmer could not be found. Miss Collett read for the former, and Mr. R. Palmer for his brother. The play had never been published, and they were obliged to use the manuscript copy. Miss Collett and Mr. Palmer, each with a candle in hand, passed the manuscript from one to the other, as their turn came. At one moment Palmer came to a passage so blotted and interlined that he could not proceed. The audience hissed violently, upon which Palmer came forward and requested the book might be examined by any gentleman in the pit, to see if the fault could be attributed to him. The gentleman who examined it declared it was illegible. The audience loudly applauded, and, the book being returned, permission was granted to pass over illegible passages.

AN OBSTINATE COUGH.

JOHN KEMBLE, once playing Macbeth when he suffered from a violent cold, was compelled actually to cough after his decease. When Bannister was informed of this circumstance, he said, "Poor fellow, it must be a *church-yard cough.*"

A USEFUL PROMPTER.

OLD Mrs. Baker, the manageress, was an excellent woman, but totally uneducated. Her company, a small one, played many parts doubled. Gardner, the leading actor, stage-manager, and prompter, playing Hamlet one night, forgot the words in some passage. Mrs. Baker on this occasion acted as prompter in his place, and the helpless actor imploringly whispered to her, "The word, the word." "What word, Jack?" calmly inquired Mrs. Baker. "I can't go on," was the hurried reply. "Come off, then," answered the provoking female prompter. "The text, woman; the text," ejaculated the tragedian in an agony. "You fool, what's a text to do with playhouses?" exclaimed Mrs. Baker, angrily. "Here's the book; take what you want;" and she hurled the play at him.

A NONPLUSSED AIDE

WHENEVER a letter is to be read aloud on the stage, it is duly copied out, so as to save the actor who has to read it the trouble of study. Gober, who long appeared in the French theatres as Napoleon I., in all the pieces in which the career of the conqueror from Toulon to St. Helena was depicted, on one occasion having received an important despatch from an aide-de-camp, was to read it to the assembled staff. The part of aide-de-camp was taken by an inveterate and merciless practical joker named Gautier, who, knowing Cæsar to be incapable of "vamping," substituted a sheet of blank paper for the written despatch. The moment came. The aide hurried in and presented the despatch. The emperor opened the paper, perceived the joke, frowned, knit his mighty brow, and, with a gesture of command, handed the despatch to Gautier, saying, "Read the despatch to the staff, Colonel, while I look at the map!" The aide paused, became flustered, broke down, and was roundly hissed.

LINKED SWEETNESS.

IN a former page a dozen actresses have been grouped together who have married into the peerage and baronetage. The male sex does not make anything like so good a show in the matrimonial line, for, under correction, I can only bring to four the sum total of happy actors who have been allowed to take to their bosom a wife drafted from the ranks of the peerage or the baronetage. It is humiliating for our sex, but the fact seems irrefutable: the actor is not so irresistible in the eyes of the so-called "softer" sex, as the actress is to the heart of what is described as the sterner part of mankind.

Barton Booth, the tragedian, in 1704, married Frances, the daughter of Sir William Barkham, Bart., of an ancient family in the county of Norfolk, now extinct. His wife died without issue in 1711. Booth was a Westminster boy, and had studied under the famous Doctor Bushby. He was an excellent classical scholar, and has translated some of Horace's odes in a tasteful manner. After the death of his first wife, Booth married Miss Santley, an actress and danceress, which marriage so annoyed Mrs. Mountford that she lost her reason. Booth died in 1733, and was buried in Westminster Abbey.

In 1746, William O'Brien, a comedian of Drury Lane, married Lady Susannah Sarah Louisa Fox Strangeways, eldest daughter of the Earl of Ilchester. He left the stage, and the happy pair soon after were despatched to America, where they obtained a grant of land in Ohio. Seven years later they returned to England, and O'Brien became a mediocre playwright. He died in 1813, Lady Susannah in 1825. This marriage caused a great flutter in Vanity Fair, and various details connected with it are chronicled in Walpole's Correspondence. O'Brien was the son of a fencing master in Dublin.

William Parsons, the original Crabtree in *The School for Scandal*, married, in 1787, Dorothy, one of the three daughters of the Hon. James Stewart, brother to the Earl of Galloway. The young lady had run away from a convent at Lisle, and accidentally meeting Parsons, an utter stranger to her, in the streets of London, implored his aid. A friendship then sprang up, and after a while Parsons offered his hand and heart. He was then a staid, asthmatic gentleman of over fifty, but possessed of considerable property.

In later times, a Marchioness (query Countess?) of Antrim

was united to a Mr. Phelps, of Drury Lane, but not the late tragedian of that name.

ALTILOQUENCE.

THE morning after Covent Garden Theatre was burnt, Mr. Boaden called on the Kemble family to offer his sympathy. He gives a curious picture of the ruined family, especially of the great John, who, in one of his mysterious moods, stood before a glass shaving himself, and presently burst into a sort of inflated speech : "Yes, it has perished—that magnificent theatre ! It is gone, with all its treasures of every description"—which he proceeded to enumerate with the minuteness of an auctioneer, in their order of importance—"That library, which contained all those immortal works of our countrymen, etc. That wardrobe, etc. Scenery, the triumph of art. . . . Of all this vast treasure nothing now remains but the arms of England over the entrance of the theatre, *and the Roman eagle standing solitary in the market-place!*" When later, on this melancholy occasion, Lord Mountjoy came in and spoke of the public sympathy and gratitude Kemble was destined to receive, the actor interrupted him in the same lofty strain : "Gratitude, my lord ! Christ was crucified, De Witt was assassinated ; so much for the world and the people !"

AN ABITATION.

AN actor in De Camp's company had the unfortunate habit of dropping his *h*'s. Being cast for Schampt in *The Woodman's Hut*, the dialogue in the last act ran thus, "I see a house yonder," to which the other assents. On the present occasion, Schampt said, "I see a *nouse*." His brother comedian, relishing the fun of the thing, exclaimed, "No, it ain't ; its only a *nut*."

FRIENDLY ADVICE.

ON Miss O'Neil's first representation of Juliet in the capital of Ireland, the following ludicrous circumstance occurred:—The balcony in the garden scene was particularly low; Conway, the Romeo of the night, was uncommonly tall, and, in delivering the lines—

"Oh! that I were a glove upon that hand,
That I might touch that cheek,"

laid his hand upon the balcony. A fellow in the gallery immediately interrupted him. "Get out with your blarney," he said; "why don't you touch her, then, and not be preaching Parson Saxe there?"

UNCOMFORTABLE "SUPER."

IN Portugal Street, Lincoln's Inn Fields, on the site now occupied by Messrs. Copeland and Spode's chinaware repository, stood the Duke's Theatre, opened in the reign of Charles II. Nightingale, in the tenth volume of the *Beauties of England and Wales*, gives the following strange account of the last performance in this house, in 1737:—"The shutting up of this structure has been whimsically accounted for by vulgar tradition. Upon a representation of *Harlequin and Dr. Faustus*, when a tribe of demons necessary for the piece were assembled, a supernumerary devil was observed, who, not approving of going out in a complaisant manner at the door, to show a *devil's trick*, flew up to the ceiling, made his way through the tiling, and tore away one fourth of the house. This circumstance so affrighted the manager, that the proprietor had not the courage to open the house ever afterwards." The origin of this story is the following:—In one of Rich's first pantomimes, perhaps *The Sorcerer*, a dance of infernals was exhibited. They were represented in black and red, with fiery eyes and snaky locks, and decked out with every appendage of horror. Among them there appeared suddenly an additional goblin: they were twelve in number, but this made the thirteenth, and from his more terrific dress he seemed to be the chief fiend. His companions grew alarmed—they knew he did not belong to them; a general panic succeeded, and the whole group fled different ways, some to their dressing-rooms, others through the streets to their homes. The confusion of the audience is scarcely to be imagined; the reality of the supernatural appearance was so thoroughly believed, that no official explanation could entirely do away with the idea. Jackson, the chronicler of the Scotch stage, who relates this story, had it from Rich himself, who told it in the presence of Bencraft, the contriver if not the actor of it. The joke was an old one. There is a popular legend that Alleyn, the Elizabethan actor, was one day performing a demon with six others in one of Shakespeare's (!) pieces. In the midst of the play, he was surprised by the appearance of another devil, and this so worked on his fancy that he made a vow to build a hospital. To this prank of one of Alleyn's companions, Dulwich hospital, we are told, owes its origin.

CANINE SAGACITY.

THE following anecdote related by Mrs. Garrick, concerning her little dog Biddy, gives a curious proof of the attention with which the canine species watch the proceedings of their masters:—"One evening, after Mr. Garrick and I were seated in our box at Drury Lane Theatre, he said, 'Surely there is something wrong on the stage,' and added, that he would go and see what it was. Shortly after this, when the curtain was drawn up, I saw a person come forward to speak a new prologue, in the dress of a country bumpkin, whose features seemed new to me. Whilst I was wondering who it could possibly be, I felt my little dog's tail wag, for he was seated in my lap, his usual place at the theatre, looking towards the stage. 'Aha!' said I, 'what! do you know him? is it your master? Then you have seen him practice his part at home.'"

A NEW ENDING TO HAMLET.

MISS HENRIETTA HODSON tells an excellent story about the manner in which she once, when in her teens, assisted in killing and murdering *Hamlet*. The troupe was a strolling company, under the management of Mrs. Glover; and the theatre a railway arch, without scenery, in a small town in Scotland. For Miss Hodson's benefit *Hamlet* was given, the *bénéficiaire* having to impersonate Ophelia, and in the last act Osric. As no Ophelia can be mad in anything but a white dress, and Miss Hodson was not possessed of such an article, a tablecloth over a white petticoat was made to do duty for the dress in the mad scene; and by means of a sword-belt buckled round the waist, this same garment might be transformed into a tunic for Osric. Unfortunately, when all was settled Hamlet had one of those sudden indispositions to which the children of Thespis are so frequently subject. In this emergency, Hamlet's landlord—a tall, rawboned Scotchman, who knew the part—volunteered to impersonate the Prince of Denmark. Among jokes of the audience, who recognized the volunteer Hamlet, all went off pretty well. But alas! when Osric was fighting the duel with Hamlet, the treacherous belt gave way, and all at once the young prince stood before the audience in the drapery of the mad Ophelia. After this it was impossible to finish the piece, and to conciliate the audience a Scotch reel, in which all the members of the company took part, was substituted for the tragic termination penned by Shakespeare. The reel was a perfect success, and was even encored.

DEROGATORY.

ON the night of the celebration of the Shakespeare Jubilee a supper was given to all the performers. At the head of the table sat the mighty Kemble family; at the foot, Messrs. Simmons and the asterisks of the drama. To be in keeping with this classification, the upper tables groaned beneath the bottles of champagne, Bucellas, Madeira, sherry, etc.; whilst the lower ones supported exhilarating but humble bowls of rum punch. On this Faucit Saville remarked with much wit and poignancy, "That it was a degradation to the regular drama to introduce *Punch* on such an occasion."

SURGICAL OPERATIONS.

WHEN Kean first played Sir Giles Overreach, he made as great an impression on his fellow-actors as on the audience, and they agreed to present him with a silver cup. For this purpose a subscription was set on foot in the greenroom, and in less than an hour £170 was raised, to which Lord Byron, then a member of the committee of management, contributed twenty-five guineas. When Oxberry, the Justice Greedy of the play, and in whom the measure had its origin, applied to Munden, who played Marrall, the latter replied, with his peculiar manner, "I have no objection to your *cupping* Kean, but I'll be d——d if you *bleed* me."

THEATRICAL DESPATCHES.

GARRICK was fond of exhibiting his skill as a writer of sharp letters, and at one time or another engaged in angry correspondence with every member of his company, from the highest to the lowest. A man of the name of Stone, who was frequently employed by him to get recruits for the "supers," had hired a fellow to perform the character of the Bishop of Winchester in Shakespeare's *Henry the Eighth.* On the night of the performance, Stone sent a note to Garrick in these words :

SIR,—the Bishop of Winchester is getting drunk at the Cat and Fiddle, and swears he will not play to-night. I am yours, etc.—W. STONE."

To this Garrick replied—

"Stone, the bishop may go to the devil. I do not know a greater rascal, except yourself.—D. G."

Some time after, Stone wrote as follows :—

"SIR,—Mr. Lacy turned me out of the lobby yesterday. I only asked for my two guineas for the last bishop, and he said I should not have one farthing. I cannot live upon air. I have a few "cupids" you may have cheap, as they belong to a poor journeyman shoemaker I drink with now and then. I am, etc.—W. STONE."

Answer: "Stone, you are the best fellow in the world. Bring the cupids to the theatre to-morrow; if they are under six and well made, you shall have a guinea a-piece for them. If you can get me two good "murderers," I will pay you handsomely; particularly the spouting fellow who keeps the apple-stall on Tower Hill—the villainous cut of his face is just the thing. Pick me up an "alderman" or two for *Richard,* if you can; and I have no objection to treat with you for a comely, portly "mayor."—D. G.

AN ECCENTRIC ACTOR.

JUNIUS BRUTUS BOOTH was born in London in 1796, but passed the whole of his theatrical life in America, where he was unrivalled for nearly a quarter of a century. As a tragedian, Cooke and Kean have only surpassed him; Charles Kemble and Macready, compared to him, were considered only "plodding, wire-drawing critics." Booth was not above playing the smallest parts, and it is related of him that once in Baltimore, during Charles Kean's engagement, he appeared as the Second Actor in the play scene in *Hamlet.* In this part he had only six lines to recite. This doggrel, usually made particularly atrocious by the way in which it is rendered by some supernumerary, was recited with such effect that the audience rose *en masse* and cheered him to the echo.

Booth's eccentricities bordered on insanity: a large volume would scarcely contain all the stories told of him. At the very outset of his career in America, he actually earnestly applied for the position of lighthouse-keeper at Cape Hatteras, at a salary of three hundred dollars a year, and would have taken it but for the interference of some theatrical manager. In 1822, he bought a farm in a most secluded spot, twenty-five miles from Baltimore, to which he constantly resorted. No trees were allowed to be cut down, and all animal life, even to black snakes, was held religiously sacred. The Rev. James F. Clarke, in the September *Atlantic* for 1861, relates a most singular story of the great tragedian calling upon him twenty years previous, and requesting him to assist at a burial. The corpse proved to be a bushel of dead pigeons, which Booth had picked up in the fields, the birds having been shot whilst large flocks passed over the neighbourhood. The eccentric actor actually had a coffin made for them, hired a hearse and mourning coach, bought a piece of ground for the interment, and went through the solemnity of a funeral, to testify, as he said, against the wanton destruction of animal life.

All forms of religion and all temples of devotion were sacred to him, and in passing churches he never failed to reverently bare his head. He worshipped at many shrines, and even had a great admiration for the Koran, which he read assiduously. Days sacred to colour, ore, and metals were religiously observed by him. In the synagogues he was known as a Jew, because he conversed with the rabbis, and joined their worship in the Hebrew tongue. He read the Talmud, and strictly adhered to many of its laws. Roman Catholic priests aver that he was of their persuasion, by his knowledge of the mysteries of their faith.

Once while playing Richard at the Park Theatre, this lunatic, sword in hand, chased the Richmond of the evening out by the back door of the theatre into the street. Another time, while playing Othello, he bore down so heavily with the pillow on the Desdemona, that she was in danger of her life, and was only rescued from suffocation by the other actors, who rushed upon the stage to save her. In Charleston, after playing Othello one night, he went to his hotel, where he had rooms with Tom Flynn, a brother actor. Assuming that Flynn was Iago, he began to rehearse the famous passage "Villain, be sure thou prove," with such terrible vehemence that Flynn in self-defence grasped the poker, and struck Booth over the nose, breaking it, and thus marring his noble countenance for ever. Such is one of the improbable versions of this accident, which happened in 1837. Miss Rosalie Booth, however, in the biography of her father, says, "The rumours of this melancholy event are so numerous and contradictory, that we never could form a definite conclusion in regard to the occurrence."

SOMETHING IN A NAME.

ONE night, in the Dublin Theatre, the play was *Hamlet*. That character was sustained by a gentleman named Butler, and the part of Horatio by Mr. H. Cooke. The "boys" in the gallery were full of their fun during the whole play, being especially facetious upon the Player King, and any of the subordinates whose tenuity of leg or peculiarity of voice gave a handle for a satirical jest or a rude witticism. On the fall of the curtain there arose a general shouting and hurrahing, in which the name "Butler! Butler!" was frequently heard. After some minutes of increasing uproar, the actor so called presented himself, and acknowledged the doubtful compliment. A voice from above then gave a fresh hint, by calling out, "We've had the *Butler*, boys, now let's have the *Cooke*." The idea was snatched at instantly, and nothing could quell the riotous vociferations for "Cooke! Cooke!" that succeeded, but the reappearance before the curtain of the actor who had played Horatio.

INVENI PORTUM.

JAMES COBB, the author of the excellent farce *No Song, no Supper*, was once strolling out with a friend a few miles from town, when a sudden storm of thunder and rain compelled them to take shelter in a roadside public-house. They called for some port wine, which was brought, when Cobb's companion complained that it was very bad. "Ah! don't grumble," said Cobb; "you know, any *port* in a storm is acceptable."

FAMILY JARS.

FOOTE being in company one evening with two dignitaries of the Church, the conversation chanced to turn on some polemical points in divinity, and the two Churchmen, with considerable warmth, took different sides of the argument. During the clerical combat, Foote took no other part in the dispute than that of "bottle-holder," filling their glasses, in order to enable nature to sustain the unusual exertion. At last one of them turned to Foote, and begged that he would take part in the discussion, as he could sometimes be as argumentative as he could be witty. "Not I," replied Foote; "I make it a rule never to meddle in *family affairs*."

COMPARISONS.

THE younger Crébillon always made it a point of decrying the dramatic works of his father. "How, now," said a friend one day, "shall you, who have produced nothing but fairy tales and other frivolous rhapsodies, pretend to criticize a man who was an honour to the age he lived in; who has produced so many grand tragedies?" "Well," replied young Crébillon, "and which of his works is it you admire so much?" "It would be difficult," was the answer, "to say which is his best work, but it is easy to see that you are his worst." Wits jump. In a like manner the elder Dumas was wont to declare that his drama, *Antony*, and his son were his two best works.

THE LESSER OF TWO EVILS.

WHEN Macklin was acting at the Crow Street Theatre, Dublin, he was on the Saturday morning frequently told that "the treasurer was out of the way, that he was ill," etc. Macklin was soon tired of these excuses, and peremptorily demanded his money. Barry, the manager, now found that he must make a new tack, and told the comedian that, "as he lived two miles out of town, the taking with him of so large a sum as £30 every Saturday night would endanger him to be robbed," and therefore he had better let his money lie in the treasury. Macklin heard this with one of his usual sarcastic grins, and, pulling a large knife out of his pocket, exclaimed, "Look'ee here, sir, here is my remedy against thieves. The man who attempts to rob me, shall have this steel in his belly first. No, no! No robberies!" "Well, but, my dear sir," replied Barry, "consider, determined as you are, you are but one man, and these fellows go in gangs, so that your knife will be nothing against numbers." "Very true, sir. But, allowing all this to be true, I have still but a *chance* of being robbed on the highway; whereas, in the other case, my dear Barry"—looking him full in the face—"*you know* there is a *certainty* of my being *robbed in town*, therefore I'll choose the least risk. Pay me my money, or, by G—d, I'm no longer your actor."

PARSON'S FUN.

THE comics of the old school frequently took most unwarrantable liberties, and abused the good nature of the audience. Parsons, in particular, was an incorrigible offender in this way. When on the stage with Palmer and Aitken, he used to make it a point to make them laugh. Michael Kelly once, whilst enjoying a dish of fried tripe with Parsons at an eating-house, opposite the stage-door of Drury Lane Theatre, took him to task for this misplaced jocularity, adding that he would never laugh on the stage out of his part. A few nights after, the two were acting together in *The Doctor and Apothecary*, and Kelly was to sing a song. Just as the orchestra had pitched the key, Parsons called out to the leader, "Stop! stop!" and putting his head into Kelly's face, whilst kicking up his heels—a favourite action of his—he drove him from one end of the stage to the other, crying out all the time, "I'll be hanged if you shall have any more fried tripe—no more fried tripe, no more fried tripe!"—completely pushing Kelly off the stage. Kelly could not resist laughter, and even the audience joined. Thereupon Parsons took Kelly by the hand, saying, "I think you must own, my serious lad, that I have conquered;" and leading him back to the spot from whence he had driven him, looking down to the orchestra, said, "Now, sirs, begin," so that Kelly might have his song.

SMALL ODDS.

SHERIDAN never gave Monk Lewis any of the profits of *The Castle Spectre*. One day Lewis, being in company with him, said, "Sheridan, I will make you a large bet." Sheridan, who was always ready to make a wager, however inconvenient he might find it to pay if he lost, asked eagerly, "What bet?" "All the profits of my *Castle Spectre*," replied

Lewis. "I will tell you what," said Sheridan, matchless at repartee, "I will make you a very small one—what it is worth." The fact is, though *The Castle Spectre* had a great run, it was a silly piece.

A CAT-A-STROPHE.

ONE of the most sensational scenes in Victor Neszler's opera, *The Ratcatcher of Hameln*, is that representing the exodus of rodents from Hameln, brought about by the tuneful spells of Singuf the Charmer. Whilst this fantastic personage is singing his incantation, thousands upon thousands of rats invade the stage, emerging from doors and windows of the houses composing the "set," from crevices in walls, and from holes in the ground. In the leading houses of Germany, no pains or expense were spared in order to impart a realistic character to this rat-episode. So excellently managed was this particular effect at the Dresden Opera House, that upon the occasion of the *Ratcatcher's* first performance in that theatre, the property rats fairly took in the worthy old cat, perpetually retained upon the strength of the establishment in consideration of her long and valuable services. This conscientious creature, whilst watching the stage "business" with placid interest from her favourite corner behind one of the wings, suddenly perceived what she believed to be a host of her natural foes in the very act of committing an audacious trespass within the sacred limits of her territorial jurisdiction. With a piercing mew of indignation she straightway bounded upon the stage, and, to the delight of the audience, furiously attacked the legion of "counterfeit presentments" that occupied the boards. No sooner, however, had actual contact with the property rats enlightened her respecting their fictitious nature than she majestically retired. In obedience to an enthusiastic recall, she was brought on a few minutes later in the arms of a super, to receive the tribute of applause her spirited conduct had so richly earned.

DAYS AND MONTHS.

IN 1767 Voltaire produced his drama *Les Scythes*, a work of considerable merit. It did not "take," however, at the first representation. Like many of Voltaire's plays, it was written in a hurry, and the author had to take it back, to correct and alter it. This fact was recorded in one of the public prints of the period in the following paragraph:—"We understand that Mr. Voltaire has sent the actors a tragedy, entitled *Les Scythes*, and informed them, at the same time, that he wrote it in twelve days. The actors, to be even with him, have returned it, with a humble request that he will take twelve months to correct it."

BLACK-EYED SUSAN.

"I discovered," writes Mr. T. F. Dillon Croker, in his "Jottings on Jerrold," in the *Era Almanac*, "on looking over Mr. Cooke's correspondence, a letter from my father, bearing no date, but which, I believe, was written in 1853, in which my father says, 'I am much obliged, and so will be my son, for your recollection of us in the shape of an order for the Princess's; and I, who never go to a theatre, actually made a pilgrimage with him the other evening to see *Black-eyed Susan*, and I have seldom been more pleased. As for a woman who sat next to me, she blubbered like a child, and in the last scene was quite audible in the house—"Oh, will they hang him, will they hang him?"' I may remark, *en parenthèse*, that the reply of Gnatbrain, when William says, 'What do you think we found in the shark?' is usually, 'What? His innards?' though the author leaves William to finish his yarn without interruption, and to say, 'We found all the watches and 'bacca-boxes as had been lost for the last ten years, an admiral's cocked hat, and three pilot telescopes.' Some latitude is, however, given to Gnatbrain. I remember hearing Mr. Toole say, when T. P. Cooke played William during a farewell engagement, 'I can't say what you found in the shark—I know what you didn't find in him.' 'What's that?' said William. 'Why, another T. P. Cooke!' During the round of applause which followed the impromptu, Toole whispered, 'Give it me back; reply that you don't care to be made a Toole of,' which was accordingly the retort of Mr. Cooke. Again, when the drama was played at the time of the farewell dinner given to Macready, Buckstone, who was the Gnatbrain, is reported to have suggested that the great tragedian's farewell speech was found in St. Domingo Billy. 'No,' said Cooke, shaking his head. 'Ah,' observed Buckstone, 'I thought he couldn't have swallowed that!' My friend Mr. E. L. Blanchard has reminded me of a humorous incident said to have occurred during a representation of *Black-eyed Susan* at Liverpool, in 1858. The jury, carried away by the cunning of the scene, when asked for their verdict, 'Guilty or not guilty?' at once exclaimed, 'Not guilty;' upon which the Admiral observed, *sotto voce*, 'Gentlemen, you know the piece cannot proceed unless you reconsider your verdict,' which was accordingly reversed, and thus prevented a lame and impotent conclusion."

AN UNINVITED GUEST.

THE first Garrick club, called the School of Garrick, was formed by a few actors, contemporaries of the British Roscius, who dined together during the theatrical winter season once a month. One night, in the beginning of this century, when Moody, the aged comedian, was in the chair, a waiter came in to tell Henry Johnstone that a gentleman wished to speak to him in the next room. In a few minutes there was a great noise and bustle, and Johnstone was heard to say in a loud tone, "Sir, you cannot go into the room where the club is—none but members are on any account admitted; such are our rules." "Talk not to me of your rules," said the stranger; "I insist upon being admitted." And after a long controversy of "I will go" and "You shan't," the door was burst open, and both contending parties came tumbling in. The stranger, an uncommonly ill-favoured person, coolly took his place at the table, commenced a rhapsodic speech about his admiration of the club, that he could not resist the temptation of joining it, and ended by filling himself a glass and drinking "To our better acquaintance." Moody, with great solemnity, requested him to withdraw, as no one could have a seat at that table unless he was a member. The stranger, who seemed somewhat elevated, replied, "I don't care for your rules; talk not to me of your regulations. I want to become a member, and won't stir an inch!" "Then," cried the infuriated Moody, "old as I am, I will take upon myself to turn you out." With that he jumped up, and took hold of the stranger, who resisted valiantly. All was confusion, and poor Moody was getting black in the face, when the stranger threw off his wig, spectacles, and false nose, and before them stood Charles Mathews the elder, a member of the club. So well had the mimic played his part that nobody except Johnstone, his accomplice in the plot, had suspected him.

SERIO-COMICALITY.

CUMBERLAND, the dramatist, had an inveterate dislike to Sheridan, which, considering the abuse Sheridan had heaped upon him in *The Critic*, was not surprising. When *The School for Scandal* came out, Cumberland's children prevailed upon their father to take them to see it. They had the stage-box, the father was seated behind them, and every time the children laughed at what was going on on the stage, he pinched them, and said, "What are you laughing at, my dear little folks? You should not laugh, my angels; there is nothing to laugh at;" and then, in an undertone, "Keep still, you little dunces." Sheridan, having been told of this, said, "It was very ungrateful in Cumberland, to have been displeased with his poor children for laughing at *my comedy;* for I went the other night to see *his tragedy*, and laughed at it from beginning to end."

NEW READING.

IN a certain garrison town theatre, *Julius Cæsar* was to be represented with considerable splendour. Supernumeraries, of course, were necessary to impersonate the Roman plebs, and some score of "Connaught Rangers"—the regiment at that time stationed in the town—were drilled into sympathizing citizens, and nightly clamoured for the production of Cæsar's will. The gallant soldiers shouted "The testament! the testament!" with emphasis and discretion in the right place during three successive enactments; after which Julius rested "i' th' capitol." Just before the company left, the Roman hero was "bespoke" by a classical patron of the drama for reslaughter. Having been so lately performed, it was deemed unnecessary to rehearse the tragedy, and its scenic illustration proceeded with due solemnity to the eventful moment of Antony's oration. At their well-remembered "cue," the practised Romanized Hibernians cried loudly for "The testament!" but superior duties having unfortunately claimed the attendance of divers members of the original mob, several of their uninitiated substitutes—instructed only to do as their companions did, and make a "row"—upon hearing their brother Romans shout for "the testament," determined not to be outdone in religious zeal, and roared long and lustily, "The Bible! the Bible! the Bible!"

WAITING.

IN 1825 Kean was engaged for nine nights at Cork, during which period he represented his best characters to almost empty houses. On the night of his benefit, however, owing partly to the entertainments, which were well calculated to "force a house," and partly to individual exertion, a numerous audience assembled. In *Sylvester Daggerwood*, he made several oblique allusions to the neglect he had experienced, but "one hit" was most "palpable." When the manager's servant in that play announced his master's exit, and Fustian complained of having in vain waited two hours for an audience with him, Kean replied, with peculiar emphasis, "O Lord! you have no cause of complaint. I have been *nine nights waiting here* for an audience, and have seen nobody." This marked rejoinder was received with enthusiastic applause.

RIP VAN WINKLE.

WHILE Joseph Jefferson was once playing Rip Van Winkle at Chicago, he went to the theatre very much exhausted by a long day's fishing on the lake. As the curtain rose on the third act, it disclosed the white-haired Rip still deep in his twenty years' nap. Five, ten, twenty minutes passed and he did not waken. The audience began to get impatient and the prompter uneasy. The great actor doubtless knew what he was about, but this was carrying the realistic business too far. The fact was that all this time Jefferson was really sleeping the sleep of the just, or rather of the fisherman who had sat eight hours in the sun. Finally the gallery became uproarious, and one of the "gods" wanted to know if there was going to be "nineteen years more of this snooze business!" At this point Jefferson began to snore. This decided the prompter, who opened a small trap beneath the stage, and began to prod Rip from below. The fagged comedian fumbled in his pocket for an imaginary railway ticket, and muttered drowsily, "Going right through, 'ductor." At this entirely new reading the audience was transfixed with amazement, when all at once Jefferson sat up with a loud shriek, evidently in agony. The exasperated prompter had "jabbed" him with a pin. The play went on after that—with a rush.

AN UNCOUTH SENATOR.

AMONG the insolent frolics perpetrated by the buffoon Joe Haines, the following will help us to a view of theatrical manners in his days. One night, when the tragedy of *Catiline's Conspiracy* was being performed, which required a great number of Roman senators on the stage, Hart, then leader of the company, ordered Joe to dress for one of the "potent, grave, and reverend seigniors," although Joe, whose salary was then fifty shillings per week, was above such parts. The comic, vexed at the slight Hart put upon him, determined to be revenged. He put on a Scaramouch dress, a large, full ruff, moustaches from ear to ear, and a fool's cap on his head. Thus accoutred, with a pipe in his mouth, and a little three-legged stool in his hand, Joe followed Hart on the stage, sat himself down behind him, and commenced smoking his pipe, making grimaces, and pointing to the actor. This comical figure put the whole house in an uproar, some laughing, some clapping their hands, others holloaing. Hart was one of those players whom nothing could disconcert; had a scene fallen behind him, he would not have looked back. He continued to play as if nothing had happened, wondering, however, at the unusual merriment of the house, now thinking that there was somebody in the house exciting this mirth, again having an uncomfortable apprehension that there was something amiss in his dress. At last, happening to turn himself towards the scenes, he discovered Joe in the aforesaid posture. This was too much even for the imperturbable tragedian, who immediately left the stage, swearing that he would never set his foot on it again unless Joe was immediately discharged, which was done *stante pede*.

A FACE OF THUNDER.

LABLACHE had the extraordinary talent of representing a thunder-storm, simply by facial expression. First, gloom gradually overspread his countenance; it appeared to deepen into actual darkness, and a terrific frown indicated the angry lowering of the tempest. The lightning commenced by winks of the eyes, and twisting and twitchings of the muscles of the face, succeeded by rapid sidelong movements of the mouth, which wonderfully recalled the forked flashes that seem to rend the sky, the notion of thunder being conveyed by the shaking of his head. By degrees the lightning became less vivid, the frown relaxed, the gloom departed, and a broad smile illuminating his expansive face, gave the impression that the sun had broken through the clouds, and the storm was over.

ACTOR AND GENTLEMAN.

THOMAS SHERIDAN, manager of the Crow Street Theatre in Dublin, once had to give evidence at a trial in the Exchequer Court, in that city. The leading counsel frequently urged the evidence of "so very respectable a gentleman as Mr. Sheridan," who came there to support his client's cause. The barrister employed on the other side, laying hold of his learned brother's repeatedly terming Sheridan a "gentleman," commenced his harangue with illiberal remarks, concluding, "My learned brother calls a stage-player, an actor in tragedies and comedies, a *gentleman!* 'Tell it not in Gath, publish it not in the streets of Askelon,' that a common player should in a high court of justice be termed a *gentleman!* I have heard of gentlemen soldiers, gentlemen sailors; but, I must confess, I never before now heard of or saw a *gentleman player*." Sheridan repressed his indignation, and, turning to the calumniator of his profession with a placid smile and his hand laid gracefully on his bosom, simply said, "I hope, sir, you see one now," accompanied by a courtly bow.

THE CLERGY AND THE PLAYHOUSE.

WHEN Mrs. Siddons made her first appearance in Edinburgh, in 1784, the General Assembly of the Scottish Church was obliged to adjourn its sittings at an early hour, to enable its reverend members to attend the theatre and witness the performance of the great tragic actress. Here was a change from the days when the production of Horne's tragedy of *Douglas* had excited a ferment in the Scottish Church which has become historical.

FRIGID FARCES.

THE crew of the American ship engaged in the Grinnell expedition in search of Franklin, performed a farce on the 14th of February, 1851, in the Arctic regions. The outside temperature on that evening, was $-36°$; in the "house," it was $-25°$ behind the scenes, and $-20°$ in the audience department. The farce was called *The Mysteries and Miseries of New York*. One of the sailors had to enact the part of a damsel with bare arms; and when a cold flat-iron, part of the properties, touched his skin, the sensation was like that of burning with a hot iron. But this was not the most arduous of their dramatic exploits. A week later, on Washington's birthday, there was another performance. The ship's thermometer outside was at $-46°$; inside, the audience and actors, by aid of lungs, lamps, and hangings, got it as high as $-30°$, *only* 62° *below* freezing point, probably the lowest atmospheric record of a theatrical representation. It was a strange thing altogether. The condensation was so excessive, that the audience could scarcely see the performers; they walked in a cloud of steam. Any extra vehemence of delivery was accompanied by volumes of vapour.

Their hands steamed. When an excited Thespian took off his coat, it steamed like a dish of hot potatoes.

CONTRACTORS FOR SUCCESS.

THOUGH the French, as a rule, do not read Shakespeare, still they unwittingly agree with the truth of at least one remark of "the divine William's," viz. that "there is something in a name." Generally, it is not the fault of the Frenchman, if he does not give as fine a name to everything connected with himself as can possibly be applied to it. Thus the gallant band of hirelings who thunder forth applause in the theatres distinguishes itself by the heroic name of "Romans;" their chief, in a plain unvarnished definition, is described "chief of clapping" (*chef de claque*), but preferably he styles himself by, a circumlocution, a "contractor for success." With such a title, a man cannot but respect himself and feel his worth. The following characteristic letter, written to Mdlle. Rachel by a success-contractor when the celebrated tragedian had expressed dissatisfaction with the exertions of the clapping fraternity, throws some light on the position the *chef de claque* considers himself to hold:—

"MADEMOISELLE,—I cannot remain under the obloquy of a reproach from lips such as yours! The following is an authentic statement of what really took place:—At the first representation, I led the attack in person no less than thirty-three times. We had three acclamations, four hilarities, two thrilling movements, four renewals of applause, and two indefinite explosions. In fact, to such an extent did we carry our applause that the occupants of the stalls were scandalized, and cried out, 'Turn them out!' My men were positively overcome with fatigue, and intimated to me that they could not again go through such an evening. Seeing such to be the case, I applied for the manuscript, and after having profoundly studied the piece, I was obliged to make up my mind, for the second representation, to certain curtailments in the service of my men. I, however, applied them only to MM."—here follow the names—"and, if the temporary office which I hold affords me the opportunity, I will make them ample amends. In such a situation as that which I have just depicted, I have only to request you to believe firmly in my profound admiration and respectful zeal; and I venture to entreat you to have some consideration for the difficulties which environ me. I am, Mademoiselle," etc.

A FALSE ALARM.

WHEN the Spanish Armada was hovering on the English coast, a company of strolling actors were performing a piece called *Sampson* in a booth at Penryn. The enemy, having silently landed a body of men, were making their way to surprise the town, when fortunately at that instant the players let Sampson loose on the Philistines. The sounds of drums, trumpets, shouts, and firing of ordnance created such a tremendous hubbub that the Spaniards fancied the whole town, with Beelzebub at their back, were pouring down upon them, and immediately turning tail, scampered off to their ships. This anecdote may perhaps have suggested the amusing incident in *Tom Jones*, where the drum of the puppet-show so terrified poor Partridge, that he fancied the Pretender, Jenny Cameron, and all the Scotch rebels were at hand, and that his dying hour was come.

OBITUARY NOTICE.

IN *The Friendly Writer and Register of Truth*, a quaker weekly paper edited by Ruth Collins, under date September 25, 1732, the death of Robert Wilks, the tragedian, is announced in these words: "Died this week, Master *Robert Wilks*, of the *Irish Nation*. He was one that showed great Behaviour of Body, and spake many quaint Words of

Vanity upon a Stage of Wood, before People who delight in vain Babbling; and they are now greatly troubled at his Loss. For, say they, where shall we find his Fellow, to yield Delight into our Ears, and unto our Hearts, in the doleful Evenings of the Winter. Those that were of his Company also mourn, and say, Our neighbouring Brethren will rejoyce, as hoping to be Gainers by his Departure."

ABOUT PANTOMIMES.

THE pantomime was introduced into England by Rich, the manager of Covent Garden Theatre. The first entertainment of this kind was produced in 1717, at the theatre in Lincoln's Inn Fields. It was called *Harlequin Sorcerer*, and is described as "A species of dramatic composition consisting of two parts, one serious and the other comic. By the help of gay scenes, fine dresses, grand dances, appropriate music, and other decorations, Rich exhibited a story taken from Ovid's *Metamorphoses*. Between the acts of this serious representation he interwove a comic fable, consisting chiefly of the courtship of Harlequin and Columbine, with a variety of surprising adventures and tricks, produced by the magic wand of Harlequin, such as the sudden transformations of palaces and temples to huts and cottages, of men and women into wheel-barrows and jointstools, of trees into houses, colonnades to beds of tulips, and mechanics' shops into serpents and ostriches." The fertility of Rich's invention in devising entertainments was extraordinary: of all the pantomimes which he produced between 1717 and 1761, scarcely one was a failure.

The "comic openings" of the modern pantomime had no place in these old pantomimes; no allusions to passing events or the follies of the day were introduced in them. It was only some fifty years ago that that change came about. Leigh Hunt writing in 1831, complained that pantomimes were not what they had been, and that the opening, which "used to form merely a brief excuse for putting the harlequinade in motion," had come to be a considerable part of the performance. Gradually, also, Harlequin lost his importance and fell into the background, before the inimitable clown impersonated by Joe Grimaldi. It was this great artist who designed the eccentric costume still worn by clowns, which originally was the same as that of the Pierrot of the masked ball. Harlequin at first wore the loosely fitting, parti-coloured jacket and trousers familiar in biscuit and china paintings of the last century. In 1800, James Byrne, the father of the late Mr. Oscar Byrne, appeared as Harlequin in the pantomime of *Harlequin Amulet; or, The Magic of Mona*, at Drury Lane. His attire in that character is described as "a white silk shape fitting without a wrinkle, into the which the coloured silk patches were woven, the whole being profusely covered with spangles, and representing a very sparkling appearance." This innovation took the stage by storm, and ere long became the costume of all harlequins all over the world.

OUT-HERODING HEROD.

EDWARD RAVENSCROFT, a writer, or rather compiler, of plays in the reign of Charles II. and his two successors, wrote a drama entitled *Titus Andronicus; or, The Rape of Lavinia*, in which he largely borrowed from Shakespeare. Instead of diminishing any of the horrors of the original, he seized every opportunity of adding to them—witness the following speech by the Moor, after the empress Tomara has stabbed her child :—

> "She has outdone me, even in mine own art!
> Outdone *me* in murder! killed her own child!
> Give it me. . . . *I'll eat it.*"

A TALKATIVE CORPSE.

TONY LEE, a player in King Charles II.'s reign, having a violent cold, could not forbear coughing as he lay dead upon the stage, having been killed in a tragedy. This occasioned a great deal of noise and laughter in the house. Tony waggishly lifted up his head, and, addressing the audience, said, "This makes good what my poor mother used to tell me; for she would often say that I should cough in my grave, because I used to drink with my porridge." This set the house in such good humour, that it produced a thundering round of applause, and made every one pardon the solecism he had committed.

CITY FREEDOM.

LITTLE Edward Knight, passing the evening among some friends in the City, was requested in his turn to favour the company with a song. He politely declined it, alleging that he was so indifferent a performer that any attempt of his would rather weary than entertain. One of the company, however, insisted that Knight had a good voice, and said that he had frequently had the pleasure of hearing him sing at the Drury Lane Theatre. "That may be," replied the witty comedian; "but, as I am not a freeman, I *have no voice in the City*."

A GOOD REASON.

BARRY was in no part so eminent as in Romeo. At the time when he attracted the town to Covent Garden by his admirable delineation of the character, Garrick found it absolutely necessary to perform himself as Romeo at Drury Lane, in order to obtain at least some share in the attention of the public, and to divert into his own coffers a driblet of the stream of gold which was rolling into the treasury of the rival house. Garrick, however, wanted the physical advantages of Barry, and, great as he was, would perhaps have willingly avoided such a competition. This, at least, seems to have been the prevailing opinion; for, in the garden scene, when Juliet exclaims, "O Romeo, Romeo! wherefore art thou Romeo?" an auditor in the pit archly gave the explanation of this fact by replying, "Because Barry has gone to the other house."

THE COMB IN THE THEATRE.

THE beaux of the period of Charles II. and William III. flaunted in costly periwigs, "more elaborately curled than a lady's head dressed for the ball." This magnificent headgear was treated with loving care, and so much was it the fashion to attend to the proper twist of the curls that it was customary for the beaux, while standing in the pit, conversing with the ladies in the boxes, gracefully to comb the silken curls of their fair periwig. The comb was lightly held between finger and thumb, the other fingers elegantly bent, so as to show off to advantage the diamond ring on the little finger and the precious lace ruffles on the wrist. An old play tells us that, on the appearance of a masked lady—it was the fashion then for ladies to wear vizard-masks—in the pit,

> "Straight every man who thinks himself a wit
> Perks up, and managing his comb with grace,
> With his white wig sets off his nut-brown face."

Wig combs, made of the most beautiful tortoiseshell, and fancifully engraved with flowers and birds, sometimes inlaid with mother-of-pearl, or with their owner's name or crest painted on them, were carried in a shagreen case in one of the side pockets, so as to have them always ready at hand.

AN UNHINGED ARMY.

THE London correspondent of a New York paper told the following story to Booth of the time when the American actor and Irving played together years ago:—"Irving tells me that he played with you at Manchester when you were in England on your first visit. The piece he remembers best was *Richard III.* The manager of the theatre was "Richmond," and he had given himself a splendid new set of armour, and had provided the best the theatre afforded for his army. He was popular with the public in front, and did not mean to have his position unduly interfered with by the star in *Richard.* He interpolated the prayer scene, the invocation to the god of battles, from *Henry V.* While Richard's army was clothed in the most ordinary costumes, Richmond's was ablaze, partially in new armour and in old armour cleaned up and polished. When the manager came on, the extraordinary display of magnificently appointed men was loudly applauded. Everything went as he could wish, till at last came the invocation to the god of battles. Down on his knees went Richmond; his army tried to follow suit. The property-men had not oiled or greased the joints of their armour. Upon going to kneel, they fell into all kinds of comic attitudes, one or two fell upon their faces, all of them looked ridiculous. The stiff joints of the armour would not work. The audience screamed with laughter. A more absurd stage-picture was never seen. The invocation over, the army attempted to rise. This was a still more awkward-looking business than trying to kneel. The men on their faces could not get up again. Those who did get up made far more to-do about it than Rip van Winkle after his long sleep, so admirably represented by Jefferson. Richmond went off, amid shouts of laughter and chaff from the gallery. Apart from any question of ability, Richard had the best of that arrangement."

A THIEF-CATCHER ON THE STAGE.

IN 1849, Vidocq, the famous French thief-catcher, gave some theatrical representations in London. He performed in a drama in five acts, *Julie d'Escars*, in which there was a rich crop of burglaries, robberies by violence and with false keys, and incidents of cracksmen's and policemen's craft pitted against each other. In one of his "*Soirées d'Imitation*," he represented an Italian quack. When the performance was over, and Vidocq had retired to change his costume for his next appearance, one of the spectators began to make remarks about the impersonations, observing that he could do the same things just as well. Others took the part of the performer, and the discussion was taking a quarrelsome turn, when all at once the discontented spectator became deadly pale, and fell down, vomiting blood. It was thought that the unfortunate man had ruptured a blood-vessel, and people called for a doctor, when the invalid declared coolly that he did not want one, for nothing was the matter with him. It was Vidocq again in another character. This anecdote is related by Charles Maurice, the theatrical critic of the *Journal des Débats*, in his *Histoire Anecdotique*, who adds that "John Bull" applauded this tasteful performance *à outrance*.

THEATRICAL PROFITS AND EXPENSES.

IN a roll of the churchwardens of Bassingborn, in Cambridgeshire, is an account of the expenses and receipts for acting the play of *St. George*, in that parish, on the feast of St. Margaret, 1511. The company collected upwards of £4 in twenty-seven neighbouring parishes for getting up the play. They disbursed about £2 in the representation. These disbursements were—to four minstrels or waits of Cambridge, for three days, 5*s*. 6*d*.; to the players, in bread and ale, 3*s*. 2*d*.;

to the "garnement" man for "garnements" and properties, 20*s.*; to John Hobard, brotherhood-priest, for the playbook, 2*s.* 8*d.*; for hire of the croft or field in which the play was exhibited, 1*s.*; for property-making or furniture, 1*s.* 4*d.*; for fish and bread, and setting up the stages, 4*d.*; for painting three phantoms and four tormentors (*i.e.* devils). . . . The rest was expended for a feast on the occasion, for which were provided "four chickens for the gentlemen, 4*d.*"

This note proves that the theatrical term "property" is of respectable antiquity. What the "properties" were in this instance cannot be ascertained; but in a mystery, founded on the story of Tobit, exhibited at Lincoln in 1563, there occurs among the properties—hell-mouth, with a nether chap; Sarah's chamber; a great idol with a club; the city of Jerusalem, with towers and pinnacles; the city of Rages, with towers and pinnacles; the city of Nineveh; the king's palace of Nineveh; old Toby's house; a firmament with a fiery cloud, etc.

THE TWO GRAVEDIGGERS.

IT was formerly customary to make the gravedigger in *Hamlet* a comic character, and all sorts of tricks were effected for that purpose. Among other comicalities, it was held sacred that he should wear an indefinite number of waistcoats. Paul Bedford, in his *Reminiscences*, relates how he acted once at Nottingham. Edward Wright was the first grave-digger, Paul the second. The first gravedigger prepared himself to take the town by storm, by having incased his person within a dozen waistcoats of all sorts of shapes and patterns. When about to commence the operation of digging the grave for the fair Ophelia, the chief began to unwind by taking off waistcoat after waistcoat, which caused uproarious laughter among the audience. But as the chief digger relieved himself of one waistcoat, Paul, the boy digger, incased himself in the cast off vests; which increased the salvos of laughter, for, as number one became thinner, number two grew fatter and fatter. Wright, seeing himself outdone, kept on the remainder of the waistcoats, and commenced digging Ophelia's grave.

BRUTUS'S APOSTROPHE.

IN 1850, Junius Brutus Booth performed the principal part in John Howard Payne's tragedy of *Brutus*, his son Edwin supporting him as Titus. In the solemn interview where the Roman consul is condemning his recreant son to an ignominious death, his countenance pourtrayed an agony of suffering, and tears streamed from his eyes, as he gathered the head of his offending boy to his bosom. The audience was breathless, but the silence was suddenly interrupted by an exclamation from a drunken man in the gallery. Booth, still enwrapt in the character he was impersonating with such truthful earnestness, raised his eyes, and, fixing them upon the man with a steady gaze, exclaimed sternly, "Beware! I am the headsman —I am the executioner." The singular effect thus produced was shown in the continued hushed silence of the audience, which at last burst forth in rapturous applause.

CALLS BEFORE THE CURTAIN.

ON the 9th of April, 1791, a singer, making his *début* in Sedaine and Grétry's comic opera *Guillaume Tell* in Paris, was recalled. He declined to show himself, and the people in the pit were so incensed at this slight that they tore the curtain. At that time already calls before the curtain were so common in Paris that the papers, commenting on this affair, observed, "To be called before the curtain is no longer an honour. It has been abused to such an extent, both with actors and with authors." Macready relates, in his *Reminiscences*, that the practice of "calling on" the principal actor was first introduced at Covent Garden Theatre, on the occasion of his first performance of the character of Richard III., on October 19, 1819. This custom was not introduced at the Italian Opera in London till 1824, when Rossini was director and composer to the King's Theatre, and his wife, Madame Colbran Rossini, *prima donna*, with Mesdames Pasta and Catalani, for a limited number of nights. Parke, the oboe-player, in his *Musical Memoirs*, relates as a novelty that after the performance of *Il Fanatico per la Musica*, "Madame Catalani was called for, when she again presented herself, making her obeisance, amidst waving of handkerchiefs and tumultuous applause." Madame Pasta also, after playing Desdemona, "had a call when the curtain fell, and was brought back to receive the reward due to her distinguished talents." The thing appears to have been overdone, however, for not more than two seasons later, Parke, in reference to Pasta's performance of Desdemona, observes, "At the end of the opera, by desire of the audience, she came forward once more to receive that reward *which is becoming so common that it will shortly cease to be a mark of distinction.*"

It was in 1836 that the composer of an opera was for the first time called before the curtain in this country. In that year the opera of *Nourjahad* was produced at the English Opera House, now the Lyceum Theatre. The late Mr. Loder, the son of the leader of the orchestra at Bath, was the composer of this work, which was a great success. "The silly practice of calling for a favourite actor at the end of a play," writes the *Athenæum* of that week, "was upon this occasion for the first time extended to a composer, and Mr. E. J. Loder was produced upon the stage to make his bow. As the chance portion of the audience could not possibly be aware that a gentleman so little known in London was present, it would have betrayed less of the secrets of the prison house if this bit of nonsense had not been concerted by injudicious and overzealous friends. The turn of successful authors will, we suppose, come next, and therefore such of them as are not actors had better take a few lessons in bowing over the lamps, and be ready. We know some half dozen whom this process would cause to shake in their shoes more vehemently than even the already accumulated anxieties of a first night."

The turn of successful authors *did* come, though history has omitted to record the name of the favourite dramatist to whom the honour of "bowing over the footlights" was first accorded. In France, Voltaire was the first author called before the curtain, after the first representation of *Merope;* the second was Marmontel, after the production of his *Dionyse.*

OLD MORTALITY.

MACKLIN'S last attempt on the stage was Shylock, which in former days had been his greatest success. He came dressed for the character into the greenroom, where all the actors were assembled. Looking round, he said, "What! is there a play to-night?" All were astonished, and no one answered. He repeated, "Is there a play to-night?" Portia remarked, "Why, sir, what is the matter? *The Merchant of Venice*, you know." "And who is Shylock?" asked Macklin. "Why, you, sir; you are Shylock." "Ah!" said he, "am I?" and sat down in silence. Every one was much concerned and alarmed. However, the curtain rose, the play began, and he got through the part, every now and then going to the side of the stage, lifting up his hair with one hand and putting his ear down to the prompter, who gave him the word. He then walked to the centre of the stage, and repeated the words tolerably well. This occurred often through the play, but sometimes he said to the prompter, "Eh, what is it? what do you say?" The play was got through, and then Macklin came forward, with a wish to address the house, but he could only utter in a tremulous voice, "My age, my age!" This was Macklin's last appearance. He died at his house in Covent Garden, the right-hand corner of Tavistock Court, and was buried in St. Paul's, Covent Garden, where an inscription to his memory may be read on the south wall. "Though many persons, at the time of his death, had been applied to in order to ascertain the period of his birth," says J. T. Smith, in *Nollekens and his Times*, "Nobody had been able to fix it with certainty. Just as the coffin was being lowered into the vault, a letter, containing a copy of the register of his birth, was put into the hands of the chief mourner, who immediately took out his penknife and scratched 107 on the coffin-plate, where the actor's age had been left in blank."

REAL TRAGEDY.

SOME time in 1880, if newspaper reports may be trusted, a madman armed with a hatchet made his way on to the stage of the Teatro del Circo, at Madrid. After slaying one of the attendants who attempted to seize him, the inconvenient supernumerary swung the hatchet about his head with such desperation that the municipal authorities dared not approach him. A squad of soldiers were at length called in, and these, under the instruction of their officer, fired at the madman with blank cartridge, in the hope of frightening him into surrender. Failing in this effort, they loaded with ball and fired once more. This time they were successful, and the intruder, his antics all over, lay upon the stage a corpse, with three bullets in his head and body. So soon as it was known that the man was dead, the audience returned to the places they had quitted in terror, and the performances were resumed at the point at which they had been interrupted by this little episode.

AN OBSTINATE ADMIRER.

G. F. COOKE, when in his cups, was what is vulgarly described as "an ugly customer." One evening he was very merry at a tavern, when Incledon came in. Cooke requested him to sing "The Storm," but, as it was late, Incledon refused, and soon after went to bed. Irritated at this refusal, Cooke was determined to have his revenge, and after musing for a few minutes, asked the waiter if he knew the man who had just been sitting in the same box with him. He replied that it was Mr. Incledon. "No such thing," exclaimed Cooke; "'tis some vile impostor! He has stolen my watch, and I insist on an officer being sent for, that we may search him." Remonstrance was fruitless, so at length the guardian of the night was summoned, and they all ascended to Incledon's chamber, with Cooke at their head. Incledon, roused from his first sleep, asked what they wanted. Cooke insisted that he was the man who had picked his pocket, at the same time observing, "If it is really Incledon, he can sing 'The Storm;' let him do so, and I shall be convinced of my error." Incledon now perceived the drift of the joke, and without further protest struck up, "Cease, rude Boreas." Cooke, having heard the desired ditty, left him once more to his repose.

CHARLES THE SECOND'S WIG.

SHORTLY after the demise of Mr. Rawle, one of George III.'s accoutrement makers, and the friend of Captain Grose, the antiquary, a sale of his effects took place. Among other historical curiosities, there was a large black wig, with long flowing curls, which was stated to have been worn by King Charles II. Suett, the actor, a great collector of wigs, was a bidder for this curiosity, and to prove to the company that it would suit him better than any of his opponents, he put it upon his head. Thus dignified, he went on with his biddings, which were accompanied by remarks sometimes sarcastically serious, at others ludicrously comic. The company, however, though highly amused, thought it ungenerous to prolong the biddings, and therefore one and all declared that it ought to be knocked down to Suett, which accordingly was done. Suett continued to act in this wig for many years in *Tom Thumb* and other pieces, till, unfortunately, it was burnt when the theatre at Birmingham was destroyed by fire.

DEMONSTRATIVE APPRECIATION.

CHARLES MATHEWS, it appears, was wont to complain of the undemonstrative habits of American audiences, apropos of which fact Mrs. Fields tells a characteristic anecdote. Her husband's acquaintance with Mr. Charles Mathews must have begun with Mathews's first visit to America, for he used to relate an anecdote of him long before the visit of 1871. Mr. Fields had enjoyed Mathews's playing sincerely; it seemed to him perfect of its kind. "Mathews," he exclaimed, when they met, "I enjoyed your performance beyond expression!" "Ah! that is just it," said Mathews, "you don't express anything. How can your people expect to get the best out of an actor, if they don't speak or try to tell him so? They will never know what we can do. It is impossible to give one's best under such circumstances."

The elder Mathews was of the same opinion. At Plymouth, during one of his entertainments, a gentleman close to him presented such a melancholy face, that Mathews could not stand it. Advancing to where the depressed one sat, he addressed him thus: "I beg your pardon, sir, but if you don't laugh I cannot go on." This was received by the audience with such roars, that the unconsciously offending gentleman throughout the rest of the evening laughed louder than anybody else.

Liston found applause of whatever kind so absolutely necessary to him, that he declared he liked to see even a small dog wag his tail in approbation of his exertions. The playgoers of York were at one time so lukewarm in their reception of popular players that, at the instance of Woodward, Tate Wilkinson, the manager, called on the chief patrons of the theatre, and informed them that the actor was so mortified by their coolness that he could not play nearly so well in York as in London, Edinburgh, or Dublin. The York audience benefited by the remonstrance, and on Woodward's next appearance, greatly to his delight, awarded him extraordinary applause.

THE TWO QUEENS.

MRS. PORTER, a celebrated actress in the time of Colley Cibber, was one night performing Queen Elizabeth in the tragedy of *The Earl of Essex*, before Queen Anne. The queen happening to drop her fan on the stage, Mrs. Porter, with great dignity, and in the full spirit of the character she was representing, immediately addressed one of the performers, and with a majestic air, said, "Take up our sister's fan." The audience received this sally with great applause, and the queen affably smiled; but the actress, the moment she had uttered the words, was ready to sink with confusion.

FOOTE'S IMPERTINENCIES.

FOOTE had little regard for the feelings of others; he spared neither friend nor foe. If he thought of a witty thing that would create laughter, he said or did it. Once he met by accident an inferior person in the street very like Dr. Arne, the celebrated musical composer, who when full dressed was sometimes rather a grotesque figure. Foote contrived not only to obtain some old clothes of the doctor's, but likewise one of his cast-off wigs, and introduced the man on the stage to bring in music books, as an attendant on the commissary. The house was all astonishment, and many began even to doubt of the absolute identity. The doctor, of course, was horribly annoyed; but Foote made money by his impertinency, which was all he cared for. Soon after he proceeded so far as to order wooden figures to be made for a puppet show, of which Dr. Johnson and Oliver Goldsmith were to be the leading characters. Goldsmith affected to laugh, though he was known to speak seriously about the matter to his friends. But the great leviathan of literature was so incensed at the report, as to purchase an immense oak cudgel, which he carried with him to the shop of Tom Davies the bookseller, where Foote frequently called, and being there asked for what purpose it was intended, he sternly replied, "For the castigation of vice upon the stage." This threat having been immediately conveyed to Foote, as it was meant to be, the comedian, it is stated, was really intimidated, and the scheme as to *them* was given up, though other well-known characters continued to be victimized.

SECOND NATURE.

"THE gods do not bestow such a face as Mrs. Siddons's on the stage more than once in a century," says Sydney Smith. "I knew her well, and she had the good taste to laugh at my jokes. She was an excellent person, but she was not remarkable out of her profession, and never got out of tragedy even in common life. She used to *stab* her potatoes; and said, 'Boy, give me a knife!' as she would have said on the stage, 'Give me the dagger!' Many pleasant stories were current at the time about Mrs. Siddons's stately fashion and tragic tone, heard in shops and at dinner-tables. Such was her question to the draper: 'Will it wash?' as though she were speaking to Macbeth about the dreadful bloodstains; her blank verse to the Scotch provost, 'Beef cannot be too salt for me, my lord!' and to an attendant at the dinner-table, 'I asked for porter, boy, and you brought me beer.'"

A SHAKESPEARE ANECDOTE.

THE following anecdote concerning Shakespeare occurs in Harleian MS. 5353, a diary, under date March 13, 1601: —"Upon a time when Burbadge played Richard III., there was a citizen grew so far in liking with him, that before she went from the play she appointed him to come that evening unto her, by the name of Richard III. Shakespeare, overhearing their conclusion, went before, and was entertained before Burbadge came. The message being brought that Richard III. was at the door, Shakespeare caused answer to be made, that William the Conqueror was before Richard III." It was not uncommon at that time for ladies of a certain class to go and sup with the actors. Thus, in Middleton's *Mad World, my Masters* (Act. v. sc. 2), the city madam tells Sir Bounteous, "O' my troth, an I were not married, I could find in my heart to fall in love with that player now, and send for him to a supper."

CHILD'S PLAY.

ORIGINALLY there was a child's character in the play of *Oliver Twist*, that of Little Dick, the sickly pauper-boy, who takes a tearful farewell of Oliver when the latter runs away from the baby farmer. Some thirty years ago, when the play was acted at the Green Street Theatre, Albany, U.S., Howard, the manager, dressed his little daughter Cordelia, four years old, as Dick, and placed her as a "dummy" behind the paling for Oliver to talk to. But when, at the rehearsal, the mother, who impersonated Oliver, went through the scene, the little thing responded just in the proper place, "Good-bye; come again." The parents thereupon thought they would teach her the proper lines, which was done accordingly. Night came, the baby's chubby face was skilfully painted to represent consumption, and, duly clad in her brother's suit, with a small spade in her hand, she made her appearance on the stage. On came the fugitive Oliver, while Cordelia, according to direction, dug vigorously at the pile of earth dumped in a corner. "I'm running away, Dick," said Oliver. "Lunning away, is you?" replied the little thing; then, with a full perception of the character, but with the most self-possessed oblivion of the written words, the child gave in her own language the sense of the scene. "I'll come back and see you some day, Dick," said Oliver. "It yon't be no use, Olly dear," sobbed the baby actress. "When oo tum back, I yon't be digging 'ittle graves; I'll be all dead an' in a 'ittle grave by myself." This in a voice trembling with feigned emotion, yet clear as a bell, and distinctly heard by every person in the building. Actors and actresses were alike affected; Oliver broke down, naturally enough, but Cordelia's reputation and her parents' fortunes were made from that very night.

FRIENDLY ADVICE.

BAUBOURG, who was remarkably ugly, performed the title *rôle* in Racine's *Mithridate*. When Mademoiselle Lecouvreur, in the character of Monimia, addressed to him the words "My lord, you changed countenance," a pitiless wag in the pit exclaimed, "Let him, let him! he can't change for the worse."

AN INTERPOLATION.

STEPHEN KEMBLE had none of the stateliness of his more famous brother John; on the contrary, he was distinguished by a certain pleasant eccentricity. At the Dublin Theatre one night, when he was playing Shylock, he was put out by the constant interruptions of a drunken man in the gallery. He silenced him at last by a ready interpolation. "Until thou canst rail the seal off this bond, thou, *and that noisy fellow up there*, but offend'st thy lungs." This funny rebuke so pleased the neighbours of the noisy individual, that they contrived to keep him quiet for the rest of the night.

MANAGERIAL ELOQUENCE.

ELLISTON was unhappily gifted with a turn for speech-making, which led him, like so many of his brethren, to turn the stage into a rostrum, from which he could communicate his grievances and opinions to the public on every occasion. His biographer, Raymond, has preserved many specimens of his eloquence, among which the following is deliciously "Ellistonian." One evening, too many persons having been admitted to the gallery of the Surrey Theatre, over which he then "reigned," occasioned much altercation, and totally prevented the performers from being heard. Elliston came forward as usual, and thus addressed the audience: "Ladies and gentlemen! I take the liberty of addressing you. It is of rare occurrence that I deem it necessary to place myself in juxtaposition with you. (*Noise in the gallery.*) When I said juxtaposition, I meant *vis-à-vis.* (*Increased noise.*) When I uttered the words *vis-à-vis*, I meant contactability. Now, let me tell you that *vis-à-vis*—it is a French term—and contactability, which is a truly English term, very nearly assimilate to each other. (*The disturbance above redoubled.*) Gentlemen! gentlemen! I am really ashamed of your conduct. It is unlike a Surrey audience. Are you aware that I have in this establishment most efficient peace-officers at my immediate disposal? Peace-officers, gentlemen, mean persons necessary in time of war. One word more. If that tall gentleman in the carpenter's cap will sit down"—pointing to the pit—"the little girl behind him, in red ribbons—you, my love, I mean—will be able to see the entertainment." This oration produced the desired effect, and Elliston, after bowing most respectfully, as he always did when he had made an impudent speech, retired to spend his *afternoon.*

MATHEWS ON THE BENCH.

THE elder Mathews was one day standing among the crowd in a Court of Assize, where Judge Alan Park was presiding. His lordship, perceiving the witty comedian, sent a message down to him, requesting him to come and take a seat on the bench. Mathews obeyed, and the judge was courteously attentive to him. Not long after, Mathews was the guest of his old friend Mr. Rolls, at whose house in Monmouthshire the judge had previously been staying. The actor asked if his lordship had alluded to him. "Yes," said Mr. Rolls, who proceeded to relate how Judge Park had been startled at seeing in court "a fellow" who was in the habit of imitating on the stage the voice and manners of the judges, adding that the presence of Mathews so troubled him that he invited the mimic to sit near him, and behaved so kindly that he hoped the actor, out of simple gratitude, would not include him in his legal portraits in comedy or farce.

THEATRICAL NURSERIES.

IT was formerly not uncommon to have plays acted by children. In 1378, the children of St. Paul's School presented a petition to Richard II., praying him to prohibit some inexpert persons from representing *The History of the Old Testament*, as the said children had been at great expense in order to represent this play publicly at Christmas. The children of St. Paul's continued acting till some time prior to 1591, when their performances, which took place in the singing-room, were suppressed. About 1600, however, they played again, and in *Jack Drum's Entertainment*, published in 1601, the following allusion to them occurs:—

> "I saw the children of Powles last night,
> And, troth, they pleased me pretty, pretty well.
> The apes in time will do it handsomely."

In 1603, the children of the chapel of Queen Elizabeth came to the crown, and were then called Children of her Majesty's Revels. Order was given that they were to be brought up for the purpose of exhibiting "plays and shows" before the queen, and they were authorized to perform at Blackfriars or any other convenient place. This infantine company performed many of Lillo's, Shakespeare's, and Ben Jonson's plays, and there is no doubt that they were that "eyry of children, little eyases that cry out on the top of question" mentioned in Hamlet, and of whose popularity Shakespeare naturally complains.

In Charles II.'s time there seem to have been two distinct seminaries where children were educated for the profession of the stage. One of these stood in Golden Lane, Barbican, and is described in Pennant's *London*, as a row of low houses of singular construction, and, according to the inscription underneath an old print in his possession, had been a nursery for the children of Henry VIII. The same author states that this building was also used as a playhouse in the reign of Elizabeth and James I. This establishment was ridiculed by Dryden in his *Mac Flecnoe:*

> "Near there a Nursery erects its head,
> Where queens are form'd and future heroes bred,
> Where unfledg'd actors learn to laugh and cry,
> Where infant punks their tender voices try,
> And little Maximins the gods defy;
> Great Fletcher never treads in buskins here,
> Nor greater Jonson dares in socks appear."

In the play of the *Rehearsal*, Bayes is made to declare that he will only write for the Nursery, and "mump the proud players" of the regular theatres. Langbaine, the critic, writing in the reign of William III., also tells us that he had seen Chapman's *Revenge for Honour*, acted many years ago at the Nursery, in Barbican.

The other Nursery stood in Hatton Garden. We learn from the Shakespeare's Society's papers that a patent was granted by Charles II., on the 3rd of March, 1664, to Colonel William

Legge, groom of the bed-chamber, giving him the privilege of instituting a Nursery for young actors, but no locality is fixed in the instrument. Perhaps this was the Nursery mentioned by Thomas Killigrew in his diary.

Pepys occasionally mentions the Nursery, without specifying either of these two establishments. On the 24th of February, 1668, the gossiping Clerk of the Acts writes: "To the Nursery, where none of us ever were before. The house is better and the music better than we looked for, and the acting not much worse, because I expected as bad as could be; and I was not much mistaken, for it was so. Here was good company by us, who did make mighty sport at the folly of the acting, which I could not refrain from sometimes, though I was sorry for it." They paid two shillings each at the door, and the money-taker cheated them with adroitness and coolness out of one shilling, Pepys tells us with high glee. It may be added that Joe Haynes, the famous comic actor, was originally a pupil of this establishment. Pepys commends him as "a capital dancer and an understanding fellow." He was then of the king's playhouse.

The idea of a training school for young actors was subsequently revived by Garrick, who organized an "infant school of actors," where children, from their earliest years, were to be trained for the stage and instructed in the histrionic art. The plan made some progress, if it was unattended by important results. In December, 1756, Garrick produced at Drury Lane his farce of *Lilliput*, founded upon the first book of *Gulliver's Travels.* "The piece," says Murphy, "was acted by boys and girls, all tutored by the manager, and the parents of not less than a hundred were most liberally rewarded." He adds that the author had, further, a moral object in view: he hoped that "at the sight of such diminutive creatures adopting the follies of real life, the fashionable world would learn to lower their pride, and the dignity of vice would be lost." It is not to be believed, however, that Garrick laid much stress upon the didactic quality of the production. *Lilliput* was excellently represented by the children, we are told, and was frequently repeated. Yet only two of the young pupils of Garrick's seminary became afterwards known to fame, and took rank among the mature members of the company. Cautherley, whom the world considered a son of Garrick's, acquired some favour at a later date, in George Barnwell and suchlike parts; also Miss Jane Pope, whose successful career upon the stage commenced thus early, and did not terminate till the year 1808.

A CURIOUS RELIC.

FRANCIS BLISSETT, the Bath actor, was quite an eccentric, but his eccentricities were harmless. William Dimond and he originally tramped unto the city of Bath together, and by the time they had reached it they were nearly barefooted. When Dimond, in after days, had become the director of the theatre, and Blissett himself was in prosperous circumstances, the latter invited his manager to a little entertainment at his lodgings, and in the course of the evening observed that this was the anniversary of their entering Bath together. "And now, friend, I'll introduce you to a couple of old acquaintances." Saying this, he produced a pair of old shoes, literally worn through. "See, here they are," cried he, "the only friends I had at that time, save yourself. They bore me safely here, and I shall keep them till I die. I could almost wish to be buried in those shoes."

FOOTE'S SENTIMENT.

IF Foote ever had a serious regard for any one, it was for Holland; yet, after his friend's funeral, he violated all decency concerning him. Holland was the son of a baker at Hampton, and on the stage was a close imitator of Garrick, who had such a respect for him that he played "the ghost" to his "Hamlet," merely to serve him at his benefit.

Holland died rather young, and Foote attended as one of the mourners. He was really grieved, and his eyes were swollen with tears; yet, when an acquaintance said to him in the evening, "So, Foote, you have been attending the funeral of your dear friend Holland?" the latter smilingly replied, "Yes, we have shoved the little baker into his last oven."

A DOUBTFUL COMPLIMENT.

MR. TERNAN, a good actor and an estimable man about half a century ago, on one occasion played Jaffir, in the now shelved drama of *Venice Preserved*, and also a character in the pantomime on the same evening, in some town in the north. The next morning, as he was walking down the High Street, he was accosted by one of the shopkeepers. "Oh, Mr. Ternan, I was delighted with your play last night!" "I am glad to hear you say so," replied Ternan, rubbing his hands with satisfaction. "And, pray, which portion did you like best?" "Why, the way in which you swallowed that bucket of water, and the manner in which you writhed and wriggled when they pumped it up again from your stomach couldn't be equalled." "There is a sort of compliment," wrote Douglas Jerrold in one of his comedies, "which comes upon a man like a cannon-ball," of which certainly this might be considered an example. It was an occurrence in the pantomime the shopkeeper had most admired, not the character of Jaffir, which was one of Ternan's favourite parts.

THE VOICE OF MERCY.

CHARLOTTE CUSHMAN, the American actress, when starring it in the old country, played for some nights in Dublin. She gives some anecdotes about the Irish in her *Life Letters and Memories*, among which the following. One night a sudden disturbance occurred among the gods, and could not be easily quieted. Of course the pit took the matter in hand: much wit was bandied about, up and down, and, as in old pagan times, a victim was demanded. "Throw him over! throw him over!" resounded from all sides. Suddenly, in a lull of the confusion, a delicate female voice was heard exclaiming, in dulcet tones, "Oh no, don't throw him over; *kill him where he is.*"

INAPPROPRIATE.

FOR the following Charles Dibdin is responsible. In his *Complete History of the English Stage*, he casts a glance at the sacred dramas anciently performed in Spain, and remarks, "We have gone yet but a little way towards this on our stage. In action we have, to be sure, now and then introduced Noah's ark, Solomon's Temple, Heaven, Hell, and other similar objects; and held up Moses, Aaron, and David as freemasons. But in our oratorios we come on pretty well. *The Messiah*, *The Redemption*, and such familiar titles, by way of companions to *The Tarantula*, and *The Cabinet of Monkeys*, are sported against all the blind walls in town. I remember in one of these sacred dramas, as they are facetiously called, which had for its title *The Ascension*, that in the moment our Saviour is supposed gradually to disappear, 'to soft music,' the orchestra in a most lively style struck up 'Deil take the Wars that hurried Willy from me.' This charming production was performed but once."

FOR THE MERIDIAN OF CAPPADOCIA.

THOMAS CORNEILLE'S drama *Laodicea* did not succeed so well as his former plays had done, at which the author could not help expressing his astonishment. "Why," said he to a friend, "the scene lies in Cappadocia, and I am sure I have pictured the manner of that people to the life." "That is the reason, perhaps," replied the friend, "why it is not relished in France. I'll tell you what to do. Send it to Cappadocia to be performed."

SLEEPING LIKE A HUMMING-TOP.

WHEN Bath still basked in the noontide of fashion, a Captain Stanley was a constant visitor there. The captain, from the rotundity of his figure and the roseate blush of his nose, bore the convivial nickname of the "Bath Bacchus." He was a habitué of the theatre, but, however great his gratification or sympathy, he could not at all times command his senses, and would fall asleep—a fact which was soon obvious to the whole of the audience, by the melody which the captain performed with his nose. One evening, the play being Shakespeare's *Twelfth Night*, when Orsino said—

> "That strain again;—it had a dying fall:
> Oh, it came o'er my ear like the sweet sound
> That breathes upon a bank of violets."

the captain replied with such a shrill blast to this invitation that he disconcerted the actor, and plunged the house in a convulsion of merriment.

A SECOND-HAND LEG OF MUTTON.

SPILLER, passing one day through Rag Fair, a noted quarter for the sale of second-hand articles, cheapened a leg of mutton, for which the butcher asked him two shillings. "No," said the comic, "I can't afford to give you two shillings for a second-hand leg of mutton, when I can buy a new one in Clare market for half a crown."

THE LIGHT FANTASTIC TOE.

LEGRAND PERROT was a celebrated dancer, who figured for some time as ballet master in Covent Garden during the latter end of the last century. His pride, presumption, and obstinacy were phenomenal. At a ballet in Vienna he only chose to appear in the last act, and when the emperor sent him a request to appear earlier in the performance, he answered the aide-camp, "that men of talent never made themselves too cheap." The emperor instantly left the theatre, followed by the court. Perrot, on being informed of this, stepped forward and thus addressed his *corps-de-ballet*: "My children, now we will dance for our own pleasure, not for that of the emperor." Strange as it may appear, the emperor forgave the insult, and when Perrot's engagement was finished, sent him a golden snuff-box, with his portrait set in brilliants. Perrot was under the hands of his hair-dresser when the present was delivered to him. He took it in a careless manner, looked at it, then broke the glass over the miniature with his thumb, and gave the box to his hair-dresser, saying, "That is the way I dispose of baubles sent to me by men I do not think worthy of my friendship." The moment after he was in his post-chaise, and was just able to make his escape from the imperial dominions, being closely pursued by a detachment of hussars sent in pursuit of the insolent fugitive.

ILL TO PLEASE.

G. F. COOKE once playing Shylock when intoxicated was much hissed; two nights after, he was advertised for Richard, but did not appear at all. On his next performance, he was received with much disapprobation, when he turned to Claremont, and said, "On Monday I was drunk, but appeared, and they didn't like that. On Wednesday I was drunk, so I didn't appear, and they don't like that. What the devil would they have?"

A LUCKY FALL.

DURING George Colman the Elder's management, a gallery visitor, in his eagerness to obtain a front seat, fell into the pit. The poor fellow broke his leg, and was conveyed instantly to a neighbouring surgeon's, when the broken limb was set. Colman humanely supported him during his illness, and, when recovered, sent him a small present. The man waited on the manager to express his gratitude. Colman received him with great good nature, and presented him with a free ticket for life to the pit, saying, "I give you this, on condition that you promise never to enter the pit again in the same manner as you did the last time."

THE SORROWS OF A MANAGER.

THE fag end of the season of a metropolitan theatre is not the most pleasing period of the year for a manager. Ducrow once from the bottom of his wounded heart gave the following graphic discription of it, which for choice, high-coloured language equals Zola:—"I don't know how you find it," he complained to a brother manager, "but as soon as I once announce the last few nights of the season, the beggars begin to show their *h*airs. I went into the theatre th' other night, and seeing a prime little roasting pig on a nice white napkin in the hall, I told 'em to take it up to Mrs. D. The fellow said it warn't for me—'twas for Mr. Roberts, who's the chap as orders the corn, and I'm the chap as pays for it; so he gets the pig, and I don't. Then those —— carpenters sneak in of a morning, with their hands in their breeches pockets, doubled up as if they had got the cholera; and at night they march out as upright as grenadiers, 'cause every one on 'em has got a deal plank at his back, up his coat. Then the supernumeraries carry out each a lump of coal in his hat, and, going round the corner, club their priggings together, and make the best part of a chaldron of it. As to the riders, they come into rehearsal gallows-grand, 'cause they have had all the season a precious deal better salary than they were worth; and at night they come in gallows-drunk, from having had a good dinner for once in their lives, and, forgetting that they may want to come back another year, they are as saucy as a bit of Billingsgate."

WHO SHOT COCK ROBIN?

A HUMOROUS circumstance was connected with one of the first representations of *Guillaume Tell* at Drury Lane. During the rehearsals, Braham proved so indifferent a toxophilite in the celebrated trial to which Tell is subjected, that at the representation the arrow had to be discharged by a skilful hand behind the scenes, Braham covering the party, and receiving the approbation due to another. On one occasion the shaft accidentally missed the apple, and Braham, finding the audience disposed to a titter, threw them in a loud roar by advancing to the foot-lights and saying, "Ladies and gentlemen, it wasn't *I* who shot at the apple."

AN EXPEDITIOUS PLAYWRIGHT.

NO dramatist, certainly, has ever produced so many theatrical pieces of one kind and another as Lopez de Vega. His dramatic works form twenty-six volumes, exclusive of four hundred religious plays. What is still more surprising, we have his own authority for the fact that his printed works formed the least part of his productions. According to accurate computation, this author is calculated to have penned 22,316,000 verses, and so extraordinary was the quickness of his fancy, that his usual time of writing a play was twenty-four hours : some of his comedies he completed in less than four hours. No wonder that he accumulated competence by his pen, and was able to leave a sum of 150,000 ducats.

WHO'S TO GO?

AT Sadlers Wells Theatre one evening during Mr. Phelps's management, the house was very full and very noisy, and there was every appearance of the performance going off in a dumb show. Just before the time for the curtain to go up, there were loud cries from the gallery of "Phelps! Phelps!" After a little delay, the green baize was drawn back, and Mr. Phelps, dressed for his part, came forward. Advancing to the foot-lights with folded arms, and looking up to the gallery very firmly, he called out, "What is it you want?" "Too full! too full!" shouted a dozen voices. "Well," answered Phelps, "why don't some of you go out?" This seemed to take the gods by surprise, for there was no response. Mr. Phelps thereupon retired, the curtain went up, and no more was heard of "too full."

MR. DIDDLER'S SONG.

WHEN Lord William Lennox was on his father's staff at Quebec, amateur theatricals were got up in that garrison, the play being Kennedy's comedy of *Raising the Wind.* Lord William acted Jeremy Diddler, and in that character was desirous of giving the song of "My Beautiful Maid," which ought to be introduced at the opening scene of the second act. Unfortunately, his lordship could not turn a tune; but one of the amateurs, Mr. Tolfrey, who acted Hardcastle, was a splendid singer, and it was agreed that he should sing the song in question. For this purpose, the supper-table was placed quite at the back of the stage, and Lord William's "double" was to sing through a slit made in the scenes behind which he was standing. All went off well. Lord William moved his mouth as if he was singing. He was rapturously applauded, and even encored. Thinking that Jerry's voice was still in waiting, the company at the supper-table joined, saying, "Bravo, Mr. Diddler! pray sing that song again." Jeremy bowed, placed himself in a singing attitude, and waited for the first note; but no notes were forthcoming. Mr. Tolfrey, after finishing his song, had retired. Nothing was left for Jeremy but to apologize to the audience. So, approaching the foot-lights, he thanked the public for the applause, begging them to excuse his not repeating the song, as he had "lost his voice," and then returned to his seat. Whilst he was still acknowledging the "bravos," he found to his surprise that his voice had returned. Tolfrey had been summoned, and began the song again. Although a little flustered at this unexpected recovery, Lord William soon gained his presence of mind, opened his mouth, and successfully carried out the deception.

"A TIME FOR SORROW."

MRS. HANNAH BRAND, the eccentric actress, wrote a tragedy, *Agmunda*, in 1794, which was acted the last night of the season and condemned off hand. At one of its rehearsals at the Haymarket Theatre, when she acted the principal part, she made a pause of considerable length. When the whole company was "in amazement lost," Hannah turned majestically round, and, in blank-verse tone, observed to the prompter, "Observe, Mr. Warren, I have stopped thus long that you may remember at night, *all this length of time I shall be weeping*."

QUAINT APPEAL.

LINTON, a musician belonging to the orchestra of Covent Garden Theatre, was murdered in the beginning of this century by footpads, who were afterwards discovered and executed. A play was given for the benefit of his widow and children, on which occasion the following quaint appeal appeared in the *Morning Herald*, on the day preceding the performance :—

"THEATRE ROYAL, COVENT GARDEN.

"*For the Benefit of Mrs. Linton, etc.*

"'The widow,' said Charity, whispering me in the ear, 'must have your mite. Wait upon her with a guinea, and purchase a box-ticket.'

"'You may have one for five shillings,' observed Avarice, pulling me by the sleeve.

"My hand was in my pocket, and the guinea, which was between my finger and thumb, slipped out.

"'Yes,' said I, 'she shall have my five shillings.'

"'Good heavens!' exclaimed Justice, 'what are you about? Five shillings! If you pay but five shillings for going into the theatre, then you get value received for your money.'

"'And I shall owe him no thanks,' added Charity, laying her hand upon my heart, and leading me on the way to the widow's house.

"Taking the knocker in my left hand, my whole frame trembled. Looking round, I saw Avarice turn the corner of the street, and I found all the money in my pocket grasped in my hand.

"'Is your mother at home, my dear?' said I to a child, who conducted me into a parlour.

"'Yes,' answered the infant; 'but my father has not been at home for a great while. That is his harpsichord, and that is his violin: he used to play on them for me.'

"'Shall I play you a tune, my boy?' said I.

"'No, sir,' answered the boy, 'my mother will not let them be touched; for since my father went abroad, music makes her cry, and then we all cry.'

"I looked at the violin—it was unstrung.

"I touched the harpsichord—it was out of tune.

"Had the lyre of Orpheus sounded in my ear, it could not have insinuated to my heart thrills of sensibility equal to what I felt.

"It was the spirit in unison with the flesh.

"'I hear my mother on the stairs,' said the boy.

"I shook him by the hand. 'Give her this, my lad,' said I, and left the house.

"It rained. I called a coach, drove to a coffee-house, but, not having a farthing in my pocket, borrowed a shilling at the bar."

SARAH BERNHARDT'S PHOTO.

SARAH BERNHARDT, suffering one day from what on the Continent is called "the spleen," attired herself in a shroud, and, with her hair undone, laid down in her famous coffin, an elegant piece of cabinet-work made of black ebony, and comfortably padded with white satin. She closed her eyes, opened her mouth, and requested an aristocratic friend to play a *Miserere* on the organ. Not content with this, she caused a number of tapers to be lit, and sent for her bosom friend, Louise Abbema. This celebrated artist was requested to assume the garb of a nun, and to kneel beside the coffin as in prayer, whilst in the background Sarah's servants were grouped, some praying, others in attitudes of despair. Liebert, the photographer, was then ordered to call with his apparatus, and to take a photograph of the scene, which was so ghastly that when young Maurice, Sarah's son, happened to enter unexpectedly, he fell forthwith in a swoon. This anecdote is related in one of the last numbers of the "*Neue Musik Zeitung*," which paper vouches for the truth as derived from one of its most trustworthy Paris correspondents.

UNCALLED FOR.

DURING forty years the sallies of Frédéric Lemaitre were a common topic of conversation in the *cafés* of the Boulevard du Temple. Like many of his colleagues, he had an insatiable craving for applause. In 1847, at one of the last representations of his famous Robert Macaire, contrary to his expectation, he was not called before the curtain at the end of the piece. Greatly disappointed, he ordered the curtain to be drawn, and, after making his bow to the public, inquired if M. Auguste was not there. M. Auguste did not answer, and the audience looked astonished. "Is Mr. Antoine here, perhaps?" inquired the imperturbable comedian. Receiving no answer, he continued, "Well, gentlemen, it is evident that I have been imposed upon by the chief and the deputy chief of the *claque*. I paid them forty francs this morning, to be called before the curtain, and neither of them is here. You see, gentlemen, I have been *done*." Roars of laughter and a volley of applause rewarded the actor for his impudence.

TOO MUCH OF A GOOD THING.

WHEN Incledon was engaged at the Bath Theatre, he one day went to Frome with some friends, where after a merry dinner they went to the theatre, where they pretty well filled the boxes. Recognizing some acquaintance among the actors, Incledon went behind the scenes, and directly after volunteered a song. This was a high treat to the pit and gallery, but his friends in the boxes were bent on fun. They encored him twice, and brought him on the stage for the fourth time. He now perceived their intention, and, making a low bow, addressed them as follows :—"Gentlemen, I sang this song for the first time to please my friends behind the scene, the second to please the public, the third to please yourselves ; but if I sing it again, may I be——" stopping as if to meditate a terrific oath. "What?" shouted a dozen voices. "Why, I'll whisper you, gentlemen, when I come round." And with these words he returned to the boxes.

A POCKETFUL OF WIT.

COLMAN the elder and Harris had a quarrel at Covent Garden Theatre one day, when Billy Bates was standing by. Colman, disdaining a war of words, walked out of the house ; and Harris, bouncing about the stage, exclaimed, "A little impudent rascal! I'd a good mind to double him up and put him in my pocket." "Then," observed Bates, "you'd have more wit in your pocket than you ever had in your head, a great deal."

A PHYSICAL IMPOSSIBILITY.

NANINE, a comedy taken from Richardson's "*Pamela,*" was put upon the French stage by Voltaire, and was a great success. The poet Piron pretended not to like it—perhaps did not like it, for Heaven knows it is dull enough. He told Voltaire so, who asked why he did not hiss it. "It was impossible," replied Piron ; "a man cannot hiss and yawn at the same time."

ENGLISH PLAYERS IN PARIS.

THE first English dramatic company which appeared in Paris during the present century, was under the management of Penley. They made their *début* on July 30, 1822, at the Porte St. Martin Theatre, with *Othello*. But the Parisian public at that time was as much excited against the English, as the London public had been against some supposed French, but in reality Swiss, dancers, who appeared in a ballet entitled *The Chinese Festival*, in the reign of George III. The interruptions, the jokes, the abuse levelled at Barlow, an actor of considerable talent, completely stopped the piece. The Moor was treated with greater indignity in Paris than of yore in Venice; he was obliged to address "the most potent, grave, and reverend seigniors" in dumb show. Towards the third act the noise became unbearable. Boxing matches took place in various parts of the pit; the stage was invaded, and the actors, unable to maintain the unequal conflict, beat a retreat. It is surprising that a second attempt should have been made, yet such was the case. *The School for Scandal*, given on the following night, was not better received. All sorts of projectiles—potatoes, eggs, coppers, and clay pipes—were thrown at the unfortunate actors. Miss Gaskill was well-nigh blinded by one of the weighty copper two-penny pieces then in use, thrown at her by a gallant Gaul with such force that she fainted. A squad of gendarmes was then drawn up on the stage. They were assailed with broken seats and benches, whilst a man took a drum from the orchestra and beat the charge. The audience prepared to storm the stage, when the officer commanded his men to prime and load, threatening to fire should the tumult continue. This brought the rioters to their senses, but the play was discontinued, and the company left the unhospitable capital of civilization.

Five years elapsed before another English company ventured

across the Channel to try its fortunes. It was under the management of Abbott, and comprised some of the greatest actors of the day—Charles Kemble, Edmund Kean, and Macready. Among the actresses were the beautiful Harriet Smithson, who eventually became the wife of Hector Berlioz, the celebrated composer, and Maria Foote. This lady, who in London was little appreciated, and, on account of her Irish accent, generally condemned to "walking ladies," became after crossing the water at once a star of the first magnitude. They performed at the Salle Favart. Among the plays acted were *The Rivals*, *Fortune's Frolics*, *She Stoops to Conquer*, and *Love, Law, and Physic.* In October, 1827, this company acted at the Odeon *Macbeth*, *Jane Shore*, and *The Stranger*. Their last night was July 25, 1828. The elder Dumas records the immense impression made on him by this first sight of real passions, moving men of flesh and blood. It opened beyond him new ranges of vision, and contributed in a great measure to the triumph of the new romantic over the old unreal, pedantic, classic school of drama.

The third English company visited Paris in 1846, but it was not more successful than the one which went over during the Exhibition of 1855. Charles Mathews made two appearances in the French capital. He went over in 1863, and acted at the Variétés in *L'Anglais Timide*, a French play adapted by himself from *Coöl as a Cucumber.* His success was so great that he returned two years later to play *L'Homme Blasé*, taken from *Used Up.* Four years later, in August, 1867, Mr. Sothern, as Lord Dundreary, drew fair houses for twenty consecutive nights in the same theatre.

GARRICK EXTINGUISHED.

GARRICK was once on a visit at Mr. Rigby's seat, Mistley Hall, Essex, when Dr. Gough formed one of the party. Observing the potent appetite of the learned doctor, Garrick indulged in some unbecoming jests on the occasion, to the great amusement of some of the company. When the laugh had subsided, the butt of Garrick's wit thus addressed the party: "Gentlemen, you must doubtless suppose, from the extreme familiarity with which Mr. Garrick thought fit to treat me, that I am an acquaintance of his; but I can assure you that, till I met him here, I never saw him but once before, and then I paid five shillings for the sight." No more jokes from Mr. Garrick that night.

A COLLISION WITH A COMET.

MISS SARAH BOOTH, the golden-haired beauty (she wore a wig), rehearsing Priscilla Tomboy to Mr. Heathcote, a provincial actor and play-writer, took great pains to instruct him in the business and tricks she intended to introduce. When she had concluded, Heathcote calmly said, "Miss Booth, I feel much obliged by the trouble you have taken, but I am sure I shall not be able to remember above half what you've told me." Once more with exemplary patience the star repeated the sitting on the chairs, the making of cat's cradles, etc., but at night poor Heathcote forgot it all. Either to fill up the scene or from the influence of anger, Miss Booth gave the forgetful actor a sounding box on the ear. "These London actresses won't do for me," subsequently remarked Heathcote. "I may be stage-struck or moon-struck, but I'll never be *star*-struck again."

AN UNEXPECTED ARRIVAL.

ON Friday, December 24, 1814, *The Stranger* was performed for the benefit of Charles Kemble. During the fourth act, Mrs. Cruse, who performed Mrs. Haller, appeared much agitated. The audience attributed it to the pathetic nature of the character, and applauded her highly. When, however, the bell rang for the fifth act, they were informed that Mrs. Cruse was very seriously indisposed, and the character was finished by another actress. In the interim, Mrs. Cruse was delivered of a child in the ladies' dressing-room. Only the night before, she had played Juliet.

THE TEMPTER.

RYLEY relates, in his voluminous *Memoirs of a Strolling Actor*, that as manager Hall was strutting one night at Taunton through the part of Castalio, an apple-woman happened to come to the theatre for the first time of her life to hawk her wares. One of the company, Jonathan Davis, a wag, directed her attention to the unfortunate manager, "who, he was sure," he said, "wanted some fruit, and was at that moment beckoning her to him." The apple-woman readily believed it, and just as Castalio was closing his grand soliloquy about the fall of mankind—

> "To his temptations lewdly she inclin'd,
> And for a paltry apple. . . ."

she walked on the stage, and, dropping a curtsey, said, "Do you want any apples, sir?" The disconcerted manager ran off, threatening vengeance; but the audience derived more amusement from this ludicrous circumstance than any acting could have afforded.

A GERMAN DESDEMONA.

ON one occasion Edwin Forrest was playing an engagement out West. The company was limited in numbers, and the leading actress, a lady of German extraction, had not as yet entirely mastered the English language; nor had she the least idea of the characters, particularly those of Shakespeare, in which she appeared. On the occasion of Forrest's playing Othello, this lady, of course, took Desdemona. Forrest's description of this performance, as frequently told when he was "in the humour," was rich beyond expression, exaggerated to a certain extent, yet, he said, the main features were strictly true. In the scene where she is called upon to corroborate Othello's story of love, and his whole course of wooing, when the father says—

> "Come hither, gentle mistress.
> Do you perceive in all this noble company
> Where most you owe obedience?"

she interpreted Shakespeare thus:

> "My noble fader, I do see here many peoples:
> You are my fader, I owe you much duty,
> Mine life, and education, and all dese things.
> But dare is mine husband, dat black man;
> I likes him de most, I prefers him to all de time. Ha! ha!"

So saying, she made a rush at the Moor, and nearly upset him; she clung to him, uttering "ha! ha!" The audience was delighted, for the actress was a great favourite.

A REFRACTORY AUDIENCE.

ON the 12th of April, 1819, the tragedy *The Italians*, by Charles Bucke—a piece damned off hand on the first night—was placed upon the boards for the second and last time. The galleries were all but deserted, the boxes and dress-circle in as sorry a condition, and the pit about half-full of people, who appeared to have come to enjoy an anticipated "row." The management, dispirited by the inauspicious aspect of affairs, brought the play to an abrupt termination with the third act. The groundlings declared that, having paid their money, they were determined to see the piece throughout. Thereupon Stephen Kemble released the hose from its privacy, carried it up into the gallery, and deluged the refractory play-goers with copious streams of water. Another moment, and a number of umbrellas were put up by way of protection, and the picture presented by the rushing water, the flapping umbrellas, and the noisy cries and gesticulations of the audience was most comical. More reasonable means eventually prevailed, and the solitary and dripping few turned their backs to the stage.

"TIME OUT OF JOINT."

THE naif anachronisms of the old plays are sometimes most amusing. In *Candlemas Day; or, The Killing of the Children of Israel*, written in 1512, the soldiers swear by Mahound or Mahomet; Herod's messenger is named Watkin, and the knights are directed to walk about the stage, while Mary and the Infant are conveyed into Eygpt. There is another play treating the same subject, *The Massacre of the Holy Innocents*, which forms part of a sacred drama represented by the English fathers at the famous Council of Constance, in 1417. Here a buffoon of Herod's court is introduced, who desires of his lord to be dubbed a knight, that he may be qualified "to go on the adventure" of killing the children of Bethlehem. This tragical business was represented on the stage. The good women of Bethlehem gave the knight-errant a warm reception with their distaffs, which they broke over his head, called him a coward and a disgrace to chivalry, and sent him home to Herod with much ignominy.

WONDERFUL TRANSFORMATIONS.

TOWARDS the end of the seventeenth century, an English traveller and critic witnessed some transformations on the stage in Italy, which showed an ingenuity and magnificence which our most gorgeous performances have never surpassed, even in the present day. In his comparison between the French and Italian music, he relates that at the Teatro Capranica, in Rome, there was the ghost of a woman surrounded by guards. This phantom, extending her arms and unfolding her clothes, was, with one motion, transformed into a perfect palace, with its front, its wings, body, and courtyard.

The guards, striking their halberts on the stage, were immediately turned into so many waterworks, cascades, and trees, that formed a charming garden before the palace. At the same theatre was given the interior of hell, in the opera of *Nerone Infante*. Here part of the stage opened, and discovered a scene underneath representing several caves full of infernal spirits, that flew about, discharging fire and smoke ; on another side, the river of Lethe and Charon's boat. On the shore of this river a prodigious monster appeared, whose mouth, opening to the great horror of the spectators, covered the front wings of the remaining part of the stage. Within his jaws was discovered a throne of fire on which Pluto sat, surrounded by a multitude of snakes. After a while the monster expanding its wings, began to move slowly towards the audience. Under its body appeared a great multitude of devils, who formed themselves into a ballet, and, their dancing finished, disappeared one after the other into the floor. All at once the gigantic monster was transformed into an innumerable quantity of large white butterflies, which flew all over the pit, so low that some of them touched the hats of the spectators, till at length they disappeared. During this occurrence, which sufficiently employed the eyes of the spectators, the stage was refitted, and the scene changed into a beautiful garden, with which the third act commenced. We do not wonder, when the author adds that "numbers of strangers came from a distance to see this performance."

A SENSATIONAL PIECE.

GEORGE DUVAL relates, in his *Souvenirs de la Terreur*, that when Saint Fargeau, the Deputy, had been murdered in January, 1793, a splendid funeral was organized in honour of this victim of royalist vengeance, and his daughter was adopted by the Convention. "Moreover, in order to bestow every kind of homage on this martyr of liberty, a ballad was composed, in which his assassination was sung to the tune of the canticle of St. Roch. The murder was also made the subject of an opera represented on the stage of the Théâtre Italien. There I had the pleasure of hearing the impersonator of the victim warble songs, duets, and solos, the chorus being formed by a score of assassins, whom the composer of this *comical* opera had brought together to slay the theatrical Deputy. Their costumes and faces were enough to make one shudder."

WITCHERY.

DURING the production of *Faust* in the Albany Theatre, U.S., in 1872, Lottie Angus, a very pretty super, had a narrow escape. It was in the temptation scene, where a beautiful witch appears, clad in—well, there was a little gauze floating about her person, and she had tiny rose-satin slippers on. This reminiscence of St. Anthony was attended with a display of fireworks, and the diaphanous drapery of the fair tempter caught fire. For a moment the audience were treated to a sensation not on the bills, but the Faust of the evening was equal to the situation. Comprehending the danger, with one sweep of his long arm he tore the burning drapery from the frightened girl, and she sprang behind the scenes, apparently unharmed and certainly—undressed. The next night she was not so fortunate. Contrary to the order of the manager, fireworks were again used. Her drapery again caught fire, and this time it was said she was very severely burned.

RIVAL THUNDER.

WHILST KEAN was manager of the Princess's, Mr. Boucicault produced a drama entitled *The Vampire*. The opening scene represented the highest regions of the Alps by moonlight, whilst a storm of thunder and lightning was raging. The Vampire (Boucicault) was seen lying dead on a mountain-peak, and as the ray of the moon touches his body he returns to life. The thunder-claps were produced at given signals by the carpenter up in the flies. One night in the height of the season, a tremendous clap startled the audience, and interrupted the Vampire in the middle of a speech. "Very well, Mr. Davids," said he, looking up at the flies, in a voice to be heard by the thunderer, but not by the audience; "you are making more mistakes. That clap of thunder came in the wrong place." Davids, bawling to the monster, replied, "No fault of mine, sir; it wasn't my thunder. Thunder's real out of doors; perhaps you can stop it there."

RESERVED SEATS.

RESERVED seats were unknown till 1829. Up to the end of the eighteenth century, people who wished to secure a good place had no alternative but to come hours before the play commenced, or to send somebody to take a seat for them, and keep it by the simple but effectual plan of sitting in it. This primitive custom was, no doubt, of old standing. It is alluded to by Pepys who occasionally used to engage a street boy to occupy a seat for him till he came. But families who were in possession of livery servants sent these in order to secure places. In the prologue to Cartell's tragic-comedy of *Arviragus*, 1672, Dryden writes, begging the public to support rather the English than the French performers, who were then visiting London—

"And therefore, messieurs, if you'll do us grace,
Send lacqueys early to preserve your place."

In 1732, when Covent Garden opened, the bill set out—"All persons who want places are desired to send to the stage-door (the passage from Bow Street leading to it), where attendance will be given, and places kept for the following nights as usual."

Here was improvement. Seats could be taken beforehand; but when once taken, had to be occupied from the commencement of the play. This little suited the taste of the leaders of fashion, for it was "ton" to come late and enter the house with considerable bustle and noise. In Fielding's farce, *Miss Lucy in Town*, 1742, when the country-bred lady inquires of Mrs. Tawdrey about the manners of the fine London ladies at the playhouse, she is answered, "Why, if they can they take a stage-box where they let the footman sit for the first two acts, to show his livery." So it continued in Garrick's time, when the following advertisement appeared at the bottom of each playbill on any benefit of consequence :—"Part of the pit will be railed into the boxes, and, for the better accommodation of the ladies, the stage will be formed into an amphitheatre where servants will be allowed to keep places." And when, in 1744, Garrick took his benefit at Drury Lane, the play, *Hamlet*, was to begin at six, and in the bills of the day ladies were requested "to send their servants *by three o'clock.*

Such a practice would now be considered an intolerable nuisance; but people in those days were less squeamish, and appear to have thought nothing of sitting for an act or two cheek by jowl with a lacquey, or even with a street Arab such as Pepys was wont to recruit for the purpose. And the conduct of these "placemen" appears frequently to have been most objectionable. In the *Weekly Register* for March 25, 1732, it is remarked, "The theatre should be esteemed the centre of politeness and good manners, yet numbers of footmen every evening loll over the boxes, while they keep places for their masters, with their hats on, play over their airs, take snuff, laugh aloud, adjust their cock's-combs, or hold dialogues with their brethren from one side of the house to the other."

"Placekeepers," however, could not assert the right to a seat for their employers beyond the end of the first act. If by that time the rightful owner for the night had not made his appearance, the proxy had to evacuate the seat, and make room for his betters. Hence curious mistakes sometimes arose. Angelo relates, in his *Reminiscences*, how the Duke of Norfolk one night went to Drury Lane Theatre, accompanied by the editor of a certain paper, and took seats in the front rows of the boxes. Neither having what Angelo calls "the exterior garb of people of condition," a gentleman behind at the commencement of the second act, tapped the duke on the shoulder, and told him that it was time to decamp, he being desirous of having the front seat.

Towards the end of the last century seats could be booked beforehand, but still on condition of occupation before the end of the first act, after which the right was forfeited. An amusing instance of the difficulties playgoers had to face in those days is told by Miss Seward, who, wishing to hear Mrs. Siddons, in 1782, could not get seats: "A gentleman of Mr. Barugh's train accidentally popped us, before the play began, into places a man was keeping in the fifth row of the front boxes, on our promise of retiring if they were claimed before the first act was over, after which we should, by the rule of the house, have a right to keep them. Our stars fought for us, the act was over, the box-keeper retired with a shilling reward for not bustling us, and in a second the people who had taken the places claimed them. Vain was their claim; our beaux asserted our right to keep them, and keep them we did."

LEAR'S MOP-ING.

AT one time Macready opened at Nottingham with *King Lear*. The property-man received his plot for the play in the usual manner, a map—perhaps rather anachronistically—being required among the many articles for Lear to divide his kingdom by. The property-man, whose education had been somewhat neglected, read *mop* for *map*. At the proper time, Macready, in full state on his throne, calls for his map, when a "super" noble gravely entered and, kneeling down, presented the aged king with a bran-new white curly mop. The astounded tragedian rushed off the stage, under immense laughter, dragging the unfortunate nobleman and his mop with him, whilst actors and audience were wild with delight.

THE PANTOMIME AT THE ANTIPODES.

SOME years since, during the run of the pantomime at the Theatre Royal, Melbourne, the clown, a native of Victoria, took his benefit. The public on this occasion were regaled with a grand procession, in which the *bénéficiaire* was drawn across the stage "by a magnificent team"—so said the advertisement—of twenty-four tom cats. The effect certainly was comical, for one poor tom would pull one way, and one another, and the triumphant march played by the orchestra was almost drowned by the terrific caterwauling of the Thomas cats. A long rope had been fastened to the triumphal car, in which the clown was seated; to this rope the unfortunate cats were attached, and the end of it carried to the other side of the stage. Thus toms, car, and clown were hauled across, to the delight of the laughter-shrieking audience.

A SUCCESSFUL PLAY.

BELLOY'S mediocre drama, *Le Siège de Calais*, had an extraordinary success, owing to its being the first purely historical French play. With great art and management, the dramatist had contrived to make not only the times which he pourtrayed resemble the times in which he wrote, but the personages also were portraits of living celebrities. The Marshal de Brissac was aimed at in one of the principal characters of this piece, and was delighted with the distinction. One evening, meeting Brizard, the actor who impersonated this part, he exclaimed, "Brizard, if you should happen to be ill some night, just make your comrades let me know, and I'll play your part." Concerning this play, it may be added that during its successful run De Belloy was almost nightly called before the curtain, when the whole house received him with deafening cries of "Long live the king and M. de Belloy." The Siege of Calais was performed in every town throughout France. The inhabitants of Calais presented the author with a gold box, and placed his portrait in the Hotel de Ville; the military voted him their thanks, from the generals down to the rank and file; and the celebrated Count d'Estaing caused the drama to be printed at St. Domingo, and distributed gratis through all the French West Indian Islands. Yet, after all these freaks of French patriotism, this once famous play is now utterly forgotten and sent to limbo.

VALUABLE ASSISTANCE.

ANDREW JACKSON ALLEN, a subordinate actor who travelled with Edwin Forrest on his professional tour as his "costumer," possessed a patent for the manufacture of gold and silver leather, much used upon stage costume. On one occasion, at some festival given to Forrest, Allen was present, and becoming very loquacious, the great tragedian said, "Come, come, Allen, you had better go home and attend to your silver leather." At this remark "the great American costumer," as he styled himself, rose up indignant, and, banging his hat upon his head, stammered out, "B—B—what ud your Bacbeth or Richard be bidout by silber leather." An impediment in Allen's speech, and his indignant manner, rendered this reply irresistible.

A LESSON.

THE late Mr. Sothern, when starring in the country, was invited by the officers of some garrison to dine at their mess. After dinner, they requested that he should give them his famous drunken scene from *David Garrick*. As they would accept no excuses, Sothern at last consented, and gave the scene faithfully, at the same time conveying a well-deserved lesson. At the close of the scene, the actor, according to stage directions, on leaving drags down a curtain. On this occasion Sothern, affecting to be carried away by his impersonation, caught hold of the tablecloth, and with one vigorous jerk swept off plates, glasses, bottles, and decanters in one collective ruin.

"LARGE AS LIFE AND TWICE AS NATURAL."

JOHNSTONE, the machinist, who flourished at Old Drury in the reign of Sheridan, was celebrated for his superior skill and taste in the construction of wickerwork lions, pasteboard swans, and all the sham birds and beasts appertaining to a theatrical menagerie. He wished on a certain occasion to spy the nakedness of the enemy's camp, and for that purpose insinuated himself with a friend into the two-shilling gallery, to witness the night rehearsal of a pantomime at Covent Garden. Among the attractions of the Christmas foolery a *real* elephant was introduced, making a prodigious figure in the procession. "This is a bitter bad job for Old Drury," said the friend. "Why, the elephant's *alive;* he'll carry all before him, and beat you hollow." "Nonsense," replied Johnstone, in a tone of the utmost contempt. "I should be very sorry if I couldn't make a much better elephant than that at any time."

"BEAT THE IRON WHILST IT IS HOT."

A*NTONY*, one of the elder Dumas's earlier pieces, had a success which, to use a suggestive theatrical phrase, "brought the house down." The story, however, is simply absurd. The author knew how audacious it was, and how important to its success was the leaving as little time as possible to the playgoer for sober second thought. At the first performance, when the curtain fell on the fourth act, there was great enthusiasm. Dumas sprang upon the stage, and shouted to the carpenters, "A hundred francs for you if you get the curtain up before the applause ceases!" By this presence of mind, he succeeded in springing his very ticklish fifth act upon the audience while they were still excited over the fourth.

WHICH IS WHICH?

AN actor of the name of Bass was the manager of a provincial theatre in England, on the boards of which Edmund Kean once appeared for a few nights. During his brief engagement *Othello* was performed three or four times, the part of the Moor and his ancient being alternately taken by the great tragedian and the manager. One evening they had been dining together, and the bottle had been passed too freely. They got through the play, however, without their condition being discovered by the audience, until they came to the scene in the third act, in which Othello seizes Iago by the throat, and delivers the speech beginning "Villain, be sure thou prove," etc. Kean, who on this occasion was the Othello, as he spoke, grasped Iago so fiercely that, being somewhat unsteady on his legs, the ancient fell, dragging his dusky chief down with him. This accident confused them both, and when they regained their feet, Kean, instead of waiting for Bass to continue the dialogue, himself uttered the exclamation, "Is it come to this?" which properly belongs to Iago. Bass, who was "letter perfect" in either part, took the cue, and went on with that of Othello. For a moment or two, the audience were not a little puzzled by this interchange of characters; but as soon as the real facts of the case dawned upon them, they appreciated to the full the absurdity of the situation, and the remainder of the scene—usually listened to in breathless silence—was greeted with frequent peals of laughter. Both actors were alike surprised and disgusted at the merriment they caused. Kean, in particular, was in a towering rage. Anger in some measure sobered him. Still, he had no suspicion of the blunder he had been guilty of, and when he quitted the stage, he made his way hastily to the greenroom. As he entered the apartment, however, the reflection of his dark visage and Moorish garments in a mirror over the mantelpiece, caught his eye, and turning to his fellow actor, he abruptly exclaimed, "By heaven, Bass, I'm Othello!" "Of course you are," was the response. "Then why the deuce did you assume my character?" was the angry query. "Because you, in the first instance, took mine; and, being as drunk as you were, I simply followed your lead." Kean was about to make a furious rejoinder, when suddenly, the humorous side of the incident striking him, the heavy frown which had gathered on his brow relaxed, and bursting into a hearty fit of laughter, he said, "Well, after all, I believe it was as much my fault as yours. But I fancy we shall find the people in front in no very appreciative temper during the remainder of the evening." In this, however, Kean was mistaken. When he next appeared upon the stage, the magnificence of his acting—he being now upon his mettle—quickly quelled all manifestations of merriment, and during the remainder of the play he never once relaxed his hold upon the audience.

INDEX.

D

E

F

G

H

I

P

Q

R

S

PRINTED BY WILLIAM CLOWES AND SONS, LIMITED, LONDON AND BECCLES.

CPSIA information can be obtained at www.ICGtesting.com
Printed in the USA
LVOW09s1032110716

495849LV00022B/459/P

9 781177 032735